# Researching Langu... ...ia

# WITHDRAWN

Social media is fast becoming a key area of linguistic research. This highly accessible guidebook leads students through the process of undertaking research in order to explore the language that people use when they communicate on social media sites.

This textbook provides:

- An introduction to the linguistic frameworks currently used to analyse language found in social media contexts.
- An outline of the practical steps and ethical guidelines entailed when gathering linguistic data from social media sites and platforms.
- A range of illustrative case studies, which cover different approaches, linguistic topics, digital platforms and national contexts.

Each chapter begins with a clear summary of the topics covered and also suggests sources for further reading to supplement the initial discussion and case studies. Written with an international outlook, *Researching Language and Social Media* is an essential book for undergraduate and postgraduate students of Linguistics, Media Studies and Communication Studies.

**Ruth Page** is a Reader in English Language at the University of Leicester, UK.

**David Barton** is Professor of Language and Literacy and Director of the Lancaster Literacy Research Centre at Lancaster University, UK.

**Johann W. Unger** is Academic Director and a lecturer in the Department of Linguistics and English Language at Lancaster University, UK.

**Michele Zappavigna** is Australian Research Council (ARC) Postdoctoral Fellow in Linguistics at the University of Sydney, Australia.

# Researching Language and Social Media

A Student Guide

Ruth Page, David Barton, Johann W. Unger, Michele Zappavigna

Routledge
Taylor & Francis Group

LONDON AND NEW YORK

First published 2014
by Routledge
2 Park Square, Milton Park, Abingdon, Oxon OX14 4RN

and by Routledge
711 Third Avenue, New York, NY 10017

*Routledge is an imprint of the Taylor & Francis Group, an informa business*

*British Library Cataloguing in Publication Data*
A catalogue record for this book is available from the British Library

*Library of Congress Cataloging in Publication Data*
Page, Ruth E., 1972-
Researching language and social media : a student guide / Ruth Page,
David Barton, Johann W. Unger, Michele Zappavigna.
pages cm.
Includes index.
1. Communication – Technological innovations. 2. Language and languages –
Usage. 3. Human-computer interaction. 4. Technological innovations – Social
aspects. 5. Social media. I. Title.
P96.T42P34 2014
302.23'1 – dc23
2013047922

ISBN: 978-0-415-84199-3 (hbk)
ISBN: 978-0-415-84200-6 (pbk)
ISBN: 978-1-315-77178-6 (ebk)

Typeset in Goudy
by Taylor & Francis Books

MIX
Paper from
responsible sources
FSC  FSC® C013056
www.fsc.org

Printed and bound in Great Britain by
TJ International Ltd, Padstow, Cornwall

# Contents

# Figures

# Tables

# Boxes

# Acknowledgments

The examples of techno-biographies given in Chapter 7 are taken from an undergraduate Language and Media course taught by Julia Gillen and David Barton. Other examples have been developed in association with Carmen Lee, Uta Papen and Karin Tusting.

Figure 9.3 was created by John Caulfield and is reproduced with permission.

Figure 9.6 was created by Michele Zappavigna using Jeff Clark's Twitter Streamgraph and is reproduced here with permission.

Figure 9.7 was created by Brice Russ and is reproduced here with permission.

# Introduction

## About this book

This book is about how to study the language that occurs in social media contexts. The platforms that have become associated with the umbrella term *social media* include sites and services that are now well known and have been adopted on an international scale. Examples include the social network site Facebook, the micro-blogging site Twitter, the video-sharing site YouTube and the wiki Wikipedia, whilst social media genres like blogs, discussion forums and chat continue to evolve across many different sites. These (and other) forms of social media provide contexts where people communicate with each other by posting messages, sharing information, uploading images and video. Our focus in this book is specifically on how you might go about exploring the language that people use when they communicate (rather than focusing on the sites and services in a more general sense). Researching the language used in these social media contexts is a growing area of interest. There are many reasons why this field is particularly attractive for researchers. The sheer amount of interaction which takes place within social media contexts means there is a wealth of material that can be considered, and that material is often available in forms that are (relatively) easy to access. The fast-paced and rapidly evolving nature of these interactions mean that there is often something new to be observed, whether that be about the seemingly 'routine' interactions that interweave social media with people's day-to-day activities, or about the variously creative ways people adapt and innovate in their communication with each other. Given the scope of what might be included in a research project about the "language in social media" it can be hard to know exactly where to start.

Our aim in this book is to provide both beginning and more advanced researchers with an introduction to the topics, methods and frameworks that will enable them to design and carry out a project about language and social media. We hope that this book will be useful to a wide range of researchers: students who might be studying in different departments and for different degree programmes in different countries; researchers who might be planning a small or perhaps rather larger project; readers who might pick up this book with a clear idea of what kind of research they want to do and readers who just want to find out more about how you could research language in social media contexts but don't yet have a project in mind. Our reason for writing this book came from our experience that often the students we have taught in recent years were very enthusiastic about carrying out research projects with a social media focus, but often had a lot of questions about how they should go about planning and carrying out their projects. While this book cannot address every issue or possible way you could start to explore the language in social media, we have tried both to include a broad range of approaches and to include more elementary and advanced topics and guidance.

## About the chapters

We have organised the chapters of the book in the following way:

### Chapters 1 and 2: introducing 'social media' and 'language'

The first two chapters provide an introduction to the areas which are brought together as the focus for potential research projects: social media (Chapter 1) and language (Chapter 2). Although both *social media* and *language* are familiar terms, they cover varied phenomena and have been used in different ways by researchers. In these two chapters we set out definitions for each term and outline some of the most well-known approaches that have been used to analyse different types of social media and different kinds of language and language use.

### Chapters 3 and 4: introducing research

Chapter 3 explains what we mean by *research*, and introduces some of the basic choices that you might need to make at the outset of thinking about a research project: identifying a focus and research questions, and outlining the different methods and approaches that might be available for collecting and then analysing material. Chapter 4 turns to the ethical dimensions of a research project. The responsibilities that a researcher has to the other people involved in their project are an important factor to consider from the outset to the completion of the research process. But in social media contexts some of the established guidelines for ethical research used in linguistics can be tricky to apply or need to be negotiated in slightly different ways.

### Chapters 5, 6 and 7: qualitative approaches

One distinction that is often made is between qualitative and quantitative research methods. Although throughout this book we emphasise the value of combining different approaches, for ease of reference, we have separated the approaches most usually associated with qualitative and quantitative research. We begin with three chapters focused on different kinds of qualitative research. Chapter 5 introduces different frameworks used to carry out the analysis of the 'talk' in social media contexts (discourse analysis, conversation analysis, critical discourse analysis, multimodal discourse analysis). Chapter 6 provides an introduction to the principles of ethnographic research and how it might be applied to social media interactions, followed by a more specific focus in Chapter 7 on how to use techno-biographies as a tool for examining how language practices are evolving in social media contexts.

### *Chapters 8 and 9: quantitative approaches*

In the last two chapters, we turn to the frameworks associated with quantitative research. Chapter 8 focuses on the principles, tools and software that you might use to gather materials for a quantitative project, including both small-scale projects and larger collection strategies needed to build a corpus. Chapter 9 covers how you might analyse social media materials from a quantitative perspective, including the use of concordancing software for corpus linguistics projects. We conclude with an introduction to the visualisation tools that can be useful for representing the quantitative analysis of the language used in social media contexts.

In some of these chapters there is a greater emphasis on providing information about the principles and methods used to do research (describing existing examples and providing background knowledge). Other chapters are framed more directly as advice and steps to follow when carrying out a research project. Depending on your reason for reading this book, you might find it useful to read all of the chapters, but if you have a specific project in mind, then certain parts may be more helpful than others. Chapters 3 and 4 are relevant whatever the focus of the research project, whilst the chapters in the 'Qualitative' and 'Quantitative' sections could be read separately. Along with the discussions, in each chapter you will find:

- An introductory section outlining the content of the chapter.
- Illustrative case studies from other researchers.
- Reflection points to apply the material to your own research project.
- A list of the resources we refer to in the chapter.

### Format conventions

The following format conventions are used in the chapters. *Italics* are used for emphasis and for mentioning rather than using words (*here* means I am talking about that word, not using it to refer to the present location).

Underlines are retained in quotations to indicate hyperlinks. **Bold** is used in examples to indicate added emphasis or to highlight a linguistic feature. Unless otherwise indicated, it was not added in the original. Where we use quoted excerpts from data, we have kept the exact spelling and punctuation used by the original authors of the material quoted from the data, not using *sic* to indicate unconventional spelling or usage. Sometimes, although not always, that unconventionality is part of the style used by the person first writing the quoted material.

## A note about the authors

One of the key characteristics of social media is its collaborative nature. In keeping with that, this book has also been a collaborative venture. As authors, we work in different departments (English, Language and Linguistics, and Media), in different universities and in different countries. We also have different approaches to researching the language of social media, and special interests in different social media sites. We have learnt a lot about each other's work and research approaches through the process of writing this book; we hope that you will benefit similarly from the variety of perspectives that we bring. Most of the time, we write using the plural pronoun, but from time to time you will find that one or the other of us refers to our own particular projects too, and then we move to use the first person pronoun and then include our individual names. From the outset, we also recognised that our combined expertise as authors was limited and we wanted to include a wider range of examples, voices and perspectives from researchers at different stages in their careers. These examples are included as case studies in the different chapters, and we are very grateful to the case study authors for their contributions. We asked the case study authors to close their contribution with a 140-character piece of advice for other researchers. You'll find these at the end of many of the case studies prefaced with the hashtag #advice.

# Chapter 1

# What is social media?

## Outline of the chapter

In this chapter we cover:

- How to define social media.
- Social media sites and their place in the wider historical evolution of computer-mediated communication.
- The relationship between social media and web 2.0.
- Frameworks used to distinguish the characteristics of social media sites and genres, drawing on the work of Kaplan and Haenlein (2009) and Herring (2007).
- The 'social' characteristics of social media.
- The 'medium-related' characteristics of social media.

## Defining social media

This first chapter considers the object of study which is our main interest – social media – and its relationship to other forms of computer-mediated communication (henceforth CMC). We use the term *social media* to refer to Internet-based sites and services that promote social interaction between participants. Examples of social media include (but are not limited to) discussion forums, blogs, wikis, podcasting, social network sites, content-sharing sites (like the video-sharing site, YouTube and the photo-sharing site, Flickr) and virtual worlds. Social media is often distinguished from forms of mass media, where mass media is presented as a one-to-many broadcasting mechanism (such as television, radio or print newspapers). In contrast, social media delivers content via a network of participants where the content can be published by anyone, but still distributed across potentially large-scale audiences.

As our definition suggests, social media is an umbrella term which groups together a seemingly diverse range of forms, with different genres (think of how blogs and discussion forums vary from each other and from social network sites), and social media sites and services which realise these genres in specific ways (compare blogging services such as Wordpress and Tumblr, or social network sites like Facebook and Weibo) and a diverse range of communicative channels and text types, some of which can be integrated within the same site. For example, Facebook is primarily a social network site, but it also allows its members to set up private profiles and to join public groups. They can also post semi-public or public updates, comments or rankings seen by a wider audience of a 'Friend list' or everyone who uses the application, and send a private email message or chat online to a single person. As time has gone by, so the convergence of media applications has made it more difficult still to state unequivocally that a particular site is or is not in its entirety an example of social media. For example, online stores can embed links to social media sites (through the now ubiquitous sharing buttons for sites like Facebook, Twitter and others) or have added options for customers to discuss and evaluate goods for sale through reviewer comments and ratings (which can sometimes resemble a blog or forum). Given the convergence of media forms on one hand and the diversity of applications on the other, it is hard to set out a definitive list of technical attributes which could be used to categorise a given application as belonging to or excluded from the set of 'social media' in a clear-cut manner. Instead, in the following sections, we begin by setting social media applications in their historical context, then move on to discuss the characteristics associated typically with these social media applications as a way of mapping out the terrain.

## Social media in historical context

Although listing the attributes of social media sites definitively is elusive, there is a general consensus that social media platforms can be distinguished historically from other kinds of digitally enabled communication. From this perspective, social media often refers to the range of tools and technologies that began to be developed in the latter years of the 1990s and became sites of mainstream Internet activities in the first decade of the twenty-first century. The chronological context of social media platforms is set out in Table 1.1 and the discussion focuses on developments in English-speaking countries.

The timeline in Table 1.1 suggests the increasingly interactive potential of social media. The conversational nature of social media sites is not exclusive to blogs, wikis or content-sharing platforms, and is also present in earlier forms of online communication. The email lists, bulletin boards and text messages of the 1980s might be seen as precursors to the communicative channels that characterise twenty-first century Internet behaviour. But the mid-1990s saw a decisive shift in the way that social media sites enabled interaction between participants, and placed that interaction in public rather than private or semi-private contexts. Blogs and wikis extended the range of interactive possibilities, with blogs allowing individual writers to

*Table 1.1* Timeline of selected social media platforms

| | |
|---|---|
| 1978 | Bulletin Board System |
| 1980 | Usenet |
| 1984 | SMS concept developed |
| 1988 | Internet Relay Chat |
| 1995 | eBay, Ward Cunningham coins the term "wiki" and launches first wiki site |
| 1997 | John Barger coins term "web log" |
| 1998 | Yahoo groups |
| 1999 | Live Journal, Blogger.com, |
| 2001 | Google groups, Wikipedia, Cyworld, Tripadvisor |
| 2002 | Friendster, Last.fm |
| 2003 | MySpace, WordPress, Del.ici.ous, LinkedIn, Second Life, Skype, 4 Chan |
| 2004 | Flickr, Facebook, Digg, Orkut, Ben Hammersly coins the term "podcasting", Tim O'Reilly launches the first "web 2.0" conference |
| 2005 | YouTube |
| 2006 | Twitter |
| 2007 | Justin TV, Tumblr, Gowalla |
| 2008 | 9GAG |
| 2009 | Foursquare, Google Wave, Chatroulette, Weibo, Klout |
| 2010 | Instagram, Diaspora*, WeChat |
| 2011 | Google plus, Snapchat |

connect to other bloggers (through blog rolls, links, comments) and wikis fostering collective contributions to a single enterprise (Myers 2010). These became mainstream examples of Internet use when sites like Live Journal, Blogger and later Wordpress made it easier than ever for contributors to publish reports and opinions, and Wikipedia was launched in 2001. The years 2003–6 saw a rapid expansion of social network sites (such as LinkedIn, Orkut, MySpace, Flickr, Facebook, YouTube and Twitter) which reframed the dialogic links between participants as a network, increasing the number, visibility and reach of an individual's connections with others in online spaces.

The scale on which social media has been adopted needs to be understood in the wider history of the Internet. The mid-1990s saw several technological developments that would enable the later social media genres to gain popularity and prominence. In 1993, Mosaic was the first popular web browser to make the web available to a wider audience. MP3 file formats became publicly available from late 1994, Real Player was launched in April 1995 and Macromedia's Flash Software was released as a browser plug-in from 1996. These technological developments facilitated digital animation and audio resources which could be created and shared with relative ease, transforming the Internet from a text-based medium to the richly varied multimodality that is now familiar. By 1997, commercial standards for wi-fi had been agreed, and 1996 saw the first smart phone (the Nokia 9000 communicator). Access to the Internet was no longer restricted to static computer terminals connected to wired power supplies. With increased possibilities for access, social media interactions could be produced and consumed in a greater range of locations and at any point in time. Further developments in markup language, like HTML5, which made it easier to include multimedia content and to access that content via smart phones, have further increased these trends for cross-platform, on-the-fly production and consumption of social media content. By 2007, 70 million blogs were indexed by Technorati. Two years later, 13 million articles had been posted on Wikipedia. By 2010, the major social network sites had millions of members each and YouTube boasted over two billion daily views.

## Social media or web 2.0?

Social media is often treated as more or less synonymous with the inter-related descriptor 'web 2.0'. However, the two terms are different. Thus Kaplan and Haenlein (2009) differentiate between web 2.0 technologies and ideologies and the social media applications that build on them (2009, p.61). The ideologies of web 2.0 are associated with Tim O'Reilly's use of the label, which attempted to demarcate a new era for online interaction, one which assumed a clear contrast between old (1.0) and new (2.0) web genres. The characteristics associated with web 2.0 reflected an apparent shift towards web users as creators (rather than consumers) of content, where software and online publications were in a continuous and rapid process of updating. The example given by *Time* magazine (Grossman 2006) as an illustration of web 2.0's characteristics compared the production of the *Encyclopedia Britannica* with the online encyclopedia Wikipedia. The print publication of the *Encyclopedia Britannica* released updated versions of its articles on a schedule where each revision was published in serial fashion (that is, with a hiatus sometimes of several years between one version and another). The authorship of these articles was and still is associated with "experts" including "subject area specialists" (Britannica homepage), a model which emphasised individual contributions selected on the basis of academic credentials. In contrast, Wikipedia articles are continuously open to public revision and can be edited by anyone with access to the Internet.

The comparison of the *Encyclopedia Britannica* and Wikipedia projects a polarised contrast between print-based production by individuals whose status as authorities is established by pre-existing systems (education or professional experience) with a rapid, transparent and online process of revision which draws collectively on the 'wisdom of the crowd' shaped by a model of democracy and open-ness. But this polarised contrast is not as straightforward as it might appear. First, the comparison elides several distinct aspects of social media sites: the modes of production and the social judgements that are made about the quality of the texts that are published (for example, what counts as authoritative). Second, the contrast between the *Encyclopedia Britannica* and Wikipedia makes a comparison between print and social media, not between earlier and later web genres, therefore cannot be taken as illustrating how web 2.0 forms are different from web 1.0: a better comparison would contrast the online Encyclopedia Britannica and Wikipedia. Third, the contrast is highly selective and ignores the points of comparison between the two encyclopedias. As Britannica's home page documents, print and online encyclopedias are both collaborative endeavours between readers, authors, reviewers and editors, which are revised over time. Other researchers have debated the relative credibility of Britannica and Wikipedia articles, finding more similarity than difference (Chesney 2006), while Oxley *et al.* (2010) show how Wikipedia contributors do not do away altogether with claims to authority based on credentials but position these alongside other criteria such as references to external sources or to personal experience.

The distinction between web 2.0 characteristics and those found in earlier forms of communication is not clear cut: the comparison of the encyclopedias point to the overlap between the practices and products that pre-date the creation of wikis, blogs and social network sites. Rather than demarcating a single, unified transition which contrasts communicative genres based on clear criteria, the term "web 2.0" is better understood as a rhetorical label which was particularly important for strategically reframing e-commerce in the early twenty-first century (Marwick 2010). Because we want to acknowledge both the points of continuity and the distinct developments in online communication, we will not use the term "web 2.0" in this book. Our alternative term, "social media", is also less than perfect, but it allows us to examine aspects of the interactions in online contexts that are reshaped in relation to their social uses and the characteristics of the media which are employed. In the next three sections, we examine more closely what 'social' and 'media' might mean, drawing on the categories used to classify computer-mediated communication more generally.

There are various classification systems which could be used to compare types of social media with other channels of communication. Working from a media theory perspective, Kaplan and Haenlein (2009) draw on social presence theory and media richness to compare the different ways in which participants might engage in interactions that are more or less direct (in time and space) and which allow a greater or lesser amount of information to be conveyed between the participants. Hence a telephone conversation would be characterised as allowing the participants to communicate vocally in real time, but mediated through the technology of a telephone system, conveying with a high degree of fidelity the communicative resources associated with speech (such as voice quality, volume, choice of words), but not conveying any of the paralinguistic resources found in face-to-face conversation (like gesture, gaze, body posture and so on). Kaplan and Haenlein go on to suggest that these media-related characteristics intersect with the choices that participants can make within particular social media sites to disclose more or less information about themselves, which can vary according to degree (whether a high or low level of self-disclosure is required) and in the modes through which the participant can represent his or herself (through words, images, sound, and whether the representation is assumed to match the identities that the participant presents in offline contexts). These options are summarised in Table 1.2.

Working from a linguistic tradition, Herring (2007) adapted Hymes' (1974) ethnography of communication model to provide a starting point for describing the factors which influence language practices in online contexts. Like Kaplan and Haenlein, Herring makes a distinction between the characteristics which are associated with properties of the medium and those which are related to the participants and the wider situation in which the interaction takes place. A summary of Herring's medium and situation factors is given in Table 1.3.

Both models recognise that in order to document the variety within forms of social media communication, classification systems need to be flexible and open-ended, and that social media platforms can be set alongside the genres of communication that take place in earlier online and offline forms. Although drawing on different theoretical perspectives, both models also make a broad distinction between the factors which characterise the discourse according to the participants (such as the number of people involved in the interaction, what demographic categories might apply to the participants, how much information people choose to convey, what language variety they use and how the purpose of the interaction influences the talk) and the factors which relate to the technology which is used to convey the interaction (such as the size of the message, how it is preserved and disseminated through the architectures of particular sites, whether the message is made available in public or private contexts, whether technologies enable participants to

*Table 1.2* Summary of Kaplan and Haenlein's (2009) factors for classifying social media types

| *Media characteristics* | | |
|---|---|---|
| Social presence | Degree of mediation | High–Low |
| | Degree of immediacy | High–Low |
| Media richness | Amount of information | High–Low |
| *Social characteristics* | | |
| Self-presentation | Extent and forms of self-disclosure | High–Low Representational mode |

*Table 1.3* Herring's (2007) medium and situation factors

| Medium factors | Synchronicity | Asynchronous–synchronous |
|---|---|---|
| | Message transmission | One-to-one; one-to-many; many-to-many |
| | Persistence of the transcript | Ephemeral–archived |
| | Size of message | Amount of text conveyed |
| | Channels of communication | Words, image, sound, video |
| | Privacy settings | Public, semi-public, semi-private, private contexts |
| | Anonymous | Extent to which the participants' identities are represented within a site |
| | Message format | Architectures for displaying interactions |
| Situation factors | Participation structure | Number of participants involved |
| | Participant characteristics | Stated or assumed demographic and ideological characteristics |
| | Purpose | Goals of interaction (either at individual or group level) |
| | Topic | Subject matter |
| | Tone | Formal or informal |
| | Norms | Accepted practices established by the group |
| | Code | Language variety and choice of script |

communicate in real time, or enable geographically and temporally remote interactions). Each group of factors is discussed in more detail in the following two sections. The first section focuses on the factors relating to 'social' factors and the second considers characteristics related to 'media'.

## Points for reflection

Where would you position the social media sites that form the focus of your research project within the chronological time line given in Table 1.1? What are the site's antecedents?

Which of the factors set out by Kaplan and Haenlein (2009) and by Herring (2007) most help you understand the distinctive characteristics of the social media sites you want to analyse?

Why is it so difficult to define 'social media'?

## *Social* media

### *Interactions between people: participation structure*

The modifier *social* draws attention to the ways in which social network sites, blogs and wikis enable people to interact with each other. This is similar to the focus of other kinds of computer-mediated communication, where the interest lies in how people use technology to communicate rather than in the systems which underpin the platforms (for example, the coding languages and systems used to create software and applications). The communication that takes place between participants in social media can be distinguished from other kinds of web genres on the grounds that they enable two-way communication between participants, emphasising the dialogic and collaborative potential of social media as opposed to mainstream media interactions. Of course, the sharp contrast between a uni-directional broadcast, like a pay-on-demand television streaming service and a multi-party discussion on a forum about a television show polarises this distinction. The language used in uni-directional broadcasts can sometimes mimic the conversational styles found in face-to-face conversations. For example, the use of second person pronouns and questions which address the audience are typical of print adverts. But this mode of address does not allow the audience to interact directly with the writer of the advert: it is an example of what Fairclough (1989) calls synthetic personalisation and has been described more widely in relation to other kinds of broadcast talk (Thornborrow and Montgomery 2010). In contrast, social media formats have participation structures that allow the sender and the recipient of the message to interact directly with each other, often within a short time frame. The ways in which mainstream media has integrated social media platforms within their productions highlights this dialogic quality of social media. For example, reality television shows may draw explicitly on examples of the audience's response by quoting tweets or Facebook posts about the show's performance as it is taking place: in doing this they position the audience as active participants rather than as passive consumers, and they do so within the time frame in which the show is aired. This contrasts with earlier models of interaction where the viewing audience might send in their responses to a show by letter or postcards which were read out in the later time frame of the next broadcast.

### *Purpose and activity: interactions which exchange information*

Participants might communicate via computer-mediated technology for a wide range of reasons, many of which can appear subjective and hard to pin down. As a starting point, analysts interested in discourse have made a bold distinction between interactions where the participants exchange physical

actions or objects (sometimes referred to as "goods and services") and interactions where the phenomena is intangible, seeking or receiving information
(Halliday 1994). From this perspective, social media interactions are oriented
towards the exchange of information and tend to emphasise interpersonal
exchanges rather than task-based transactions. In this sense, they are distinct
from sites where the primary purposes might allow a customer to purchase
goods (for example, goods from an online store, making a hotel reservation
or buying tickets for a journey) or to carry out a financial transaction (such as
the activities included in online banking services). Instead, descriptions of
social media platforms emphasise the ways in which they allow members
to share information with each other: this can be information about the
member's activities or feelings, about breaking news, gossip or other discourse
genres such as jokes.

However, once again, a blunt, wholesale dichotomy between information-
sharing social media and the goods and service exchanged in other forms of
computer-mediated interactions can be blurred. For example, the exchange
of information which takes place on social media sites when members
discuss their shared interests and activities can in some cases become a
form of 'goods' with economic value, exchanged with online advertisers
who may use data mining applied to social media sites to target campaigns
to particular customers. Conversely, as sites which emphasise the exchange of
goods and services (such as online shopping stores) have evolved, some
have embedded within them aspects of social media. For example, sites like
eBay and Amazon include customers' comments in the form of product or
seller reviews and rankings. Nonetheless, identifying the purpose of the
participants' interactions can help distinguish between the social media
aspects of a platform and other kinds of exchange. For instance, you might
compare visiting Amazon to purchase a book, versus visiting Amazon to
write a review or read about a book you want to purchase. The two activities
are interrelated but separable: you could complete one without the other.
But Amazon is not primarily a review-sharing site: its primary function is to
exchange goods and services. On the other hand, visiting a blog or forum to
read a review of a book would enable the audience and reviewer to share
information about their opinions, but it would not enable the person
reading the review to purchase the book.

### Participant characteristics and self-disclosure

In order to enable interaction between participants, most social media
platforms allow members to display information about the site member's
identity in the form of a profile page. The kinds of information included in
a social media profile can vary from site to site. As Kaplan and Haenlein
point out, one distinction rests on the extent to which participants self-disclose
information about their offline identities: conventions for representing a

member's identity as anonymous, pseudonymous or representing aspects of the member's offline identity in a more or less transparent fashion. Although, as Rak (2005) notes, conventions for self-representation have shifted over time towards authenticity, the range of choices between anonymous or clearly nominated options for members of social media sites varies considerably. At one end of the spectrum, the terms and conditions of Facebook require that its members use their "real names" when registering for the site, and the relationship between Facebook members and their Friend list can often overlay offline and online interactions. Of course, this does not mean that all information posted to Facebook is necessarily truthful or eschews playful or ambiguous modes of self-presentation. Facebook members can be highly selective in the information they choose to disclose about their personal identity. At the other end of the spectrum, the profiles created in Wikipedia tend to contain limited autobiographical information about the users and focus instead on information relevant to their contributions to the site (for example, listing which articles a user might have contributed to, how long they have been a contributor to Wikipedia and so on). Although these profiles are among the more static aspects of social media (they may be presented on a separate page within the site from the areas in which interactions with others take place), the norms for self-representation and the extent to which particular demographic characteristics of participants come to the fore can influence the ways in which interactions between members of the site then take place.

Self-representation in social media sites is distinctive because of the ways in which individuals can present their relationship with others. Anthropologists, linguists and media scholars have long documented the ways in which identities are negotiated through interactions with others, and how identities are created on personal, collective and social levels. In social media, the profile information can also document information about the audience with whom a person might connect. boyd and Ellison (2007) describe social network sites as platforms which allow a member to display their network of contacts (for example as a Friend list on Facebook, Follower list on Twitter, or Contact list on Flickr). Blogging platforms also enable their authors to display connections to other blogs, for example through a blog roll or the communities that they belong to. These displays of networked connections might signal the communities with which the person is associated, but can also be valued as an indication of status or authority.

The impact of interacting via social media has been assessed in positive terms (as a potentially democratising context) and in negative terms (in relation to moral panics). These judgements move the concern to macro-level discussions of media and social change. The relationship between technology, culture and society has been long debated in many different fields and in relation to many different kinds of technologies. As Crystal (2008) argues, the moral panics surrounding social media are nothing new. However, the relationship between technology and social change is not straightforward. When technological change is represented as the cause of social change, this is sometimes described as technological determinism. Technological determinism is often problematic because it represents the relationship between technology and social change in terms that are too simple and reduce the complexity of the wider situation. For example, claiming that SMS messages (the technology) damages teenagers' spelling ability (their language practice), presents the technology as the cause of the change and does not take into account the actions of the people using the technology. In so doing, this claim is also able to bypass a number of other social factors that might influence spelling practices, such as the choice of genre where teenagers might choose to use non-standard spelling in some contexts (when writing an SMS message) but use standard forms adeptly in others (such as when writing an essay), and the role of spelling in signalling social identity, such as indicating that a person is (or is not) a member of a particular community or 'in group'.

The rather simplistic association of technology and social change can be seen in debates about SMS communication and literacy, or in the assumption that the relationships enabled through online interactions are of a lesser quality than those enabled through face-to-face interactions (more shallow) or lead to undesirable outcomes (loss of trust, authenticity). Other social changes which have been related to social media include the relationship between the amount of time spent communicating through social media (especially through mobile devices like smart phones) as a form of emotional labour with negative outcomes for the individuals concerned (Turkle 2011). In this book, we avoid the claims of technological determinism. Instead, our interest lies in how research can help bring to light people's interactions with social media, which in turn may have different kinds of social outcomes for them (such as how they perceive their identity, their relationship with other people and the role of language in this).

## Social *media*

Social media platforms can also be differentiated according to their technological characteristics. Here the term *media* is slippery and has at least two separable but overlapping senses. One use of the term refers to the texts produced by the technology (Couldry 2010). In this sense, media in the sense of *multimedia* is often treated as synonymous with semiotic mode including images, movement, sound, touch, gesture and words. A second use of the term refers to the technologies used to transmit messages from one participant to another, including devices with digital components such as mobile phones, tablets, laptops, televisions and so on, as well as the different sites. The extent to which these different modes can be considered as 'language' and how far 'language' itself functions as a distinct mode is taken up in

Chapter 2. Here we discuss how both meanings of 'media' can categorise social media platforms, beginning with the factors which relate to media as a semiotic mode.

### Media as mode: channels of communication and media richness

Herring's (2007) classification describes different semiotic modes as channels of communication, thus distinguishing between platforms according to whether the participants rely on conveying meaning through image, sound or written words, for example. The range and prominence of particular channels of communication also underpins Kaplan and Haenlein's (2009) use of media richness to distinguish one platform from another. Social media genres have often been distinguished from their predecessors on the grounds of their increased range of multimodal resources and hence greater media richness (where earlier genres relied more upon a narrow range of resources, especially written text). In this respect, the primarily verbal resources of technologies like email contrast with the integration of visual and audio-visual elements in social network sites like Facebook. But there is still considerable variation across different social media platforms in terms of which semiotic modes predominate. For example, in the video-sharing site, YouTube, audio-visual channels dominate but are accompanied by written text (in the comments and in profile information). In comparison, on the photo-sharing site, Flickr, images are the main focus, but again written words take a subordinate role in framing and commenting on the images. The templates used by Twitter do make use of visual resources by way of colour, layout and profile avatars, but it is the words typed into the updates which carry the primary meaning: at the time of writing, images posted to other sites (like Instagram, yfrog or TwitPic) can only be viewed by clicking on a link posted as a string of characters in the post itself.

The complexity of the multimodal ensembles used to communicate in social media sites has also increased as the layout and architecture of the templates have evolved. In its early years, Facebook archived photo sharing and updating discretely in separate parts of a personal profile, but after the introduction of its timeline in 2011, uploaded images and uploaded text were streamed through the same feed. Similarly, the updating template in Facebook was a text box, but now allows site members to share links, add GPS information through a 'Check in' function, and to indicate their activities through a range of visual icons (which at the time of writing include Feelings, Eating, Drinking, Watching, Reading and Listening to). Such possibilities will continue to change over time.

These various semiotic resources sometimes make it difficult to find the right language to describe how people interact on social media sites. Early studies of computer-mediated communication signalled the varying ways in which communication via digital technologies might use written words, but simultaneously employ interactional structures (such as turn-taking) and stylistic choices (such as formality and discourse markers) that are more typical of spoken conversation. The result is that sometimes social media sites blur modalities in their description of interactions or interactive spaces. For example, some sites have a 'chat' function (such as Facebook or IRC) and the discussions which are used to debate the evolution of Wikipedia articles are called 'Talk Pages', even though participants write their contributions rather than speak them aloud to each other in both these cases. Of course the use of communicative terms associated with spoken discourse as synonymous with communication more generally is not new to social media: much literary criticism endows written texts with this kind of communicative potential (seen in phrases such as "the book says" where the text is taken metonymically to represent the author's communication).

The blurring of spoken and written modes can be found in the labels which linguists have used to describe communication in social media and other kinds of digitally mediated communication. As Androutsopoulos (2006) points out, these labels have often exoticised computer-mediated communication as a distinct language variety, such as 'Net speak', 'Internet Slang', 'Txt speak', 'Digital Discourse' or 'Language Online'. Part of the difficulty with this proliferation of terms is that researchers struggle to find a modifier which includes all the media that are used to produce the material they are interested in studying in a single term. In the list of titles given here we find particular media (digital) as well as modes of publication (online) and particular domains of publication (Internet). A second area of confusion arises in relation to the second term: the words speech, slang, discourse and language all appear. There is no clear consensus about which of these terms is most suitable. For the purposes of this book, we retain the established term *computer-mediated communication* which can be used to include social media genres as those that can be used via a computerised device (including smart phones), and which covers all modes of communication (both spoken, written and hybrid forms).

### Media as technology: message format

Herring (2007) uses the heading "message format" to list the technological characteristics of media important for describing social media contexts. These include the layouts, templates, archiving principles and architectures used to publish messages within a social media site. Once again, there is variation in how one site might use message formats as compared with another. However, social media archives tend to use architectures that promote recency (for example, through timelines which present the most recently added material at the top as the default view) or rankings (for example, through architectures which make the most endorsed contribution the most visible) or interaction (for example, highlighting the terms or material which has been interacted with the most, such as trending topics in Twitter).

Both the semiotic modes and the tools and technologies used to communicate via social media sites are important influences on the choices people make when communicating with each other. For example, the restrictions on a Twitter update to 140 characters controls the length of the message that can be conveyed. Or the absence of facial expression and tone of voice when using written words in a message can require people to create other resources to convey emphasis or pragmatic nuance (for example through emoticons). The enabling and constraining nature of modes and media are sometimes described as its affordances. James Gibson's (1977) ecological theory of perceived affordances has been applied in a number of fields of study, including media scholarship and CMC. The action possibilities in a particular social media context relate to the features which give rise to a particular kind of capability. Thus video-conferencing tools (such as Skype or Facetime) harness the potentialities of audio-visual display and two-way channels of communication. The affordances are then the ways in which people take up and create the possibilities which they perceive (see Barton and Lee 2013, pp.27–9 for further discussion of this important concept).

The affordances associated with social media are not exclusive properties of a single genre or set of genres. They are to do with how people actually make use of them. As we have seen so far, social media platforms and genres are not homogenous, and they also have points of similarity with other, earlier forms of communication which took place in online contexts, as well as forms of communication which use other technologies (such as print or face-to-face speech). More often, the possibilities of social media genres exaggerate the characteristics found in antecedent forms, or blur distinctions that have been used to contrast different forms of communication. This is particularly true in the case of the affordances of social media associated with time.

### Time and immediacy

Traditionally, CMC research has contrasted synchronous and asynchronous systems. In synchronous systems, the participants in an interaction are co-present in the same time frame. Pre-social media examples of synchronous systems include face-to-face conversation (where participants are also co-present in the same physical space) or telephone calls (where participants are geographically remote). In social media contexts, synchronous systems require participants to be logged on to the system at the same time (regardless of whether they are geographically co-present or not), as in the case of a Skype call or some instant messaging services. In asynchronous systems, the participants engage in the interaction in separate, sequenced messages. For example the sender might write a letter which is completed and then received some time afterwards by the recipient, or a caller might leave a message on an answering service which is later retrieved by the addressee. In social media contexts, asynchronous systems allow one participant to post a message, to log off and for the recipient to respond at a later point in time, as illustrated by the process of sending an email message.

The asynchronous systems of computer-mediated communication have resulted in distinctive patterns of turn-taking, where conversational turns within contexts like a discussion forum thread are no longer sequenced in adjacent units. The asynchronous disruption of turns can also be found in social media platforms, such as replies to a publicly addressed message in Twitter which can be separated by a number of other updates in the updater's timeline. The interactions found on social media sites can be positioned separately on the synchronous–asynchronous spectrum. Posting a comment in response to a blog post is by necessity asynchronous: it can only take place after the blog post has been published by the first author. Other kinds of social media interactions are synchronous, like the chat facilities in the virtual world, Second Life. But other examples of social media trouble a straightforward distinction between asynchronous and synchronous categories. Some sites, like Facebook, are multifaceted and contain many different options for their members to participate, some of which are asynchronous (like wall posts and comments) while others can be synchronous (like messages). The perceived scale of timeliness for responding to a post on a social networking site has become increasingly compressed. For example, although commenting on a Facebook wall post is asynchronous (the recipients do not need to be online at the same time to engage in the interaction), the patterns of interacting with sites like Facebook or Twitter where some members may spend periods of time logged on mean that they may respond to an asynchronous post with the rapidity that mirrors synchronous genres (like chat). As Erika Darics' case study points out, the binary opposition of 'synchronous' and 'asynchronous' forms of communication is difficult to sustain.

## Box 1.1 Synchronicity and asynchronicity in computer-mediated discourse

### Erika Darics

Until recently the distinction between synchronous and asynchronous computer-mediated communication (CMC) modes has been relatively straightforward: for synchronous modes, the conversational partners needed to be logged on simultaneously, and the interaction took place in real or almost-real time (for instance chatting or instant messaging (IM)). For asynchronous modes, such as bulletin boards, forums and email, considerable gaps were allowed between interactional turns. The synchronicity/asynchronicity dichotomy was a useful framework for linguists and communication scholars to capture the difference between the language use in various CMC modes: synchronous modes were described as resembling spoken discourse, whereas asynchronous modes were characterised as being closer to written discourse.

Nowadays, with CMC modes becoming a common part of our everyday communication repertoire, both for social and work purposes, and with the appearance of integrated communication technologies and convergent media platforms, the previously clear distinction between synchronous and asynchronous genres has become blurred. Social media sites, for instance, allow for real-time discussion if both participants are present, and automatically switch to embedded message sending if one of the participants is not online. These practices, naturally, have an impact on the discourse of CMC, not only at the level of grammatical complexity, but also at the level of the pragmatics of the interaction and communicative norms. At the virtual workplace, for instance, IM is often utilised as an 'asynchronous' communication mode, which means that minutes – or sometimes even hours – may pass between two conversational turns. Often colleagues use IM in a 'post-it note' function for messages that do not require immediate attention, as in the following excerpt:

1) Asid | 09:36 am | Hi, were you trying to reach me?
2) Fay | 09:36 am | yes
3) Fay | 09:36 am | but on call now
4) Asid | 09:49 am | okay, leaving for office now ... will be con-
   tactable on my cell ... and after about 20 minutes on my desk
   line too.
5) Asid | 10:26 am | Hi again ... on my seat now ... let me know
   if you still wish to speak, else I will be getting into a long call
   with Jasmine soon.
6) Asid | 10:26 am | thanks.
7) Fay | 10:26 am | its fine settled.

In this excerpt, which was collected as a part of a large scale study on IM interactions in the business environment, we can see that after learning about Fay's unavailability for interaction in line 3, Asid waits for about ten minutes before sending the next messages intended to be picked up at a more convenient time. The utterances in lines 4–5 display language use different from the preceding and following utter-ances in this interaction: the messages are considerably longer and the grammatical complexity of the sentence fragments increases.

Such 'intermittent' use of IM (previously thought of as an asynchronous form), and other 'blurred' uses of CMC force us to re-think previously well established norms of conversation. Further research, therefore, should explore these new norms, for example, the role of (the lack of) opening and closing rituals, or the participants' expectations regarding timing.

#advice: (A)synchronicity was a robust predictor of language use in CMC. Nowadays the synchronous/asynchronous dichotomy is not clear-cut any more.

Time also influences the second medium-related facet taken from Herring's (2007) classification: the persistence of the transcript. The extent to which the language used to communicate via computer-mediated genres is preserved as a tractable product (sound file, string of text characters, image, video file) can vary. At one end of the scale, computer-mediated interactions can be ephemeral, and similar to speech. Examples include use of Skype, but also typed interactions that disappear as soon as the interaction between participants is completed, such as chat interactions. At the other end of the scale, interactions can be preserved for varying lengths of time. Here further distinctions rest on whether the archiving remains under the control of the user (as in the case of email, which can be archived until the user deletes the message) or under the control of the system's architecture (where messages can be deleted without action on behalf of the site member). Again, social media genres can vary in the extent of their persistence. Wikipedia's archives date back to 2002 and provide a rich repository which documents each and every revision to its articles. Facebook's timeline format added in 2012 made it easier to return to posts added by members in earlier years, but the posts that appear in the timeline are not stable and over time are not displayed in their entirety. Other sites, like Snapchat, allow their members to determine how long a message can stay visible, but only within a time span of up to three hours. These differences have various implications for the site users, such as the extent to which they can use a search mechanism to access and interact with previous content. Knowing that a message will be preserved and viewed later in a public format may influence both the selection and style of the messages posted to a site.

Both the synchronicity and the persistence of the transcript help distinguish different types of social media platforms and genres and to show their points of continuity with other kinds of communicative media. While there are many variations in different kinds of social media examples considered in this book, there are overarching trends which suggest that the increasing rapidity of online interaction is reducing the scale of asynchronocity, but at the same time the persistence of texts is also reducing as the size of timelines becomes unwieldy as a framing architecture to enable archiving and search mechanisms.

### Publishing contexts: audiences and privacy settings

The affordances of social media can also be compared with other forms of communication in terms of how the interactions between participants can be made visible to those interacting directly with each other and a wider 'overhearing' audience. In Herring's classification (2007), this brings together two key facets of communication which are important for social media genres: the relationship between the speaker(s) and their audience and the public or private nature of the communication. As Herring points out, the number of participants involved in an interaction can vary from one-to-one, one-to-many or many-to-many. This points to the contrast between communication between two individuals (as in one-to-one email correspondence, or Direct Messages in Twitter), one-to-many broadcasts (such as a post to a mailing list, a wall post on a personal Facebook account) and many-to-many interactions (exemplified by contributions to a collective forum like a discussion thread, or a public Facebook group page). The number of participants involved allows us to see points of continuity between particular social media genres (such as blogging and micro-blogging), and social media genres and earlier forms of mass media (such as television news broadcasts and Twitter updates). However, the multiple audiences which are found in the participation structures of social media sites are often characterised by collapsed contexts (Wesch 2009). This further differentiates the one-to-many participation in formats like blogs, Facebook wall posts and Twitter updates where the audience on a Friend or Follower list may bring together different social groups who would usually be kept separate when the sender of the message communicated with them in offline contexts.

The communicative norms which emerge in a given social media site can also be influenced by whether the context of the interaction is private or public. Once again, social media genres can be located on a spectrum between interactions which take place in public domains (such as Wikipedia articles and their page histories, or the Twitter timeline) or private communication like Direct Messages in Twitter and chat exchanges in Facebook. The complex, convergent nature of many social media sites means that participants can adopt one set of privacy protocols for one aspect of their communication, whilst using others elsewhere within the same site. Both the collapsed contexts and varying expectations of privacy can coincide to produce unexpected effects on the language that people use in social media contexts. The case study from Caroline Tagg and Philip Seargeant explains how the collapsed contexts of Facebook are negotiated by multilingual speakers.

## Box 1.2 Researching language choice as an audience design strategy on social network sites

### Caroline Tagg and Philip Seargeant

Our research explores how multilingual Facebook users switch between languages as they attempt to target individuals or groups and how they thus construct and maintain communities within the site. To explore language choice as a community-building strategy, we adapted Allan Bell's 'audience design' framework, which was originally conceived with face-to-face and broadcast spoken interactions in mind. Bell's framework offers an explanation for how different members of a speaker's audience shape their speaking style. According to Bell, speakers design utterances not only to accommodate their *addressee(s)*, but also others whose participation is either ratified (*auditors*) or not (*overhearers*). An adaptation of this model has obvious potential for understanding how users negotiate the seemingly chaotic environment of Facebook.

As with other social network sites, 'private' Facebook pages are more aptly described as 'semi-public' in the sense that people often have hundreds of 'Friends'. Crucially, it is often impossible to know who from among this assorted audience will respond to a post. In our adapted framework, status updaters are likely to address those they consider to be their *active Friends* – Friends who can be expected to respond to the update – but their posts will also be shaped by their awareness of their *wider Friends* (employers, parents, acquaintances). The resources available to Facebook users in targeting others differ from those in face-to-face situations – while speakers have recourse to body language, positioning and tone of voice, Facebook users can exploit graphic and text-based affordances such as the @ sign which draws other users' attention to a post. Another strategy, encouraged by the way in which social media often brings together people from across the world, is language choice. This is the case in the following example, where a Dutch Facebook user updates her status (largely) in English, signalling that the status is for Friends across language communities.

Eva is missing a certain man (hint: it is not Sinterklass)

In doing so she uses language that is sufficiently vague (low in context) to be comprehensible only to those who know her well (they can understand the references to "a certain man" due to personal knowledge of her biography), while at the same time it is accessible on a different level to Friends familiar with the Dutch tradition of *Sinterklass* (a reference lost on international Friends unfamiliar with Dutch culture).

To explore these practices, we engage in textual analysis of status updates and comments posted by multilingual users in various countries, supplemented by participant interviews. This approach allows observations to be backed up by participants' insights into their language practices and motivations. For example, one Thai participant's asserted belief that she and her Thai friends never use English when speaking with each other in face-to-face situations or by telephone gave a new dimension to their frequent, conscious language mixing (involving a great deal of English) online. At the same time, informant accounts must be evaluated as post-hoc interpretations – although Eva, for instance, explained that she posted about Dutch topics in Dutch, this did not resonate with her actual behaviour (as the Sinterklass example shows).

## Points for reflection

Which set of characteristics (those related to "social" factors or those related to "media") do you think are the more compelling as a means of distinguishing social media sites from other forms of communication?
What other factors might be important for understanding CMC as a distinct form of communication?

## Summary

In this chapter, we have placed social media in its chronological context and compared it with other web genres. We argue that the affordances of social media are best understood as developing from and overlapping with earlier forms of communication. Although the boundaries of social media as a subset of heterogenous web genres is somewhat fuzzy, there is a general tendency for social media to emphasise recency and real-time communication, for participation structures to emphasise collective groups where the site member is positioned within a wider network of contacts, for communication to be highly contextualised and to use an increasingly wide range of multimodal resources which are often embedded in complex semiotic groups rather than distinctly separated.

## References

Androutsopoulos, J. (2006) 'Introduction: sociolinguistics and computer-mediated communication', *Journal of Sociolinguistics*, 10 (4), 419–38.
Barton, D. and Lee, C. (2013) *Language Online: Investigating Digital Texts and Practices*, London: Routledge.

boyd, d. and Ellison, N. (2007) 'Social network sites: definition, history, and scholarship', *Journal of Computer Mediated Communication*, 13 (1), available: http://jcmc. indiana.edu/vol13/issue1/boyd.ellison.html [accessed 26 April 2010].

*Britannica Homepage*, available: http://Britannica.co.uk/Britannica-editorial.asp [accessed 5 November 2013].

Chesney, T. (2006) 'An empirical examination of Wikipedia's credibility', *First Monday*, 11 (11), available: http://firstmonday.org/ojs/index.php/fm/article/view/ 1413/1331%3C/ [accessed 8 October 2013].

Couldry, N. (2010) *Media Consumption and Public Engagement: Beyond the Presumption of Attention*, Basingstoke: Palgrave.

Crystal, D. (2008) *Txting: The Gr8 Db8*, Oxford: Oxford University Press.

Fairclough, N. (1989) *Language and Power*, London: Longman.

Gibson, J. (1977) 'The theory of affordances', in Shaw, R. and Bransford, J., eds, *Perceiving, Acting, and Knowing: Toward an Ecological Psychology*, Hillsdale: Lawrence Erlbaum, 67–82.

Grossman, L. (2006) 'Person of the year: you', *Time Magazine*, 25 December, available: Time.com [accessed 26 November 2013].

Halliday, M.A.K. (1994) *Introduction to Functional Grammar*, 2nd edn, London: Edward Arnold.

Herring, S.C. (2007) 'A faceted classification scheme for computer-mediated discourse', *Language@Internet*, available: www.languageatInternet.org/articles/2007/ 761 [accessed 9 October 2013].

Hymes, D. (1974) *Foundations of Sociolinguistics: An Ethnographic Approach*, Philadelphia: University of Pennsylvania.

Kaplan, A. and Haenlein, M. (2009) 'Users of the world unite! The challenges and opportunities of social media', *Business Horizons*, 53, 59–68.

Marwick, A. (2010) *Status Update: Celebrity, Publicity and Self Branding in Web 2.0*. PhD thesis, New York University, available: www.tiara.org/blog/wp-content/ uploads/2010/09/marwick_dissertation_statusupdate.pdf [accessed 9 October 2013].

Myers, G. (2010) *The Language of Blogs and Wikis*, London: Continuum.

Oxley, M., Morgan, J.T., Zachry, M. and Hutchinson, B. (2010) '"What I know is … " Establishing credibility in Wikipedia talk pages', paper presented at WikiSym 10, 7–9 July, Gdansk, Poland, available: http://dub.washington.edu/djangosite/media/ papers/wikisym2010_submission_69.pdf [accessed 9 October 2013].

Rak, J. (2005) 'The digital queer: weblogs and Internet identity', *Biography*, 28 (1), 166–82.

Thornborrow, J. and Montgomery, M., eds (2010) *Discourse and Communication*, 4 (3). Special Issue: Personalisation in Broadcast News.

Turkle, S. (2011) *Alone Together: Why We Expect More from Technology*, New York: Basic Books.

Wesch, M. (2009) 'YouTube and you: experiences of self-awareness in the context collapse of the recording webcam', *Explorations in Media Ecology*, 8 (2), 19–34.

# Chapter 2

# What might a linguist say about social media?

## Outline of the chapter

In this chapter we cover:

- Social media as an object of study for linguists.
- A working definition of 'language'.
- Different levels and aspects of language which can be studied.
- The distinction between text and context.
- Emoticons as a language resource.

## Social media as an object of study for linguists

Although seemingly transparent, the term *language* needs to clarified, especially in relation to the study of multimodal social media texts. In this chapter, we review the place of language within a wider semiotic system that also involves image, sound and kinetic resources found typically in digital interaction. Much mainstream linguistic research has largely ignored social media to date. This may have something to do with social media being a relatively recent phenomenon and the relatively slow pace at which academic research moves through cycles of making new discoveries, attracting funding, and publication. Social media adoption was driven by younger users, and some scholars (e.g. Prensky 2001) argue that there is a distinction to be made between "digital natives", who grew up using social media and have never known a world without, and "digital immigrants", who adopted social media only as adults. We think this distinction is problematic for various reasons (see also White and Le Cornu (2011), who talk about a spectrum of users from "digital residents" to "digital visitors"). However, it is true that a linguist who is not an active user of social media (someone who is perhaps a "digital visitor") may struggle to see its relevance as a communication medium, and may thus not be inclined to consider it as a useful site for academic research. This kind of gradual awakening of interest in particular discourse communities has often occurred in the history of linguistics, for instance with regard to women's language, gay and lesbian language, youth language, or language in the workplace. Given the levels of Internet penetration and social media use in many societies, we feel that linguists ignore social media at their peril. And fortunately, building on earlier research in computer-mediated communication, the range of linguistic research which explores social media platforms is both rich and broad, including analysis of how elements of the language system are reconfigured in online contexts (such as variations in non-standard orthography and creative examples of word formation processes) and how the dynamics of inter-personal communication are managed. In this chapter, we provide a brief introduction to the key areas of linguistic work in social media.

## What is 'language'?

As we showed in the previous chapter, it is not easy to come up with a watertight definition of social media. Given how relatively new social media is in human societies, this may not be particularly surprising. It is more surprising that linguists, philosophers, biologists, psychologists and other scholars are still arguing about what exactly language is, especially given the commonly-held view that language is what defines us as human (Pinker 1994). It is not the purpose of this book to revisit this debate in any great depth, but we do need to arrive at a working definition of language, so that we can decide what exactly it is about language in social media that we are interested in researching. We therefore briefly outline two different ways of describing language, which are based on rather different assumptions about the nature of communication.

According to more traditional understandings of the role of language in communication:

1  Language is seen as a semiotic system, a system of signs used to encode meaning that senders intend to communicate to recipients.
2  The signs themselves may be abstract (such as the letter 'Q'), but take on conventional meanings over time, and are used in often highly structured ways to convey more complex meanings.
3  Meaning can be conveyed in spoken, written or signed (in the case of languages often used by deaf people) forms, or a combination of these. Each of these forms of communication develops conventions over time (e.g. spellings, accents), but there is considerable variation within each form.
4  Other kinds of signs (e.g. sounds, images, typographic elements, colours, body movements) are also used to communicate meaning, and cannot be entirely divorced from language. For instance, spoken language always involves sounds, and written language always involves particular letter shapes and colours, which may affect the way meaning is

communicated to a greater or lesser extent. All communication is there-fore multimodal, and different social media channels (see Chapter 1) make use of different modes to varying degrees (Kress and Van Leeuwen 2001).

More progressive understandings of the role of language in communication argue that:

1   Language is a way for individuals to interact with other individuals or groups.
2   Language is not an abstract system, but is always situated in a particular context. It can be seen as a set of practices that arises from commu-nicative needs in specific contexts and situations. Every bit of language has a purpose.
3   Linguistic practices are used alongside non-linguistic practices to communicate meaning.
4   Language acquires meaning only in and through its context. This explains how the same words (e.g. the phrase "oh really") can have many different meanings, depending on what has just happened or been said, the relationship between the interlocutors, the intonation used, and so on.
5   Language is used to 'perform' identity, and particular ways of using language (e.g. orthographic conventions in instant messaging) can be used to signal orientation towards shared norms and values.
6   Almost all uses of language are linked with past and future uses of language. For instance, this may happen through direct quoting (e.g. telling a friend about something you read in the news) or through anticipating future arguments against what you are saying (e.g. "Some people will call me crazy, but ... "). Some scholars (Bakhtin 1986) go as far as to argue that no utterance is ever truly original, because it is always influenced by what has come before.

Each of these approaches is to a varying degree the basis for much of the research we cite in this book. The notion that communication packages and sends little nuggets of information between participants seems at first to sit rather well alongside the technological affordances of social media. For example, when we chat on Skype or other forms of instant messaging service, we type our message, hit 'send', and then it pops up on the receiver's screen. And for some types of analysis, this kind of more decontextualised understanding of language which isolates just the messages which are sent and received is necessary. For instance, when counting tweets for automated quantitative analysis, we need to treat each tweet as a separate instance, e.g. to make claims about how many tweets are in a given language, or how frequent taboo words are in YouTube comments, or we couldn't possibly deal with huge volumes of data (see Chapters 8 and 9). However, if we were to look at a small subsample of these tweets or YouTube comments one by one and analyse them in detail, we would quickly realise the importance of context (such as the time at which the post was published), and the relationship of each tweet or comment to other tweets and comments (those which come before or after, or how they are addressed and responded to by particular users), or even to texts on other platforms (such as linked material or memes which circulate across sites).

Recent changes coming from sociolinguistics in how to conceptualise language have important implications for the study of social media. Basic concepts including the notion that there are stable, discrete systems that can each be described as 'a language' are being called into question. There has been a move away from the idea of there being distinct languages and distinct varieties, even to the extent of questioning whether language can be separated into distinct 'languages', such as 'English', 'Spanish' and 'Chinese'. The boundaries between languages are not clear; they are fuzzy and there are overlaps. Also, there are many different aspects to a language which people can draw upon. In social media, the multifaceted nature of what might count as one language variety becomes particularly blurred, in part because there is a great deal of mixing of different semiotic resources. Meaning making is done partly through the verbal contributions of language, with many aspects of language acting as resources. As well as styles and registers (indicated through words or grammatical choices), potential resources include choices of script, punctuation and font, all of which we can change when we read and when we write. These become resources for the user to express meaning. In social media, we find examples of when one language is written in the script of another, such as Greeklish, the Greek language being written in a Latin script. Some of the visual resources in particular cannot be classified as belonging to one language rather than another. For example, emoticons can be used across multiple language varieties (of course with a range of different potential meanings): it makes no sense to say that a 'smiley' face is in English, Greek or Thai. Whilst there are Asian emoticons such as ^_^ which contrast with those more typically found in Western contexts such as :-) they do not 'belong' to particular languages in any strong sense. So from the researcher's point of view, it can be important to be clear about what different aspects of the communication resources are being studied, and sensitive to the creative and multilayered manner in which linguistic resources can be combined by different participants when they interact with others.

Alongside this, there has been a movement from seeing language as a 'thing' (a product which can be isolated and studied) to seeing it as an activity (a process, which is often harder to capture and pin down). As a result, researchers are developing new ways of conceptualising language. Some researchers talk in terms of 'languaging', turning the noun 'language' into a verb. The word 'languaging' has been used to capture this idea of there being many different resources to draw upon (see Garcia 2009). Others have used the idea of 'polylanguaging' (Jørgensen *et al.* 2011) which refers to the ways in which users simultaneously draw upon features associated with different languages – this can happen even when they know very little of these languages. Choosing a style from one language and using it in another has been referred to as 'crossing' (Rampton 1995). Another term, 'translingualism' (Canagarajah 2012, 2013), with the idea that it is the practices which cross languages, fits well with a literacy studies approach with its focus on practices. Links are also made back to Bakhtin's (1981) work on 'heteroglossia'. These notions highlight the ways in which resources from different language varieties and registers can intermingle, often so closely that it is either difficult or inappropriate to separate out one variety from another, or where so doing would seem to be at odds with the ways in which the participants are using language to communicate with others. Examples of this approach being applied to social media include Leppä-nen's (2012) studies of young people's interactions around creating and using fan-fiction and Androutsopoulos's (2011) work on profile pages on various sites.

Some researchers have focused on the changing view from clearly defined and separable language varieties around the notion of "superdiversity", arguing that traditional notions of diversity in sociolinguistics do not work in the contemporary world (Blommaert and Rampton 2011). There is so much travel and movement and so many forms of communication and interaction that traditional notions of 'diversity' are no longer adequate to describe contemporary life. Superdiversity is closely related to changes in communications media and it means that long-held notions of diversity and links to language, migration and identity, at least in the United Kingdom and similar countries, are difficult to sustain, especially in the face of the complex and creative ways in which participants communicate in their online activities. One important aspect for someone doing research on social media is the lack of stability in these practices: in many ways, there is constant change online. Texts are no longer thought of as fixed objects with clear boundaries but can be constantly changing, and some of the standard communicative genres (such as 'conversation') become less stable as they are reconfigured in social media contexts. All these ideas about the fluid and potentially blurred nature of what counts as 'language', 'varieties' and 'languaging', are still being developed. This can make the search for clear definitions and the boundaries of 'language use' and 'language practices' open to discussion as we seek to take into account the fluid, mobile use of language in social media contexts. In the following section, we explain how more traditional and more recent approaches to the analysis of 'language' set out the different objects of interest that can be analysed in research of this kind.

### *What do we look at when we analyse language?*

Language can be analysed at different levels. These are sometimes cate-gorised in slightly different ways, and they partially overlap, but some of the common units of analysis you will find referred to in this book are:

- Linguistic practices: what people do with language, the regular behaviours that develop within particular communities, and the ways in which language is used to perform particular identities (for instance, linguists might analyse how a forum community uses narratives/stories to enhance group cohesion, or how Facebook friends code-switch between different languages to signal their linguistic identities).
- Texts/utterances: collections of words, clauses and sentences arranged deliberately in a structure with a clear communicative function. When a certain type of text becomes easily recognisable, this is often referred to as a genre, e.g. a comment thread on a newspaper site. This level of language is also sometimes referred to as discourse (see Chapter 5).
- Clauses and sentences: strings of words arranged in a structure, often described as syntax or grammar.
- Lexemes or words: units of meaning consisting of one or more morphemes, like *eggs*.
- Morphemes: the smallest units of meaning, e.g. *egg*, which calls up a certain concept in our minds, or '-s' to indicate plurality.
- Phonemes: individual sounds/signs that make up spoken or signed words; and graphemes, e.g. letters or characters in writing.

While the features described above are features of language (as a semiotic system or a set of practices), researchers also talk about *a* language, or languages (plural), or particular language varieties, despite the difficulties in defining and delimiting those we discuss above. From this more traditional perspective on language, users of different languages and varieties will display regular patterns of usage at these different levels, so that for instance the graphemes used to write down in Mandarin Chinese differ from those used for Romanian, or certain syntactic features are less frequent in American English than in British English (present perfect verb forms, for instance). Users in many social media contexts code-switch using several different languages or varieties in the course of an interaction, or style-shift, for instance using formal and less formal language in different parts of a text. And varieties are rarely static or monolithic – they contain a lot of variation within them (for instance, a "New York accent" will differ slightly from speaker to speaker, but will still be recognisable as such by people who have heard a number of New Yorkers speaking before) and they also change over time. Finally, it is also important to pay attention to what people say about language use in social media, and how they say it.

The study of metalanguage is becoming increasingly important (Barton and Lee 2013).

These seemingly rather abstract considerations are important, because they help us define what aspects of language in social media we are able to research, and moreover what elements it is worthwhile and interesting to research.

---

**Points for reflection**

What aspects of 'language' or 'languaging' are you interested in researching?

What are the advantages or disadvantages of focusing a research project on a micro-level language feature?

How might the study of language practices either contrast with or incorporate the study of micro-level language features?

---

## Text and context

Whether linguists are interested exclusively in the more micro-level features described above or more broadly in language practices, they need to collect their data systematically from social media texts. However, the relationship between different forms of communication within social media can sometimes make it hard to identify the boundaries of the textual units you need to collect. This relates particularly to another pair of key terms which are often negotiated and renegotiated in linguistics: *text* and *context*. Deciding what counts as the text is not always straightforward: is it just the words typed into a template box, or are the information, layout and icons in the template also important? Do you need to consider material appended to your primary textual unit, such as material that might be linked to from a blog or update, or the comments below an online news article? What criteria might you apply to decide whether this additional material is necessary (or not)? What might analysing the fragment without the full contextual material miss? Can the fragment make sense on its own, or does its meaning depend on the linked context? Deciding on what counts as your textual unit is important for many reasons. First, this decision will guide what material you might gather for a research project in the first place and the ethical considerations you might need to address (see Chapter 4). Second, your choice of textual unit will be linked closely to the ways you choose to analyse that material, what methods might be practical or appropriate (see Chapter 3). There is no hard and fast rule about what kinds of unit will work best for analysing language use: different researchers choose different units depending on their interests. But drawing your boundaries around a particular kind of text means that you need also to consider what lies beyond that unit: where and how that text is situated within particular contexts.

Early linguists sometimes ignored context entirely (see Malinowski 1923 for an early critique of this). But since then, many of the more socially oriented approaches to language use have suggested that context is extremely important, even if it is hard to work out exactly what counts as "context" and where it begins and ends (Duranti and Goodwin 1992). Just as researchers have treated 'language' as a dynamic process, so context is also sometimes thought of as multilayered and fluid. From the earliest studies of CMC onwards, linguistic and sociological researchers have repeatedly drawn attention to the contextual factors that might be important when interpreting data (Baym 1995; Herring 2004a and 2004b; Thurlow *et al.* 2004; Jones and Norris 2005; Jones and Hafner 2012). The contextual factors identified in other forms of CMC which remain important for analysing the language in social media sites include:

- Participants: the people who take part in the interaction and their relationship to others in the group.
- Imagined context: the projected contexts created cognitively by participants on the basis of their world knowledge and the cues provided in CMC. This can include the projected audience that the participant addresses and the community they assume they are part of.
- Extra-situational context: the offline social practices in which the partici- pants are involved, which might be shaped by cultural values relating to demographic factors such as age, gender, ethnic or national identity and to specific values relating to their involvement in particular communities (such as friendship groups, educational cohorts, hobby or interest groups, members of the same workplace, fan communities and so on).
- Behavioural context: the physical situation in which the participants interact via social media (e.g. where and when the social media interaction takes place, what devices are used and so on).
- Textual context: sometimes referred to as *co-text*, the textual context can include the surrounding interactions (the text published in preceding and subsequent posts or comments); semi-automated information such as timestamps, location-based information like 'check ins'; screen layout and resources.
- Generic context: the social media site in which the communication takes place including the site's stated purpose, rules and norms for conduct. These are often stated explicitly (such as Wikipedia's core content policies, or can emerge from the participants' activities which recognise certain forms of interaction as appropriate or not).

The different aspects of contextual information can be important depending on the kind of research project you design. For instance, someone studying the use of non-standard orthography (spelling) in newspaper websites would be able to produce much richer findings if the data was divided into articles and user comments – this would allow a comparison between the two types of data within a single newspaper, which could be extended in turn to comparison language use across different newspapers. How these contextual factors are recorded, described and used in different kinds of linguistic projects can also vary considerably. In Chapter 5, we return to the role of extra-situational context when interpreting what might count as 'discourse' for discourse analysis, and the role played by textual context when interpreting what might count as a 'turn' in a 'conversation' and how imagined contexts can shape the participants' sense of their audience. In Chapters 6 and 7, we describe how the layers of cultural, generic and behavioural contexts which shape the literacy practices can be used in research projects. In Chapters 8 and 9, we explain how features found in the extra-situational, textual and generic contexts can be described as different kinds of variables and used in quantitative projects.

Sometimes, especially in work on digital media, the distinction between texts and context is reframed as the distinction between 'data' versus 'metadata'. The metadata of a newspaper article might thus include information which crosses between different aspects of the contextual picture in which a particular text is situated, such as the text's author, date and time of publication, URL, name of the newspaper, type of article (e.g. editorial, feature, etc.), whereas the data will be the words in the article itself (the text). Fortunately, this matches the way texts on the Internet are produced rather well – authors use templates or content management systems to upload texts, and the information is recorded in databases that separate out these different aspects of the text. For some social media sites, much of this metadata is freely downloadable, though it is always important to consider the ethical implications of using data (which are further discussed in Chapter 4). And for some linguistic investigations, particularly those employing quantitative methods (Chapters 8 and 9), this metadata may be detailed enough to help researchers answer questions about language with the use of semi-automated search tools. In some kinds of research projects, it may not be practical to annotate the additional contextual information as a form of metadata if large numbers of texts are involved. However, for research employing ethnographic (Chapters 6 and 7) or qualitative (Chapter 5) methods, the pre-existing metadata automatically appended to particular texts may not be sufficient to allow you to answer your research questions, and might need to be augmented with further contextual material collected from participant observation, interviews, manual coding or other methods.

The importance (and difficulty) of capturing the textual context of YouTube interactions is described by Stephen Pihlaja in his case study.

## Box 2.1 The development of 'drama' in YouTube discourse

### Stephen Pihlaja

My project aimed to understand how and why YouTube 'drama' (i.e. antagonistic debate) between users developed. Following a two-year observation of about 20–25 users in a YouTube community of practice discussing Christianity and atheism, I identified and transcribed 20 video 'pages' (including talk from videos and text comments) from an incidence of 'drama'. I then analysed the use of metaphors in the videos in an attempt to understand and analyse how the drama developed over time. By looking very carefully at how metaphors developed in the disagreements among users, I could describe how users saw the social world and how differences in expectations about right and wrong behaviour led to drama developing for months at a time.

The key challenge for me was users posting, and then taking down, videos. Whenever drama occurred, a rich dataset would appear and then immediately disappear when users took down their most offensive videos and reposted more diplomatic videos. My dataset was full of interesting holes with users talking about videos that had been posted and taken down, creating a whole new sort of narrative about the past interactions they had. The more I observed the community, the more I realised it would be incredibly difficult, if not impossible, to recover a whole series of videos in any given episode of drama.

To solve this, my analysis then included recovering what may or may not have happened, based on the very biased reporting of different users. I treated the drama as arguments and stories which were told and retold, changing as different users weighed in and told their version of events. Instead of trying to understand what happened in any given drama episode, my analysis became about how people position themselves within a community, using drama as a tool to talk about the social world. The project became less about recovering any 'truth', but instead, users' perception of the truth.

Although YouTube videos are copyrighted content, subject to the rules and laws of copyright, when videos are taken down, researchers have a difficult choice to make about how to treat the content. They can either download the videos using software which contravenes the YouTube Terms of Service or only do analysis of videos which are online at the time a researcher is transcribing them. I chose to transcribe the videos and comments while they were online, leading me to look at videos which were more stable and had been online for more than a year when I came to do my analysis. Although I did miss out on some of the more controversial videos which had been taken down, it did ensure that the videos would remain up while I was transcribing and analysing them.

If you want to analyse YouTube drama, you have to spend some time 'in the field', observing users over time, before you can do any analysis. YouTube channels are completely maintained by users and they control what content is available at what time. As disagreements and fights between users stretch on for years and years, you need to know the history of any interaction to analyse why users are speaking or acting in a particular way at a particular time.

#advice: Context, context, context: unless you know everything you can about the context, you can't do analysis.

---

**Points for reflection**

What aspects of context did Pihlaja include in his case study?

What can you learn from the difficulties he encountered in collecting his materials?

Where would you place his approach within a spectrum of research which focused on micro-level language features and language practices?

---

## Emoticons: language resource or 'social media stereotype'?

Much of the early research into computer-mediated communication was exclusively concerned with written language, because this was the only mode in which language could initially be used on the early Internet. Nevertheless, some groups of users circumvented these limitations by using the affordances available to them, particularly by combining punctuation marks in quite creative ways to indicate tone of voice or other kinds of meaning not easily reduced to words alone. These later came to be called emoticons, such as :-) or ;) and are often seen as the epitome of CMC language including text messages (Crystal 2008) and email (Baron 2000). Some other typical orthographic features of written computer-mediated communication in English identified by Barton and Lee (2013, p.5) are:

- acronyms and initialisms (e.g. GTG for *got to go*, LOL for *laugh out loud*);
- word reductions (e.g. *gd* for *good*; *hv* for *have*);
- letter/number homophones (e.g. U for *you* and 2 for *to*);

- stylised spelling (e.g. I'm sooooooooooo happy!);
- unconventional/stylised punctuation (e.g. '!!!!!!!!!!!!!', '.........').

These are the kinds of features that tended to interest early computer-mediated communication researchers, and continue to prove of interest, for example, tracing how these resources might be used by different groups of participants (Herring and Zelenkauskaite 2009), or the different meanings that emerge from different emoticons in use (Dresner and Herring 2012). The interest in emoticons and in other visual resources (like hashtags) is no doubt at least in part because they are so visibly different from written language as used in other contexts, such as print media, formal education or religion. But there are a number of problems with focusing only on these features when looking at computer-mediated communication. First, many written texts found on the Internet do not include these features at all. This is because many of the non-social media texts consist of more formal genres such as government reports, academic journal articles, news reports, informative websites about institutions, and so on. These are often similar or even identical to printed versions of the same texts. Second, even in social media texts, there are large differences between particular communities of users and platforms. Some forums, for instance, may develop norms that lead to strong discouragement of some of the features identified above (even to the extent that language use is 'policed' by zealous protectors of these norms, and transgressors are censured or even barred from the forums as Pedersen and Smithson (2013) describe in relation to the parenting forum Mumsnet). Other groups may embrace and even encourage creative and playful orthographies, or may develop norms that involve deliberate and strongly marked differences to formal written standards (such as Leet speak, see Blashki and Nichol 2005). And third, some of these features pre-date the Internet by a considerable margin. In English, spelling even in formal genres was rather variable until around the eighteenth century. The affordances of technologies like the telegram and postcards led to abbreviations and word reductions. And finally, poetry and other literary genres often used playful orthography as a stylistic element.

Thus while emoticons are a good example of a resource which helps expand our notion of what might count as 'language', it is by no means synonymous with "Internet language" as a whole, nor are they the only aspect of language in social media that we deal with in this book. The widespread stereotypes associated with Internet language are, however, of great interest (see for example Crystal 2011), as is the history of research into different linguistic features and their relationship with social media. Asta Zelenkauskaite's case study illustrates how the contextualised analysis of non-standard orthography continues to be of interest, and how the analysis can draw on multiple levels of context in order to interpret the specific feature that the researchers were interested in.

## Box 2.2 Standardness (non)bias: Facebook and SMS message filtering by a radio TV station

### Asta Zelenkauskaite

Radio and TV not only produce their content, they strive to engage their audiences through active participation. In addition to traditional call-in participation, which has been popular for several decades in various media genres, among which radio talk shows represent the exemplar case, social media have become an additional back channel that serves to establish a two-way interaction with listeners. Due to programming space and time constraints, not all messages get selected for broadcast.

Given that social media are notorious for non-standard typography, contrasting with standard variety of a given language, the question that was driving my research regarded the levels of acceptance/rejection of messages using non-standard typography by the radio station during their filtering process. In other words, were messages posted to the Facebook group for the radio station which included non-standard typography less likely to be broadcast, compared to the ones that do not bear non-standard typography? This question was particularly pertinent considering that my case study – the Italian radio station RTL 102.5 – broadcasts viewer/listener content on a televised version, in addition to social media outlets. Given that the RTL 102.5 content is produced by professionals, and the programming is based on a micromanaged scheduling, it would seem possible to predict that non-standard typography would be disfavoured.

The linguistic feature I explored was typography, which I contrasted in terms of standardness. Given that non-standard typography influences length, messages were also coded for structural features such as length. For the analysis, broadcast and non-broadcast messages were compared for standardness, by ideally comparing the received and broadcast contents. Non-standard categories including emoticons were extracted from the wall posts, particularly pertinent to Italian linguistic variety (e.g. k for Italian ch; cn for con (with), etc.). The variables were coded if present.

Data were collected from the Facebook wall of RTL 102.5 and recordings of the programme made for a composite week from 1 January 2011 to 30 April 2011. A total of 308,339 SMS messages were analysed. The results were contrary to those expected: RTL 102.5 did include non-standard typography elements in their programming, even if only 33 per cent of messages were included in the programming.

Challenges related to this research were multifold. First, they reside in the data collection and sampling of multimodal data. Messages had to be collected from multiple sources – TV, Facebook wall and the RTL 102.5 website which contained SMS messages. Second, even if all datapoints were collected in an automated way, only a part of recordings could be processed due to time and space constraints. Third, it was necessary to make decisions about the number of categories to be included.

Given that this study was conducted on a specific case, it was really helpful to talk to various stakeholders on RTL 102.5 who provided insights about their practices – the insider sociotechnical context – as well as giving me the basis to cross-check the sample I collected. Given that automated data analysis is challenging, I benefited from collaboration with computer science colleagues who helped me with automated data collection and parsing. Even if challenging, multimodal data analysis is rewarding because it allows for data triangulation and a better understanding on a given phenomenon – which in my case study was filtering processing practices of various data sources.

#advice: Contextualise your case, talk to key actors, seek skill-based collaboration, and buy a new hard drive to store and back-up your data.

## (Re)configuring language: social media as spoken or written?

What many of the studies mentioned in this chapter, particularly the earlier ones, have in common is an emphasis on the differences between patterns of language use in social media contexts and patterns of language use in other contexts. Each new social media platform seems to generate descriptions of how language is used, and how language use has changed or is changing as a result of particular technologies and affordances. However, Herring (2004a, p.33) warns against the dangers of following the latest fads in technology:

> CMC researchers would do well to take a step back from the parade of passing technologies and consider more deeply the question of what determines people's use of mediated communication.

She further argues that technological innovation is mostly superficial in computer-mediated communication. For instance, blogs are quite similar to earlier personal websites, and Facebook chat is (at the time of writing) quite similar to earlier instant messaging platforms like IRC. A further focus of earlier work on computer-mediated communication, which has to a large extent carried over into both scholarly and public perceptions of language use in social media, is the distinction between spoken, written and

*Table 2.1* Adapted from Herring's (2013) "Four levels of CMDA" and "Multimodal communication as an additional level of CMDA"

| | *Issues* | *Phenomena* | *Methods* |
|---|---|---|---|
| **Structure** | Orality, formality, complexity, efficiency, expressivity, genre characteristics, etc. | Typography, orthography, morphology, syntax, discourse schemata, formatting conventions, etc. | Structural/ descriptive linguistics, text analysis, stylistics |
| **Meaning** | What is intended, what is communicated, what is accomplished | Meaning of words, utterances (speech acts), exchanges, etc. | Semantics, pragmatics |
| **Interaction** | Interactivity, timing, coherence, repair, interaction as co-constructed, etc. ethnomethodology | Turns, sequences, exchanges, threads, etc. | Conversation analysis |
| **Social behaviour** | Social dynamics, power, influence, identity, community, cultural differences, etc. | Linguistic expressions of status, conflict, negotiation, face- management, play; discourse styles/lects, etc. | Interactional sociolinguistics, critical discourse analysis, ethnography of communication |
| **Participation** | Affordances, norms of the community of practice | Participation patterns over time | Statistical analysis, ethnography |
| **Multimodal communication** | Mode effects, cross-mode coherence, reference and address management, generation and spread of graphical meaning units, media coactivity, etc. | Mode choice, text-in-image, image quotes, spatial and temporal positionality and deixis, animation, etc. | Social semiotics, visual content analysis |

"in-between" language use, as suggested by Crystal's (2004) term "netspeak" for written language in digital contexts. Linguistic research has often sought to define language use in digital contexts with reference to earlier spoken or written genres, such as conversations compared with instant messaging, or letters compared with emails (Baron 2000). However, initially these classifications rested on very monolithic assumptions about spoken and written texts, for instance that the former were generally informal, and the latter formal. There are of course many examples of more formal spoken texts (such as graduation speeches at universities) or more informal non-digital written texts (such as postcards).

The focus on differences was thus a good starting point, but more recent approaches (Barton and Lee 2013) have emphasised instead the many and varied linguistic practices within particular social media contexts and the way people use language to construct and negotiate their identities. One particularly influential approach has been Susan Herring's computer-mediated discourse analysis. The differences between discourse analysis and other forms of linguistic analysis are further discussed in Chapter 5, but actually Herring's approach is rather broader than the inclusion of 'discourse analysis' in her label suggests. Table 2.1 shows the four different domains of language (and two additional domains), which relate to the levels described above and can be studied by linguists.

Crucially for our purposes, Herring (2004b, p.342) does not suggest that every analysis should incorporate all these domains, or that there is a single method that is always suited to studying a particular domain. Rather, she argues that computer-mediated discourse analysis,

> as an approach to researching online behavior provides a methodological toolkit and a set of theoretical lenses through which to make observations and interpret the results of empirical analysis.

Table 2.2 includes examples of how the different language issues and phenomena itemised in Herring's table have been analysed in different social media sites. Of course, this list is not exhaustive, but gives an overview of the different sorts of linguistic and other semiotic features analysed and platforms from which data are drawn.

The range of sites, linguistic phenomena and language practices covered in Table 2.2 indicate the rich and diverse range of research that has begun

*Table 2.2* A selected summary of linguistic studies which examine social media sites

| Author(s) and date | Feature(s) analysed | Main platform(s) studied |
| --- | --- | --- |
| Herring (2004b) | Computer-mediated discourse | Forums, instant messaging |
| Crystal (2006) | Emoticons, orthography, turntaking | Email, chat groups, virtual worlds, websites |
| Androutsopoulos (2011, 2013) | Self-presentation, identity, variation | YouTube, Facebook |
| Myers (2010) | Stance, argumentation | Blogs, Wikipedia |
| Page (2012) | Narrative | Facebook, podcasts, YouTube |
| Seargeant *et al.* (2012) | Codeswitching | Facebook |
| Zappavigna (2012) | Hashtags, lexical choice | Twitter |
| Barton and Lee (2013) | Language choice, stance-taking, multimodality | Facebook, Flickr, instant messaging |

to emerge in these contexts. Although many of these studies consider verbal forms of language as the primary feature for analysis (for example, word choice, register, evaluative forms) they also include multimodal resources (such as gesture and image) used in communication, and are interested in both language units that are recognised from established fields of language study (word formation processes, turn-taking, politeness forms) and language practices and more recent approaches to 'languaging' and creative use of multilingual variation. Each study also varies in the kinds of questions it seeks to address and in the methods of analysis that are used. These can serve as useful models which illustrate the variety of research designs which can help examine the language used in social media contexts, and which is the topic of our next chapter.

# References

Androutsopoulos, J. (2011) 'From variation to heteroglossia in the study of computer-mediated discourse', in Thurlow, C. and Mroczek, K., eds, *Digital Discourse: Language in the New Media*, London: Oxford University Press, 277–98.

Androutsopoulos, J. (2013) 'Networked multilingualism: some language practices on Facebook and their implications', *International Journal of Bilingualism*, published online 11 June 2013.

Bakhtin, M. (1981) *The Dialogic Imagination: Four Essays*, Austin: University of Texas Press.

Bakhtin, M. (1986) *Speech Genres and Other Late Essays*, Austin: University of Texas Press.

Baron, N.S. (2000) *Alphabet to Email: How Written English Evolved and Where it's Heading*, New York: Routledge.

Barton, D. and Lee, C. (2013) *Language Online: Investigating Digital Texts and Practices*, London: Routledge.

Baym, N.K. (1995) 'The performance of humor in computer-mediated communication', *Journal of Computer-Mediated Communication*, 1 (2), available: http://onlinelibrary.wiley.com/doi/10.1111/j.1083–6101.1995.tb00327.x/full [accessed 23 November 2013].

Blashki, K. and Nichol, S. (2005) 'Game geek's goss: linguistic creativity in young males within an online university forum (94/\\ 3 933k'5 9055oneone)', *Australian Journal of Emerging Technologies and Society*, 3 (2), 71–80.

Blommaert, J. and Rampton, B. (2011) 'Language and superdiversity: a position paper', *Working Papers in Urban Language and Literacies 70*.

Canagarajah, S., ed. (2012) *Literacy as Translingual Practice*, London: Routledge.

Canagarajah, S. (2013) *Translingual Practice: Global Englishes and Cosmopolitan Relations*, New York: Routledge.

Crystal, D. (2004) *A Glossary of Netspeak and Textspeak*, Edinburgh: Edinburgh University Press.

Crystal, D. (2006) *Language and the Internet*, Cambridge: Cambridge University Press.

Crystal, D. (2008) *Txtng: The gr8 db8*, Oxford: Oxford University Press.

Crystal, D. (2011) *Internet Linguistics: A Student Guide*, London: Routledge.

Dresner, E. and Herring, S.C. (2012) 'Emoticons and illocutionary force', in Riesenfel, D. and Scarafile, G., eds, *Philosophical Dialogue: Writings in Honor of Marcelo Dascal*, London: College Publication, 59–70.

Duranti, A. and Goodwin, C. (1992) *Rethinking Context: Language as an Interactive Phenomenon*, Cambridge: Cambridge University Press.

Garcia, O. (2009) *Bilingual Education in the 21st Century: A Global Perspective*, Oxford: Wiley.

Herring, S.C. (2004a) 'Slouching toward the ordinary: current trends in computer-mediated communication', *New Media and Society*, 6 (1), 26–36.

Herring, S.C. (2004b) 'Computer-mediated discourse analysis: an approach to researching online behavior', in Barab, S.A., Kling, R. and Gray, J.H., eds, *Designing for Virtual Communities in the Service of Learning*, New York: Cambridge University Press, 338–76.

Herring, S.C. (2013) 'Discourse in Web 2.0: familiar, reconfigured, emergent', in Tannen, D. and Trester, A.M., eds, *Discourse 2.0: Language and New Media*, Washington, DC: Georgetown University Press, 1–25.

Herring, S.C. and Zelenkauskaite, A. (2009) 'Symbolic capital in a virtual heterosexual market abbreviation and insertion in Italian iTV SMS', *Written Communication*, 26 (1), 5–31.

Jones, R.H. and Hafner, C. (2012) *Understanding Digital Literacies: A Practical Introduction*, London: Routledge.

Jones, R.H. and Norris, S. (2005) *Discourse in Action: Introducing Mediated Discourse Analysis*, London: Routledge.

Jørgensen, J., Karrebæk, M.S., Madsen, L.M. and Møller, J.S. (2011) 'Polylanguaging in superdiversity', *Diversities*, 13 (2). Available: www.unesco.org/shs/diversities/vol13/issue2/art2 [accessed 23 November 2013].

Kress, G. and Van Leeuwen, T. (2001) *Multimodal Discourse: The Modes and Media of Contemporary Communication*, London: Bloomsbury.

Leppänen, S. (2012) 'Language choice and linguistic heteroglossia in web writing', in Sebba, M., Mahootian, S. and Jonsson, C., eds, *Language Mixing and Code-switching in Writing: Approaches to Mixed-language Written Discourse*, London: Routledge, 233–54.

Malinowski, B. (1923) 'The problem of meaning in primitive languages', in Ogden, C.K. and Richards, I.A., eds, *The Meaning of Meaning*, London: Routledge and Kegan Paul, 296–336.

Myers, G. (2010) *The Discourse of Blogs and Wikis*, London: Continuum.

Page, R. (2012) *Stories and Social Media: Identities and Interaction*, London: Routledge.

Pedersen, S. and Smithson, J. (2013) 'Mothers with attitude—how the Mumsnet parenting forum offers space for new forms of femininity to emerge online', *Women's Studies International Forum*, 38, 97–106.

Pinker, S. (1994) *The Language Instinct*, New York: William Morrow and Company.

Prensky, M. (2001) 'Digital natives, digital immigrants', *On the Horizon*, 9 (5), available: www.marcprensky.com/writing/Prensky%20-%20Digital%20Natives,%20Digital%20Immigrants%20-%20Part1.pdf [accessed 26 November 2013].

Rampton, B. (1995) *Crossing: Language and Ethnicity among Adolescents*, London and New York: Longman.

Seargeant, P., Tagg, C. and Ngam Pramuan, W. (2012) 'Language choice and addressivity strategies in Thai-English social network interactions', *Journal of Sociolinguistics*, 16 (4), 510–31.

Thurlow, C., Lengel, L. and Tomic, A. (2004) *Computer-mediated Communication*, London: Sage.

White, D. and Le Cornu, A. (2011) 'Visitors and residents: a new typology for online engagement', *First Monday*, 16 (9), available: http://firstmonday.org/article/view/3171/3049 [accessed 26 November 2013].

Zappavigna, M. (2012) *The Discourse of Twitter and Social Media*, London: Continuum.

# Chapter 3

# What does it mean to research?

## Outline of the chapter

In this chapter we cover:

- The basic principles that underpin research design.
- Differences in research across academic disciplines.
- Methodology.
- First steps in the research process.

## Research: basic principles

Research means investigating a particular phenomenon – here the language used in social media contexts – in order to bring new knowledge to light. The fast-changing, seemingly ever-increasing forms of communication that take place via social media sites provide attractive source material for researchers: there is often something new to be observed about how language is used in these contexts, often available to researchers in various forms that can be gathered relatively easily. But while our experience working in higher education institutions has been that students at all levels and across a number of disciplines find social media an exciting source of material to study, they are not always well equipped to carry out research projects that make use of this material. On the one hand, research is an exciting activity – a chance to make discoveries about how people take up the affordances of social media when they communicate with each other – but on the other hand, acquiring the skills needed to undertake 'research' can seem overwhelming, especially given the highly varied ways in which both language and social media can be investigated.

A core principle is that research should involve systematic inquiry. There is a difference between identifying that a topic or phenomenon is interesting and designing a research project about that topic or phenomenon. For example, noticing that a hashtag in Twitter has begun to be used in a humorous or creative way is not the same as conducting research about that hashtag. Of course, there are many ways in which the research about the hashtag could proceed. Research can be descriptive. For example, the project might observe the patterns of distribution as the hashtag was taken up across messages in Twitter, how long the hashtag remained in use, or categorise messages according to the lexical and grammatical contexts in which the hashtag occurred. The research might be explanatory, seeking to understand why hashtags become popular, or how they function for particular groups of users (say as marking social identities for young people, political activists, viewers of a television show or so on). Research might be experimental, where a researcher creates a hashtag and observes its effect on pre-selected participants, or where participants might be asked to read messages with and without hashtags in controlled conditions (such as a research laboratory). As all these examples suggest, the kind of research that this book is interested in is primarily empirical: that is, it involves researchers developing their ideas in relation to evidence of some kind, rather than in a purely conceptual fashion.

Research requires careful planning, and includes an iterative process of deciding on a project's aims and question(s) and then the most appropriate means of addressing those aims and questions. The planning process can take time, and involve making decisions which are then revisited, revised or sometimes rejected. For example, the researcher might want to start with broad research questions and then refine them, carry out a pilot study to test if the project is viable, discover that the data they collected is not as rich as they first thought and need to collect more, or conversely find that only a smaller subset of examples from the data are needed for analysis. There are many excellent guides to research methods for students of linguistics. Some cover a range of methods (Litosseliti 2010), while others are rooted in particular research traditions (see Dornyei 2007; Paltridge and Phakiti 2010), and guides for designing projects which consider online materials from different perspectives, including the social sciences (Hewsen et al. 2002; Markham and Baym 2009). In many respects, our book should be regarded as complementary to these existing resources. We share with them a common interest in research methods, but bring together a specific focus on linguistics (the study of language and its use) and a specific type of online interaction (those taking place in social media). At certain points, readers with particular emphases in their projects may find it helpful to turn to the longer guides for detail on particular aspects of the methods they might need to tackle a particular stage in their intended project. But at the outset it is helpful to set out the progressive stages involved in the research process and think about how and why these might be shaped by the challenges of studying the language of social media.

This book covers a wide range of approaches to researching social media. Although the types of research can be varied and they can be rooted in different philosophical positions, the research process usually contains the same elements, which are summarised in the following list:

- identify an area of interest;
- define the aims of the research;
- formulate research questions;
- select an appropriate methodology/approach;
- select and gather data;
- analyse the data;
- interpret results and draw conclusions;
- present the research.

Research might begin with identifying a key topic that will form the focus of the investigation, but the next stage is to formulate a question about that topic, or to identify a particular problem which the research intends to solve. Returning to our example of research about hashtags, the difference between the first two stages can be illustrated by a researcher who might describe their interests: "I want to do a project about hashtags used on Twitter", and a researcher who has identified a question about hashtags that they want to answer, such as: "How do hashtags influence readers' eye movements?" or "How do companies and celebrities use hashtags?" or "What kinds of sentiment are expressed in tweets with hashtags related to political events?" Describing your interests in social media is not a bad thing, and each of us has different ways of answering the question, "What is your research about?"

> *Ruth*: Often I begin by responding that I am interested in how people tell stories about themselves in social media, and how the language people use on social media sites can differ.
> *David*: Similarly, when I am asked the same question, I talk about my interest in how people make sense of the Internet and how they use language to get things done in new ways.
> *Michele*: My response to this question is usually that I am interested in how people negotiate values and enact interpersonal bonds with social media. I then go on to explain how crucial it is to look at the role of language in social bonding and begin to describe how my work currently focuses on this concern in relation to micro-blogging.
> *Johnny*: I am interested in how ordinary people use social media to engage in politics, and how their use of language plays a role in negotiating differences in power and other aspects of identity.

As our responses indicate, we have different research interests. We have investigated different kinds of social media sites and different kinds of language use and practices, using a range of methods that are taken up in the chapters that follow. Our research is similar though, in that our work is empirical (we gather or observe data of different kinds) in order to answer research questions that we set ourselves.

Deciding the questions you want to answer and the aims you want your research to achieve can determine your research design, that is, how you might choose to select and analyse materials, how you might choose to represent your results and the kinds of conclusions you will reach at the end of your project. Given the diversity of social media contexts, and the broad range of phenomena that "language" and "language use" might entail, it will come as no surprise to find that there are many different ways you might want to design the research. Again, this is at once very exciting (as researching the language of social media is not narrowly confined to a single way of doing things) but it can be quite confusing, as different approaches, tools and values which underpin different kinds of research often carry with them particular expectations of how research should be conducted, or what makes "good research" (Dornyei 2007, pp.16–17).

## Research and academic disciplines

The differing expectations about what counts as "good research" is often related to the discipline in which the research is taking place. Academic disciplines can be thought of as communities of scholars who develop particular norms and practices for their scholarship. The differences in these norms can be reflected in boundaries, such as which department you are studying or working in, how knowledge is categorised (for example in library class mark systems or how publications are listed in search engines), how research communities gather together (in conferences and organisations), and in micro-level choices such as the formats used to write up research (style guides and templates). One of the great advantages of researching how language is used in social media is that it is highly relevant to a range of different disciplines, including education, psychology, anthropology, sociology, management studies, computer science, media studies, journalism, literature, language and applied linguistics (and more). Some of these disciplines might be regarded as belonging to the social sciences, whilst others align more readily with the arts and humanities. Linguistics itself draws on methodologies from across these disciplines. The trans-disciplinary scope of research about the language in social media contexts can open up conversations and collaborations with scholars across different subject areas. These collaborations can result in interdisciplinary research, where the differing perspectives or practices from more than one discipline are integrated in the research process. The result can be a richer, more multifaceted set of results and conclusions than would have been possible if the work had been carried out within a single discipline.

However, the trans-disciplinary scope and interdisciplinary potential of researching how language is used in social media contexts is not always easy to handle. The boundaries which demarcate one discipline from another, or one part of a discipline from another, can sometimes act as barriers which make research more difficult. These boundaries can operate at all stages of the research process. The indexing systems used by different databases can mean that certain journals are not included, so that potentially relevant research carried out by others can be missed when reviewing earlier studies. The methods used for selecting and gathering data might vary in one discipline compared with another. Different scholarly organisations can have different guidelines for ethical procedures (for example, not telling people about the point of a research project might be acceptable practice for some projects, but be considered as bordering on deceit for others). The frameworks used for analysis, and choices about how you represent data when publishing your research, can also vary from one discipline to another. For the beginning researcher, this can be difficult to negotiate: if you model your research design on an earlier study from a different discipline from the one in which you might be studying, will this result in a mismatch between the perspectives and values in your choice of research design and that valued by the department where you are submitting your work for assessment? For more advanced students, presenting research to an audience from another discipline (for example in a conference paper) can mean that you need to be very careful in how you use language to define and frame your work. Even for more experienced researchers, trans-disciplinary boundaries can persist. For example, I (Ruth) recently submitted a paper for review to a journal firmly positioned within linguistics. The reviewers (rightly) pointed out that there was a body of research I had not taken into account: research I had not even been aware of as it belonged to the field of Management Studies and published in journals not cited by the search databases I had used to inform my initial overview of the subject area. Integrating the perspectives from the Management Studies research allowed me to provide a more nuanced interpretation of my results, to correct some gaps in how I had presented material, and as a result make my work relevant to a wider range of readers.

At best, negotiating the boundaries that exist in scholarly practices across disciplines can be a helpful means of reflecting on the choices that you make as a researcher. Seeing your own work from another perspective can bring to light its limitations and value systems that are sometimes left implicit or taken for granted. The process of critical reflection from one discipline's perspectives to another can help you define your object of study, approach and analytical terms. And boundaries in scholarly practices are not impermeable, but often porous with gaps which allow exchange of ideas and for researchers to find points of common ground. As authors, we work in different departments (literature, language and linguistics, media studies) and our research interests emphasise different aspects of language study (discourse analysis, linguistic ethnography, corpus linguistics). As we have written this book, we have had discussions about our different assumptions and priorities as they shape our research practices. The authors of the case studies in the different chapters represent a wider range of interests and expertise still. We are aware that the readers of this book will likewise come from a range of different disciplines and be at different stages in the research process: you may have a specific research project in mind that will take place within a specific academic context, or you may want to explore a range of possibilities for researching social media in a way that takes into account language. While our focus is on providing guidance for the research which would be most obviously situated in language studies or applied linguistics, we hope that this book will be useful to researchers in other disciplines and to open up the possibility of interdisciplinary work.

---

**Points for reflection**

What academic discipline(s) would you say your research project belongs to?

How does this influence your research interests, aims and questions?

What might your research look like to someone working in another discipline but also interested in social media?

---

## Methodology

Methodology refers to the rationale for a particular approach to research and is distinct from the methods that are used to carry out the research itself (that is, the specific tools used to elicit, gather and analyse data). There are three key paradigms which are often used to describe differences in methodology: quantitative, qualitative and mixed methods. Historically, some academic fields have favoured particular kinds of methodologies. In practice, all three paradigms are used across different disciplines, but can be applied in different ways and for different ends. Given the multidisciplinary appeal of social media and of language, and the potential for interdisciplinary research, the methodologies which are explained and exemplified in this book include all three paradigms.

In simple terms, quantitative methodologies tend to be interested in examining the phenomenon in question in a way that measures it. In contrast, qualitative methodologies are more interested in uncovering particular patterns or perspectives. This distinction will become clearer as we discuss particular examples. The following extract from a public Facebook group to support the British television programme *Britain's Got Talent* could be explored from either a quantitative or qualitative perspective. The comments followed an embedded video clip of a young, female singer who competed in the show.

Commenter 1: I know she is a great singer and everything but serious question and I don't mean to be rude or anything but ... how on earth do you get to be that size?
11 May, 20:48

Commenter 2: Doesn't matter. Who cares? And you are rude!
11 May, 20:53

Commenter 1: I wasn't being rude I was just saying its unhealthy, that's all and i'm curious how people do it
11 May, 20:54

Commenter 3: By shallow minded comments like that making them feel bad about themselves so they turn to food for comfort ... think before comments like that.
11 May, 20:55

Commenter 1: I wasn't being rude, I have an eating disorder myself so I know what it's like to crave food but even after all the 4000 calories I eat every day I still don't get to that size, just saying, it's kinda impressive, that's all ☺
11 May, 20:57

Commenter 4: her size or her voice?
11 May, 21:23

A quantitative methodology might count the number of comments made by the contributors to the thread, or measure the frequency of particular words, where *rude* is repeated four times, *size* is repeated three times, and so on. A qualitative approach to this excerpt might be more interested in how the interaction is organised; for instance, how different adjacency pairs are organised within the thread, where some textually adjacent pairs operate as conversational pairs (comment 2 answers the question posed in question 1), but other adjacency pairs are non-sequential (so commenters 3 and 4 appear to be responding to the first comment, not to the subsequent interactions which have taken place after that). Or a qualitative approach might be interested in the pragmatic choices made by the participants in this thread: what is perceived as impolite (what counts as "rude" in this case) and how speakers position themselves as similar to or different from one another. However, rather than thinking of qualitative and quantitative paradigms as mutually exclusive, they are better understood as opposite ends of a spectrum which contrast in various ways, and that all research includes elements of qualitative and elements of quantitative research.

One of the main concerns of quantitative research is to trace overarching trends which relate to macro-level perspectives: they may be helpful as a means of allowing a researcher to generalise from their study. For example, studies which survey the use of social media platforms might compare the behaviour or attitudes of particular users and analyse that data in order to make broader claims. One such survey was carried out by Hargittai and Litt

(2011) who surveyed the adoption of Twitter by different groups of American students, and on the basis of the evidence they gathered went on to offer suggestions about the factors which might predict the uptake of Twitter (which in Hargittai and Litt's study included an interest in celebrity and entertainment news). As such, quantitative approaches often gather quite large samples of material for analysis, and use procedures for analysis that can be standardised and so re-applied to measure other sets of data.

Alongside large-scale studies, smaller experiments can also take a quantitative approach. In experimental design, the researcher assigns participants to particular groups and then asks them to engage in tasks that will test the participants' responses to particular phenomena. An example of an experimental research design is the study carried out by Shultz et al. (2011) who wanted to test the effect of the medium (mainstream news, blogs or Twitter) on the perception of apologies by companies. In this study, the researchers created fictional scenarios in which a car company made an apology to its customers in different media: either a news report, blog post or Twitter post. The participants in the study were then asked to evaluate the messages from the company by answering a series of questions with scaled responses.

The results of a quantitative study usually involve numerical outcomes, and are calculated using mathematical operations, including statistical tests. These factors are important, because quantitative work values reliability in terms of consistency. Quantitative work can also give the appearance of greater objectivity (this does not mean the research is completely free from subjectivity, though), and may approach the analysis of data to test a pre-determined concept (or hypothesis) and use categories that are already established by the researcher to sort and order the collected data. Examples of quantitative studies of social media from a linguistic perspective include the sociolinguistic studies and corpus linguistics discussed in Chapters 8 and 9.

In comparison, qualitative work tends to deal with a smaller number of people but in greater detail and with more concern for the context. It is more openly interpretative about the data. While a quantitative approach might require hundreds of participants to take part in a survey, a qualitative approach might be interested collecting more data from a much smaller number of people concerning their use of social media. Qualitative approaches aim to take into account the perspectives of the research participants, for example by collecting and reviewing data and results with the participants in an iterative cycle. This kind of practice would be impracticable with a large number of participants. Qualitative approaches can also be emergent, that is, the researcher does not set out with a clear hypothesis to test, but rather gathers data, and then sees which features emerge as prominent from the collected material (for example, in the form of repeated themes and patterns, or conversely in phenomena that seem unusual because they are at odds with patterns found in the material). In qualitative research, consistency and reliability are not measured in numerical tests or the sampling techniques used to gather data, but rather by the accuracy, depth and documentation of the researcher's account, using respondent feedback to check for the researcher's stance in interpreting results, and including critical reflection which shows awareness of the interpretative nature of the research and its findings.

In recent decades, a sharp contrast between qualitative and quantitative paradigms has been rejected and there are many studies which include elements from both, sometimes referred to as mixed methods (Angouri 2010). There are different ways to combine qualitative and quantitative approaches, for example by including a range of questions (some of which have a quantitative emphasis whilst others are qualitative), using different types of data collection, or by analysing material using different but complementary methods and so on (Tashakkori and Creswell 2007). These decisions will be driven by the research questions being pursued. There are many advantages for using mixed methods: a quantitative analysis may be able to provide contextualising information about large-scale trends in language use, while an in-depth, qualitative analysis can allow the researcher to focus on just one aspect of the larger dataset. In another instance, the researcher might choose to check their interpretation of their data with a numerical test (to confirm whether the scale of a difference observed in the results was significant or not), but this may not show how that feature was meaningful to participants: a follow-up interview to check how phenomena are perceived would be more useful. For example, in my – (Ruth's) – study of Facebook updates (2012), one feature I was interested in was the frequency of markers which signalled affect (such as emoticons). Although a statistical test would signal whether the differences I observed in the frequency of these features in my dataset was likely to be generalisable or not, it could not tell me whether women and men perceived the use of these features as conveying similar or different pragmatic meanings. Ashraf Abdullah's case study on researching the language used in the virtual world, Second Life, points to the value of a mixed-methods approach.

## Box 3.1 An ethnographic sociolinguistic study of virtual identity in Second Life

### Ashraf Abdullah

Second Life (SL henceforth) is an online 3D virtual world imagined and created by its *Residents*. SL has millions of registered users and tens of thousands online at any one time. This study explores the use of language by Second Life residents in their pursuit of a virtual identity. This is accomplished by introducing SL, defining its attributes and history, discussing current research in general and that of a linguistic nature specifically, discussing research methods and data collection techniques, building a corpus of 200,000 words and 12 hours of video data, and investigating linguistic features at three different levels: at word level, SLifers must use creative vocabulary; at phrasal level they must interact within the deictic field of the virtual environment, using appropriate indexical expressions; and at clausal level, the final step towards becoming 'virtual' is acknowledging and fulfilling a speech act in all of its felicity conditions.

One of the most important things to consider is how to collect the data. In such a virtual environment that has the ideology of living up to its name and being a 'second life', one has to realise that users are there to play, learn, socialise and even earn a living. It is vital that a participant observation data collection technique is not carried out arbitrarily, but in a systematic fashion. One has to think about a data population that is representative of a virtual community and not merely one aspect of it. In this case, an avatar was acquired and my avatar (Ashy Viper) starting *living* virtually, having a personal and professional life, and an academic existence. Ashy had a virtual family, a job as editor-in-chief in a fashion company, and was an active member in an academic discussion roundtable. Conversations were collected as data from various cyber-geographic locations such as social gatherings in clubs, parks and beaches, at Ashy's virtual home with family members, in a business institution, and at academic discussions. Interviews supplemented the data also, which included questions specific to the research aims. This type of data formed a corpus that allows quantitative as well as qualitative analysis. The use of text analysis software such as *Wordsmith Tools* facilitated observation by formulating keyword lists and enabled a search for concordances and linguistic patterns. Wordsmith also made observing the data qualitatively a less tedious task. New and creative words and word-formation techniques were found, along with their frequencies, which gave insight about unique SL vocabulary. Searching for specific deictic expressions and base forms of verbs allowed the formation of an idea of the deictic field and how instructive speech acts are formed. All these linguistic features contribute to the formulation of an account of virtual identity.

The most important things to consider when conducting such a study are being systematic about collecting the data and the data population which is representative of the community and the context, and familiarising oneself with text-analysis software to enable quantitative and facilitate qualitative analysis.

#advice: Always be systematic when building a corpus through participant observation, ensure your data is 'representative' of the media.

One of the advantages of combining multiple perspectives is sometimes described as triangulation. Triangulation uses more than one source of information in the research design and co-ordinates the perspectives which result from each source to provide a fuller picture of the phenomenon under investigation. Examples of triangulation might include the use of multiple sources of data, including multiple methods in the research design or having multiple researchers compare their findings on the same project. Sometimes this triangulation can be used to assess whether the same results apply across different contexts and so confirm how representative the research outcomes of a project might be. But triangulation can be used also to provide contrasting, sometimes quite different perspectives on a research problem. In this case, the outcome would not be corroboration but rather a richer, fuller picture of how language is used in a particular context. For example, teenagers' perceptions of what privacy means in social media contexts might be quite different to how their parents perceive it: the discrepancy between the two perspectives does not mean the results of each group's contributions to the project are invalid, but rather shows different aspects of a complex interactional situation.

The methods used in research do not group neatly into mutually exclusive categories which map onto quantitative or qualitative groupings. For example, a survey can be designed to produce quantitative data, by asking participants to respond to items with closed options, or by providing answers which can be rated on a scale (for example, by grading the extent to which a participant might agree with a statement). Alternatively, a survey might incorporate open-ended questions which are more suited to a qualitative analysis. Other methods are more closely aligned with one paradigm rather than another: statistical tests are of most use in quantitative studies, while using the researcher's interpretation of the data to code themes in observation notes draws on the characteristics of qualitative work. Different methods are also useful at different points in the research design: some methods will elicit data, others will gather data, yet others still will be important for analysing and interpreting material. Some of the most frequently used methods are summarised in Table 3.1, along with an indication of the chapters in this book where each method is discussed in more detail.

## Points for reflection

How might your research design take account of the strengths and limitations in qualitative and quantitative approaches? Will you use mixed methods and if so, why?
What research methods will you use?

*Table 3.1* Methods for gathering, eliciting, analysing and presenting data

| *Methods for gathering data* | *Methods for eliciting data* |
| --- | --- |
| **Chapter 8** | **Chapters 6 and 7** |
| Sampling strategies | Surveys |
| Scraping tools | Interviews |
| | Focus groups |
| | Diaries |
| | Observation notes |
| *Methods for analysing data* | *Methods for presenting data* |
| **Chapter 9** | **Chapter 9** |
| Concordancing tools | Visualisation packages |
| Statistical tests | |
| **Chapter 5** | |
| Transcription | |
| Textual analysis | |

## Next steps

In this chapter, we have outlined what it means to undertake research, and considered some of the key factors that might influence your decisions as you plan a research project (academic discipline, methodological paradigm, field of study). It may be useful to start from the courses you have done and to think about the research methods they draw upon. Depending on the nature of your research, the choices you make in research design may be more or less fully articulated in the presentation of your work: a doctoral thesis might contain a much lengthier account and evaluation of the research design than an undergraduate assignment. Regardless of whether you are a more or less experienced researcher, it is good practice to document the choices you make about research design. The process of self-reflection can help you articulate clearly the position that your project will take in relation to different research traditions and communities. This is always important in any academic research: as Sunderland (2010, p.25) points out, mapping out your research methodology in a chart can be a useful measure for cross-checking the alignment of your questions, aims, methodology and methods for collecting and analysing data. But given the interdisciplinary complexity of researching the language of social media, it is perhaps even more important to understand the assumptions and rationale for your research so that you can make your work as relevant as possible to those who will read and make use of it afterwards.

## References

Angouri, J. (2010) 'Quantitative, qualitative or both? Combining methods in linguistic research', in Litosseliti, L., ed., *Research Methods in Linguistics*, London and New York: Continuum, 29–48.

Dornyei, Z. (2007) *Research Methods in Applied Linguistics*, Oxford: Oxford University Press.

Hargittai, E. and Litt, E. (2011) 'The tweet smell of celebrity success: explaining Twitter adoption among a diverse group of young adults', *New Media and Society*, 13 (5), 824–42.

Hewsen, C., Yule, P., Laurent, D. and Vogel, C. (2002) *Internet Research Methods: A Practical Guide for the Social and Behavioural Sciences*, Thousand Oaks: Sage.

Litosseliti, L., ed. (2010) *Research Methods in Linguistics*, London and New York: Continuum.

Markham, A. and Baym, N. (2009) *Internet Inquiry: Conversations about Method*, Thousand Oaks: Sage.

Paltridge, B. and Phakiti, A. (2010) *Continuum Companion to Research Methods in Applied Linguistics*, London and New York: Continuum.

Shultz, F., Utz, S. and Goritz, A. (2011) 'Is the medium the message? Perceptions of and reactions to crisis communciation via Twitter, blogs and traditional media', *Public Relations*, 37, 20–7.

Sunderland, J. (2010) 'Research questions in linguistics', in Litosseliti, L., ed., *Research Methods in Linguistics*, London and New York: Continuum, 9–28.

Tashakkori, A. and Creswell, J. (2007) 'The new era of mixed methods', *Journal of Mixed Methods Research*, 1 (1), 3–8.

# Chapter 4

# What are Internet research ethics?

## Outline of the chapter

In this chapter we cover:

- Why ethics are important.
- Regulatory ethics.
- Ethical access and the right to privacy.
- The researcher's relationship to their project's participants.
- Informed consent.
- Ethical aspects of archiving and using materials.

## The importance of ethics

Researchers have responsibilities to the other people with whom they engage during the research process: the participants in the study, the audiences who will make use of the research and those who might have oversight for the research (such as an academic institution or funding body). The research design, implementation and dissemination of results must take into account those responsibilities, which can be summed up in the following general principle: avoid harm to yourself and to others. While this principle is in one sense very simple, what it means in practice is often more complex. In the case of researching social media from a linguistic perspective it may not always be clear who all the participants in a study are, what harm they might come to from the research and what steps might need to be taken in order to respect their rights at different points in the research process.

Some research practices are obviously unethical, such as making up results or using fabricated data to draw quantifiable conclusions. Within linguistics and in the social sciences more generally, such practices are considered unacceptable. There can be serious consequences for unethical research, which can range from being dismissed from an academic post (as in the case of former professor, Diederik Stapel, who was convicted of fraud in 2011 for falsifying data), to penalties applied to marked work (at the

University of Leicester, student work receives a fail grade if it does not comply with the university's code of conduct for ethical research). But other scenarios are less clear-cut. For example, does observing and then analysing interactions in an online, publicly available forum or chat room require a researcher to make their presence known to the people whose interactions are observed? Might the possibilities for pseudonymous online representation obscure the status of participants in need of special consideration as members of a vulnerable group (such as children or young adults)? What happens if you want to quote from an online interaction which is taken down from the web during or after the course of your research? The answer to these (and other) ethical questions about the practicalities entailed by Internet research is often, "it depends", and based on principles that have to be applied in relation to individual contexts. The purpose of this chapter is not to provide a single solution that will meet all ethical dilemmas, but instead to outline the key principles and questions you need to consider when making decisions about how to conduct your research with appropriate ethical responsibility.

One of the challenges for researchers interested in the language of social media is that the fundamental principles of ethical research were developed in relation to the medical sciences and to guide research that took place in offline contexts. The legacy of these disciplinary differences is still felt in the forms that students may be expected to complete in order to gain approval for their projects and carry out their research (at least in certain countries and certain educational contexts). At the institutions where the authors of this book are employed, the ethics review forms include questions such as, "Will blood or tissue samples be obtained from the participants?" and, "Is pain likely to result from the study?" It is unlikely (though not impossible) that these questions will appear directly relevant to studying linguistic phenomena in social media contexts. But this does not mean that we should dismiss ethical considerations as irrelevant to research that deals with social media. Harm to participants may appear in forms that are not immediately tangible but nonetheless may be significant. Inhibiting a person's participation in a particular online site (such as a support forum), having a negative influence on a player's interaction in an online game, quoting material which might overtly or inadvertently expose some part of a person's identity or activities that they had wished to keep private, analysing publicly available posts without a person's consent or knowledge are all potential sources of distress to the people whose interactions might be the object of linguistic scrutiny.

A first question in deciding what kinds of ethical considerations need to be put in place is whether the research involves "human subjects" or not (McKee and Porter 2009, p.37). Sometimes this question is framed in a way that poses a clear-cut distinction between whether a researcher considers the object of analysis to be people (their identities, behaviour and interactions) or text (as a decontextualised object). But the distinction between a 'person' and a 'text' is not straightforward when we consider social media materials. Although a research project might focus on textual interactions, those social media materials are produced (at least in part) by people, and people use these interactions to construct their online identities.

The methods of researching the language used in social media contexts can place different emphasis on the extent to which "human subjects" are important to the project in question. Methods include a wide range of activities, from directly interacting with people through interviews and surveys, to collecting examples of materials which have been published online by people (including publications which may be anonymous or written under a pseudonymous user name), to programming tools that will scrape large sets of text and metadata that are selected without any regard for the text's authorship. Sometimes the methods of linguistic inquiry will focus more on the experiences of the participant (for example, through the ethnographic accounts of digital literacy), while other methods may not pay attention to the authorship of a text at all (as in the large-scale datasets where texts are coded for type, not authorship). These alternatives exist on a sliding scale where, at one end, the qualities of the participant are central to the research design, process and results and, at the other, the qualities of the participant are peripheral. The point at which a particular project is positioned on that scale will then influence the ethical choices that the researcher needs to consider, such as:

- how to deal with aspects of the text that might contain details of the participant's identity (details in the text itself, or material gathered automatically as metadata);
- whether or not informed consent will be required;
- the extent to which the participants can be involved collaboratively in the research process and its outputs.

The complexity of the ethical considerations which shape a research project is also influenced by the variety in national and institutional practices and guidelines. At the time of writing, there is no single, international set of regulations which govern the choices made by a researcher who wants to explore social media interactions. Instead, there are guidelines for good practice informed by the practices of different disciplines, which operate within different national contexts, and which are employed in different ways by different institutions even within the same country. As the latest set of guidelines from the Association of Internet Researchers suggest (Markham and Buchanan 2012), there is no single set of recommendations for ethical research that can be prescribed universally to cover each and every research project. Instead, decisions made about the ethical aspects of the research design most often have to be assessed on a case-by-case basis. In that light, the discussions and questions raised in this chapter should not be taken as a set of definitive rules that can be substituted for localised regulations that may govern the processes by which projects are designed. Instead, the topics that follow, along with the reflective questions at the end of each section, are intended as a series of prompts to help researchers reflect on the ethical issues that need to be considered at the outset, during the project itself and after the project is completed.

## Regulatory ethics

Although there is no single set of regulations which govern the ethical decisions, there are several sources of information and advice that researchers can (and in some cases, should) consult. In some countries, if research is conducted within an academic institution, a researcher may be required to gain approval for the project from a regulating committee (such as a Research Ethics Committee (REC) or an Institutional Review Board (IRB)). Usually, this process takes place at the start of the research design, and before any data collection takes place. Although it can appear daunting, preparing an application for ethical approval is more than just ticking boxes, and can be used as a reflective opportunity to consider carefully the researcher's responsibilities to the people involved in the project. The exact procedures required by IRBs and RECs can vary, and can be shaped by the local arrangements organised by individual tutors and supervisors, but are underpinned by the principles codified in key international documents which have set out the foundations of human rights.

After the atrocities of the Nazi experiments in the Second World War, review procedures and international guidelines were documented to protect human rights including the *Nuremberg Code*, *The Declaration of Helsinki*, the *UN Declaration of Human Rights* and the *Belmont Report*. The principles included in these documents focus on people's right to autonomy (their right to participate in research without coercion, and with appropriate information about the project), fairness and inclusivity, respect for privacy and confidentiality, and the mandate to avoid harm and maximise benefits for the research participants. These super-ordinate principles have also shaped the guidelines developed to encourage best practice in the research across the disciplines, including those that embrace study of language and linguistics (such as education, applied linguistics, psychology). So although the subject specific nature of these guidelines is further refracted across different national contexts (such as the American Psychological Association, British Psychology Association, American Association for Applied Linguistics, British Association of Applied Linguistics, British Educational Research Association, American Educational Research Association, and so on), these guidelines often reflect the same core responsibilities which are discussed in the later sections of this chapter but are united by the same foundational value to protect human rights.

There are also governmental laws with which research must comply, such as data protection legislation, and copyright laws. Legislation can vary from one country to another, and can change over time. Given the global reach of social media, it is important that researchers are aware not only of the regulations that hold sway in the country where they are situated, but also of those that govern interactions for the countries in which the material they are studying is owned. For example, I might conduct my research in a British academic institution, but be analysing posts to a Korean dating site. There are also different legislative implications that vary according to whether the social media texts being accessed, archived or reproduced are words, images or sounds. Although the details vary, the issues at the heart of data protection legislation concerns people's rights to be able to access information which is stored about them, and to be assured that any data collected about them during the research process will be stored securely. Copyright laws address the researcher's responsibility to the creators of texts that might be reproduced and reused in the course of research. You must not appropriate texts authored by others and represent the text (words, image or sound) as if it were your own work. A researcher might also need to consider how copyright laws govern the reproduction of the texts they have analysed, especially if the results of the research are to be disseminated publicly. There are differences between the fair use which governs the reproduction of material in academic research which is not intended for publication (such as a student essay), and materials which will be reproduced for commercial ends (such as a journal article or monograph). A detailed account of the different national legislation in these areas is beyond the remit of this chapter, so you are advised to seek further advice about data protection and copyright laws from the relevant authorities in your national and academic context.

The governmental regulations, institutional ethics codes and protocols, and subject-specific guidelines for good practice have all been developed to account for research that takes place primarily in offline contexts. The documents issued by organisations recognise this limitation, and may contain specific sub-sections which deal with online materials (such as the guidelines for good practice published by the British Association of Applied Linguistics, which deal with Internet research in section 2.9). Other academic organisations focus entirely on the research practices for Internet inquiry, like the Association of Internet Researchers, who published their first set of guidelines for good practice in 2002 (Ess and the Association of Internet Researchers 2002), and reissued an updated set of recommendations in 2012 (Markham and Buchanan 2012). The Association of Internet Researchers is an international, interdisciplinary organisation. The topics covered in this chapter thus draw on their recommendations, along with other key work in the growing field of Internet research, but focus more specifically on the questions raised for the study of social media language in particular.

The publications of Internet researchers are a further resource for finding information about how academics have negotiated ethical dilemmas in their own work. The practices of existing research projects do not carry the same weight as regulatory guidelines, but nonetheless often provide helpful examples of effective research practices that have been treated as precedents for subsequent work. Studies which have allowed researchers to reflect on the limitations of the ethical choices made in their studies are just as important as a resource for helping to consider the contingent nature of research (Whiteman 2012). These studies can highlight the potential (and sometimes previously unforeseen) risks that arise in the process of undertaking research in social media contexts and remind us that ethical choices do not stop at the point at which you are planning your project, but are important both during and after the research process has been completed.

The terms and conditions which govern the membership and interactions for specific social media sites provide a further set of regulations which must be considered in the research design. The conditions may indicate who researchers should seek permission from in order to interact with other site members, who has ownership rights to the materials that are posted to the site, what restrictions govern how site members may or may not represent their identities, how data from the site must be represented and the researcher's ability to share it with others. For example, at the time of writing, Twitter currently prohibits academics from sharing corpora built from archives of harvested tweets; Instagram prohibits the use of automated scraper tools to export material from the site; Facebook's terms and conditions tells its members that if they wish to collect information from other users, they must obtain consent and explain how the information is going to be used.

In summary, although there is no universal set of regulations which govern research projects that consider the language used in social media contexts, there are a number of resources which can guide a researcher's decisions about ethics. These include national legislation (data protection and copyright laws), institutional protocols and codes of conduct (IRBs and RECs), best practice guidelines developed for different academic communities (often published for specific national contexts), precedents established by existing research practices as documented in peer-reviewed publications, and terms and conditions which govern your interaction with particular social media sites. These resources are check points which help you to hold your work accountable to others. As researchers we work within academic communities (such as institutions, disciplines). The regulatory ethics help us to have conversations with others (such as a researcher's tutor, supervisor or academic colleagues working in the field) about the design and practice of Internet research. The following questions help you consider how your research project might relate to regulatory ethics.

---

### Points for reflection

Are you carrying out your work in a context which requires your project to be approved by an institutional research committee or review board?

Will you be collecting data which is subject to data protection or copyright legislation?

Have you consulted the best practice guidelines for your discipline?

What ethical decisions did other researchers make about similar projects, and was this satisfactory?

Is the material you want to study governed by platform or site-specific regulations? Do these regulations restrict how you represent yourself, interact with others, collect or reuse data from the site?

Who are the people in your academic community with whom you could discuss ethical decision-making?

---

## Ethical access to materials: the right to privacy

At the start of the research design, the researcher must consider where the materials or interactions they want to analyse are situated because the context in which the social media materials are produced or published influences the ethical aspects of accessing that material in the first place. The researcher's right to access material is closely related to whether the material is made publicly available and considered to be free from privacy restrictions. But the definitions of the terms *public* and *private* have been debated in relation to interactions which take place via the Internet (including social media environments). These debates inform ethics because of the right to privacy online, which Elm (2009, p.69) describes as follows: "The basic idea is that each and all individuals should have the right to decide for themselves what and how much others get to know about them."

There may be regulatory aspects to privacy. As McKee and Porter (2009, p.46) point out, most countries have privacy laws. These laws might protect particularly vulnerable groups of people (such as children or young adults) and sensitive types of information (such as religious affiliation or matters relating to a person's health). However, even collecting public, apparently non-sensitive information about participants and making it available in the outputs of a research project can compromise other ethical aspects of the research design such as the anonymity of participants. Zimmer (2010) describes the problems that were caused when a dataset of Facebook material was released by an American social science research project (the *Taste, Ties and Time Project* (Lewis 2008)). Although the material in the dataset had been publicly available to the researchers and was carefully anonymised, it was still possible to deduce the identity of the college involved (and hence in some cases individual students) from innocuous information such as geographical location or the academic course for which a student was enrolled.

The regulatory aspects of privacy are also determined by site-specific terms and conditions and the architecture of particular online contexts. Many sites like blogging platforms, forums or social network sites offer their members the opportunity to control the visibility of the material they post through mechanisms like password protection. On the surface, these affordances appear to set up a binary contrast between material which is publicly available and that which is not (based on whether or not a password is needed to access the material). Some approaches to computer-mediated communication have perceived the Internet as a publicly available archive (McKee and Porter 2009, p.82) and on those grounds, use the extent to which privacy mechanisms are activated by participants as the criteria for judging the public or private nature of the material. In turn, that judgement can inform other choices about whether the researcher can ethically access the material and whether or not they should seek informant consent from the participants to do so. However, privacy and public-ness are not absolute qualities that can be so easily demarcated. The relative nature of privacy means the ethical decisions about how access to site might need to be managed may be rather more complex.

Elm (2009) points out that there are degrees of privacy or open-ness that hold in different online environments, and sets out a more nuanced set of categories: public environments (open and available for anyone with an Internet connection to access), semi-public environments (sites which are in principle publicly accessible, but require site registration), semi-private environments (which are available only to certain people, such as the intranets which are shared by all those belonging to a particular company) and private environments (whose access is restricted to the creator of the content). Different social media sites and areas within certain sites vary in the extent to which they are public or semi-public, private or semi-private. Thus Flickr is a public environment; Twitter accounts can be either public or private. The pages of Facebook operate different levels of privacy: some semi-public groups are open to all members of Facebook, other personal pages may be private or semi-private, and interactions within those areas increasingly more or less private (where the visibility of Facebook chat and messages is, by default, limited to the interacting participants alone, while varying constraints can be placed on updates, comments and wall posts).

The relative nature of privacy is not limited to the varying affordances of different social media sites. It is also influenced by the perceptions held by participants. As such, perceptions of privacy can vary from one culture to another (see McKee and Porter 2009, pp.78–9). In a more localised sense, there can be discrepancies between the affordances of a site as public and the participants' individual expectations of how visible the materials they post to that site might actually be. Just because material is publicly available, it does not mean that the person who authored that material fully anticipates the scale or reach of their readership, or expects it to be reused without their knowledge or consent. The dilemma of how far the author's expectations of privacy can hold as protection of their privacy rights has been debated in legal controversies (see Grodzinsky and Tavani 2010 for an overview). From the researcher's perspective, this should remind us that the affordances of a site are not the sole criteria that should be applied when assessing the ethical dimensions of accessing the material to be studied.

Nissenbaum's (2011) concept of contextual integrity is sometimes used as a way of explaining the additional factors that apply when determining the privacy of an online interaction. The first dimension of contextual integrity is what she calls the appropriateness of a situation. Expectations of what is appropriate to disclose to whom are not confined to material barriers (such as a closed door in the physical world, or a privacy control such as a password in online environments). Additional factors include the norms which are shaped by the purpose of an interaction and the roles that participants adopt relative to each other. For example, it is appropriate to disclose certain physical information to your physician that it would not be to tell your accountant, while you might disclose financial information to your accountant but not to your physician, even while both types of interaction might take place in confidential settings that protect the interactants' privacy. Similarly, in a research context, there will be constraints on the kinds of information that a participant might want to make available to others, and that can vary independently of whether a site on which they are interacting is public, private or somewhere between those end points.

The ways in which participants use certain areas within a given social media site can also vary in terms of the expectations of privacy. Rosenberg (2010) describes the different ways in which the members of the virtual world Second Life created spaces with varying expectations of privacy, even within publicly available areas of the site. Hence creating a space which is normally associated with a higher expectation of privacy (a bedroom space compared with a living room or lounge, for example) can create levels of privacy determined within a given community rather than the architecture of the site (here the virtual world). The uses to which such spaces are put can in turn change expectations of privacy in a fluid and transient way. For example, a lounge used by two partners for watching television is more private than the same lounge space used to host a party.

The difference between a site's affordances and the participants' expectation of privacy also rest on the participants' perception of their audience. Even

while acknowledging that a site might allow anyone with an Internet connection to read the material posted therein, there are many cases where it is
clear that the person posting the material did not expect that "anyone with
an Internet connection" would read what they had written. Baym and boyd
(2012) describe this difference in terms of a visible and imagined audience.
A participant may write with a specific, imagined audience in mind (for
example, a circle of known friends or contacts). But that imagined audience
need not map onto the actual audience who do read their posts. The actual
audience can make themselves known to the author (for example, by writing
comments on a blog post, or responding to a forum thread), but there may
also be invisible audiences who only leave a digital trace of their presence
through the information logged as a page view. This means that researchers
may need to take into account not just the affordances of a site, but the
extent to which the participants who are authoring social media materials
indicate that their writing is publicly available.

The second aspect of contextual integrity conceptualises privacy as a flow
of information. Privacy rights extend beyond access to material alone to
include how that material is used. boyd and Marwick (2011) describe a
situation where teenagers who had posted material to Facebook with full
knowledge that they had done so in a way that made this publicly available,
but objected to the reuse of the material they had posted in a talk given to
other students about online privacy. In terms of research ethics, gaining
ethical access to a site is only one aspect of the privacy rights you may need
to consider and does not automatically guarantee that the people who have
posted material to the site would be happy for their material to be used in a
research project or included in public or semi-public dissemination of that
research. Informed consent (see below) can be used to negotiate the extent
to which a participant is willing to contribute to a particular project.

The expectations of privacy may vary from person to person. Some
people state their expectations clearly on their profile pages (such as the
profile to a blog), for example by indicating what the purpose of their blog
is or by setting out constraints on how material can be used. In other cases,
expectations of privacy might be inferred from the way in which participants manage their interactions. For example, Elm (2009, p.82) noted how a
Swedish web community intentionally attracted attention from a wider
audience by placing prominent invitations for people to visit their personal
web pages. In contrast, McKee and Porter (2009, p.86) describe how Munt
et al.'s (2002) study of a lesbian community's web pages relied on the community members' rhetorical construction of an implied audience to judge the
perception of the site as a private space. But the most certain way to be
clear about a participant's expectations of privacy is to discuss this with
them directly. Whether direct communication of this kind is necessary and
how the communication might take place, depends in part on the
researcher's relationship with the participants in their study, and to some

extent, on whether an IRB or REC needs to grant approval before you might contact any of the participants in the first place.

## The researcher's relationship with the project's participants

Based on the premise that the textual content of social media is produced (at least in part) by human participants, a researcher might ask who the participants involved in the project are and how the researcher will relate to them. The nature of the researcher's relationship to the participants in their project is a matter which has been discussed in research methods more widely. A key issue is the extent to which the researcher's interventions will influence the behaviour of the research participants (for example by creating the observer's paradox), and how far this will be explicitly acknowledged and integrated within the research design and process. At one end of the spectrum, a researcher may not ever directly interact with the person who authored a social media text, as in cases where a researcher creates a large-scale dataset from posts which are randomly selected when scraped by an automated tool from publicly available sites. At the other end of the spectrum, a researcher may spend long periods of time throughout a project interacting with the research participants through ethnographic interviews and focus group discussions. A researcher may be an outside observer of the social media site, or they might be a co-member of a particular community, and involved more or less closely with that community (for example as a participant in a special interest forum, or as a social network site member with a known network of members, like a Facebook Friend list or Twitter Follower list). Even if a researcher chooses to become a site member, they may elect only to observe the interactions between others, or they may choose to participate in those interactions. These choices bear on the ethical responsibility that a researcher has to the study's participants, and how those responsibilities may change over time.

The ethical responsibilities entailed by the researcher's relationship to the participants begin with the overriding need to respect the human right to autonomy. In this case, we might consider how far the research design allows the participants the choice to participate (or not) in the project. The first step in granting participants autonomy is to make sure they know that the research is taking place: they cannot choose whether or not to participate in a project if the material they post has been analysed without their knowledge. In earlier studies of computer-mediated communication, publicly available interactions, such as those posted to discussion boards, were considered an ideal solution to the observer's paradox: interactions which were publicly available and so could be observed by the researcher without making their presence known and so influencing the 'natural' quality of the data produced by the participants. But if the research project intends to move beyond observation to analysis of those interactions, it may become necessary for the researcher to make their intentions known to the participants on the grounds of simple courtesy, if not academic integrity. On one hand, the guidelines for ethical research point out that in offline contexts, covert observation (gathering data for analysis without the participants' knowledge) is unacceptable and regarded as a form of deception, but, as Whiteman (2012, p.109) argues, the norms of online interaction are somewhat different where "lurking is a normal state of being", and does not always hold the same problematic assumptions or unwarranted surveillance or deception. On the other hand, as the debates about public-ness outlined earlier suggest, the public nature of online material as determined by site affordances does not automatically guarantee that the participants who created the online material would wish it to be reused in a research project.

Whether or not the researcher should make their identity known to the participants (and in turn gain informed consent) may depend on a number of factors: the conventions and constraints of privacy which operate in the contexts from which data is gathered, the practicalities of informing participants and the potential disruption which might be caused by researchers identifying themselves. The processes by which researchers can make their presence and intentions known to potential participants can vary from site to site. Sites like special interest discussion forums may use authorised figures like moderators to oversee the behaviour between site members. Although the site owners or moderators may not be the participants whose interactions are of interest for a research project, they may function as gatekeepers whom you could first approach to discuss the ethical implications of researching interactions that take place in that site. In other cases, there may not be a gatekeeper to the site, and it might be more appropriate to approach participants directly to invite them to participate in your project.

However, it is not always possible or practical to notify each individual of the researcher's presence. In chat rooms, for example, the fast-moving interactions between pseudonymous participants would be disrupted unhelpfully if a researcher introduced his- or herself to each new participant every time someone entered the room. In other cases, a participant may no longer be actively maintaining an online account, in which case it may not be possible to contact them to let them know about your project. Where participants are likely to be recipients of many social media interactions (such as bloggers or members of Twitter who receive hundreds of comments each day) it is difficult to guarantee that a personal message to a participant has been received or understood. Lastly, in exceptional scenarios, covert observation has occasionally been considered acceptable where the subject matter being discussed by participants is of a sensitive nature, and knowledge of a researcher might potentially cause harm to the participants. However, failing to respect the participants' autonomy through covert observation can run the risk of causing later distress to those involved if the researcher later needs to make their presence known.

The researcher's relationship to the participants in their project can change over time. At the start of her doctoral research on the interactions of fan-fiction discussion boards, Whiteman (2010, 2012) chose not to disclose her presence as a researcher to the participants she observed. However, during the course of her research she chose to declare her status as a researcher to them, as her relationship and responsibilities to the participants changed when the site was hacked and she was able to offer the participants a preserved archive of the materials that had been lost from the main site. Other researchers have found that their previously undetected presence and research projects have been disclosed without their knowledge when the results of their research have been published and disseminated in the public domain. While some participants may be glad that their work is valued through academic study, not all people will necessarily feel that way and there may be unforeseen outcomes from choosing to remain an undisclosed, outside observer to the social media interactions that form your object of interest.

Choosing how to represent yourself when you interact with the participants in a study has ethical implications for the researcher too. McKee and Porter (2009, p.99) report on the range of strategies that researchers have used in online contexts in order to present their research projects with credibility and authenticity. Important factors include the tone of an interaction, the level (and mode) of self-disclosure and the longevity of the researcher's relationship with the community they wish to study. Some researchers choose to create specific accounts used only for their research on particular sites in order to demarcate clearly the boundaries between their professional interactions with the participants in their study. For example, there are advantages and drawbacks to interacting with research participants by 'friending' them on a site like Facebook which allows reciprocal access between the accounts of site members who accept 'Friend requests'. The extent to which a researcher might wish to reveal details of their personal life in relation to a research project can vary. Karin Tusting's case study at the end of this chapter explains the choices she made when representing herself as a researcher on the discussion boards of Mumsnet.

The ethical responsibilities entailed by a researcher's relationship with participants can sometimes carry potent social consequences, whether or not they have made their presence known to the participants. If a researcher observes a participant putting his- or herself at risk (for example, threatening physical harm), they face the dilemma of whether or not to intervene. Senft's (2008) ethnographic study of cam girls describes what happened when she was faced with information about a participant threatening to commit suicide. McKee and Porter (2009) outline the choices made by other researchers in similar situations who have chosen not to intervene.

In summary, the rights to privacy and the rights to autonomy influence the ethical decisions that a researcher will need to consider at the outset of the research process, such as whether they are able to access and collect material from a particular social media site, and whether or not they should make their presence known to the participants in their study. A researcher may need to revisit these questions as their project unfolds: sites can change their privacy settings and regulations, material that was once publicly available can be taken down, and the relationship with participants can change through the course of the research. The following check list of questions outlines the ethical choices that relate to privacy and the researcher's relationship with the study's participants.

---

**Points for reflection**

Does the social media site you intend to study use controls to protect its members' privacy?

What are the regulations which govern privacy rights in your national context?

How do the participants you wish to study perceive the privacy of their interactions? What evidence do you have for their perceptions?

Will the use of material in your study compromise the privacy rights of the participants at some later stage?

How might making known your presence as a researcher influence the social media interactions you wish to study and influence the people who post the interactions?

As a researcher, are you a co-participant in the study? Do you have membership of the site you are studying, and do you interact with others on the site or not?

Is there a moderator or site owner you should consult about accessing the material you want to study and using it in your project?

Can you contact the participants in your study directly?

How will you represent yourself as a researcher: using a personal account or one created for your project?

What check points can you build into your project that will allow you to monitor the rights to privacy and autonomy during the course and at the end of the research?

---

## Informed consent

Informed consent is the process by which researchers can allow participants to negotiate, document and agree their contribution to a research project. As the term suggests, there are two aspects to this process which need careful consideration: how you inform participants about the project, and how participants might express their consent to participate. The question of whether or not informed consent is necessary is dependent on a number of contextual factors. Some of these factors have already been considered, such as regulatory constraints which might require informed consent to take place (such as the terms and conditions which govern Facebook), whether or not the material you want to study is publicly available and perceived as such by the participants, and the methods that will be used in the study (which could be more or less intrusive and involve participants to a greater or lesser extent). Additional factors concern the content of the material. Although material might be publicly available, sensitive subject matter might prompt the need for informed consent. Of course, what counts as 'sensitive' can vary according to individual perception and cultural context, but personal topics such as health, sexuality or ideologically controversial topics such as religious or political opinion can require additional consent in order to ensure that the participants understand the implications of their online material being included in a research project and are adequately protected from potential harm.

The requirements for informed consent can also increase or become more complex if the participants in your study might be considered as vulnerable. Vulnerable groups or individuals can include those who might be open to exploitation. Examples might include those in ill-health or who are disempowered (for example by their age or minority status). Within the online contexts of social media, vulnerability can also take into account technological competence, where those unaware of or unable to change site affordances (like privacy settings) may unwittingly disclose information to researchers that they might otherwise wish to control. Vulnerability may then impinge on perceptions of privacy and the participant's autonomy. In some countries, additional regulations protect vulnerable groups. For example, in the United Kingdom and in other European countries, the parent or legal guardian must give informed consent for a minor (a person under 18 years of age) to participate in a research project. In online contexts (and in certain offline contexts too), it is not always clear whether a participant's stated age is their physical age. Particular care must be taken when the research population might be likely to include young adults.

The decision of whether or not to seek informed consent can also depend on what kind of analysis the researcher wishes to conduct. Here the criterion focuses on whether the research will focus on an individual and their behaviour (for example, interacting directly with them in interviews, or quoting directly from a person's online posts), or whether the research avoids directly identifying individual participants (for example, commenting on the practices of a group as a collective whole, or using data gathered only in an aggregated form for quantified comparisons). These options exist on a cline, where the more closely a project is likely to identify a particular individual the more likely it is for informed consent to be required. If the social media context you wish to study is overseen by an administrative authority such as a moderator, you may need to approach a number of people for informed consent: the site owner, the group as a whole (such as the people who post to a forum thread or to a mailing list), or the individual people whose posts you want to analyse. How you approach those people, and how you choose to describe your research plans to them, will also vary according to whether you are an outsider to the group, or someone who has been an active member of the site, and so is more familiar with the expected norms of privacy and the purposes of the interactions that take place in the site. Deciding how to inform participants about your research project will depend in part on your relationship with them, and is best understood as a dialogic process rather than a mechanistic, one-off act of notification.

Informed consent is an important stage in helping your participants to understand your research plans. The British Association of Applied Linguistics' guidelines for good practice suggest that the information offered at this stage should include "the objectives of the research, its possible consequences, and issues of confidentiality and data security" (p.4). Obtaining consent is an ongoing process, and the European directive for Data Protection requires researchers to provide participants with a contact point so that if they wish to withdraw from a project at a later point in time, they can do so. Conveying information about your research project at an appropriate level of detail and in terms that the participants will understand requires careful thought. Information about your project needs to be clear and transparent: sometimes linguistic terminology may not be helpful at this point. It is not always clear that participants read or fully understand informed consent documentation (Buchanan 2009, p.92). As technology used to carry out research advances, more complex, multimedia applications can be used to supplement written information sheets, and bespoke platforms integrate quizzes to gauge how far participants have engaged with the information given by researchers in a meaningful way (Chalil Madathil et al. 2011).

In offline contexts, participants usually record their consent with a signature on a written document (or verbally record their consent in the case of sight impaired participants). In social media contexts, obtaining written signatures on paper consent forms is not always possible. Some research contexts still require full signatures on consent documents, or require that if digital signatures are used, they are provided with additional verification in order to ensure authenticity. However, in other cases, purchasing electronic consent systems may not be feasible. Lower-cost alternatives have included creating consent forms that allow a participant to use a click box to indicate their consent to participate. Whether you devise a paper-based or electronic form of consent, if your research is taking place in a context which requires institutional approval from an IRB or REC, these documents are likely to be required as part of the review process. Even when a researcher repeatedly attempts to gain informed consent, it may not be able to possible to do so. When this happens, and if informed consent would be regarded as necessary (for example, if the interaction takes place in a private or semi-private domain, or involves sensitive information), then you may need to change your research design.

---

**Points for reflection**

Are there contextual factors in your project which might make the need for informed consent likely (e.g. privacy, sensitive subject matter, inclusion of vulnerable participants, focus on individuals rather than a group)?

Whom do you need to approach for informed consent (site owners, communities, individuals)?

What information do you need to include for participants about your project?

How will you enable participants to withdraw from the project later if they wish to?

How will you record informed consent?

---

## Archiving and using materials

The responsibility to protect the privacy rights of participants extends beyond accessing material to include the researcher's decisions about how to store and use data. Again, regulatory restrictions may guide a researcher's decisions. The Data Protection guidelines in the United Kingdom recommend that you keep your data securely, and only for as long as the research project requires. Once you have extracted the data you need for your project, you will need to prepare it so that any personal information contained in the materials is protected adequately. For example, file names and personal information should be treated in a way that allows the participants' identities to remain anonymous (for example by replacing them with a code). This may include removing or blurring out identifying content from images or video footage. If you have extracted contextual data from a social media site (for example, in the form of a screenshot) further care may be needed to remove material if information from participants other than those who have given informed consent has also been captured. For example, a screenshot of a Facebook wall post including the whole screen might include posts or comments from the Friend list who extend beyond the participants who had granted informed consent.

Choosing which features of the data to anonymise requires careful thought. Formal indicators of identity such as a participant's name, date of birth, telephone numbers, registration numbers, postal address are straightforward features which should be anonymised (Tagg 2009, p.88). Other information, such as a reference to a person's occupation, or to publicly available information such as a place name may not need to be anonymised. However, exceptions occur, and if localised knowledge of more generic details (such as a person's occupation, or the name of a restaurant or local district) could compromise confidentiality or put a participant at risk, then these features may also need to be anonymised. With data taken from social media sites, links to additional material might need to be substituted if they lead to sources which might in turn reveal a participant's identity (for example, links to a personal blog or to an account on a photo-sharing site). Paratextual information like GPS locations may also need to be removed, depending on the extent to which this data might compromise the privacy of a participant's information too.

Personal information can be replaced by using pseudonyms, but this may generate further ethical dilemmas such as whether the participant or the researcher chooses the replacement fictional names. An effective option is to replace personal information with a system of codes which allows the researcher to represent the type of information that has been deleted (such as a first name or a surname, place name and so on). If you are dealing with a large dataset (such as compiling a corpus), using an automated system for anonymising material can reduce the labour involved, but as Tagg (2009) points out, this requires careful checking to ensure that the data is not altered incorrectly or in ways that make it difficult to use.

The responsibility to protect the participants' privacy rights also influences how to represent their material when writing up the results of a study. The extent to which a participant's identity might need to be protected depends in part on whether a researcher chooses to quote excerpts from the gathered data. In some cases, the results of a study could be represented as aggregated figures derived from the analysis of the data. In this case, the information quoted directly from the data might be minimal, such as a specific linguistic variable (a type of emoticon, lexical item or similar), from which it would be difficult to trace back the identity of individual participants in the study. However, in linguistic study, and often in qualitative linguistic research, it is commonly accepted as good practice to provide quoted examples from your data as illustrative material. If a study is likely to include quoted excerpts, then both informed consent and anonymisation should be used to protect the privacy rights of participants. If the data has been anonymised during the process of preparing it for analysis, the codes used to replace identifying information can also be used when quoting from this material. However, again, care must be taken to ensure that any codes are not too obscure (and hence disruptive to making sense of the data). The following check list can be used to help consider the ethical issues related to storing and publishing examples from your data.

**Points for reflection**

Will you quote excerpts from your data in the report of your research?

What actions do you need to take to anonymise your data?

Do your participants wish to be exempt from anonymisation and treated as authors (and so represent them by name)?

How long do you need to store your data?

Where will you store materials?

**Box 4.1 The language of Mumsnet**

**Karin Tusting**

Mumsnet is "the UK's biggest social network for parents", started in 2000. In recent years, Mumsnet has become not just an online space in which for parents to interact, but an influential and often-referenced voice in the public sphere. My research will explore the discourse and style of interactions found on the site and requires collecting a dataset of threads for detailed analysis. But gathering the data raises some difficult ethical questions.

Mumsnet is a public arena, but there are places where people may discuss personal, private or challenging issues. Some members engage regularly with a small group of people and seem to orient to their posts as private conversations. Other areas seem much more 'public' in tone. How should I decide which areas would be out of bounds?

Questions arise about anonymisation, too. Should people's online pseudonyms be used in publications referring to their words, to recognise their intellectual property? Or should their pseudonyms be altered to preserve their anonymity? And how does informed consent work in such a setting – should I post on a thread every time I look at one, to make my presence as a researcher visible; or would this be invasive and problematic?

Mumsnet own the copyright of words published on the site, so the use of quotations needs to be negotiated with them. And then there is the question of my own identity on the site, and the extent to which I might be risking making discussions of my own private and family life, under a pseudonym, public property ...

I discussed these questions with other people doing similar research, and contacted the people I knew well from Mumsnet offline for their thoughts. The Association of Internet Researchers' guidelines on ethics helped confirm my belief that I needed to work out how to position my research in a way that was appropriate for the context.

As I wanted to develop a collaborative position with the people whose words I would research, I planned to post a thread to open up a conversation about my research and its aims. I contacted the site owners to ask their opinion about this. They replied quickly and were enthusiastic about the research, but they made it very clear that posting up a thread would not be the best way to go about things! Instead they advised contacting members individually for consent if I wanted to reproduce their words, and offered support to me in doing this.

My most important lessons learnt are to identify gatekeepers and get in touch with them from early on, to get advice and get their take on how best to go about the research in the setting that they know best.

#advice: Don't make too many assumptions about how to do the research before you get in touch with key people and talk to them first! @karinpt

As Karin Tusting's case study shows, ethics influence the choices made at all stages of the research design, from initial choices of how to access material, how to represent yourself as a researcher and interact with participants, gaining informed consent, archiving material and preparing it for use in your project and potential publication of results. Given that research is a process, it is important to build points of reflection into the research design which allow the researchers to check whether the decisions made when planning the work at the outset are still appropriate or need to be modified. Given also that social media is a fast-changing environment, from the outset it is important to remember that researchers may need to be responsive to changes (foreseen and unforeseen) that occur as they collect and analyse material.

The complex and contingent nature of making ethical decisions is best negotiated through dialogue with others, and as discussed earlier in this chapter, a healthy mechanism by which researchers can make their work transparent and accountable to the other people involved in the research (the participants in the study, colleagues in the field, people who might make use of the research findings). Although this book is aimed primarily at those with an interest in linguistic research, the interdisciplinary potential of social media means that often conversations about how to conduct research ethically can bring to light differences in practices. Those differences can help us learn how to refine our practices and to examine our own assumptions about what benefits and harm might arise from our research and how best to protect the participants whose language we want to examine.

We close this chapter with the advice that when making ethical decisions, it is worth considering how you would wish to be treated as a research participant. That personal judgement cannot override regulatory constraints (for example, to suggest that informed consent is not needed if an IRB or REC requires that it is), but rather may help tease out some of the intricate choices required when deciding how to protect the rights of the people whose discourse may be the subject of your research project.

## References

Baym, N.K. and boyd, d. (2012) 'Socially mediated publicness: an introduction', *Journal of Broadcasting and Electronic Media*, 56 (3), 320–9.

boyd, d. and Marwick, A. (2011) *How Teens Understand Privacy*, unpublished manuscript, available: www.danah.org/papers/2011/SocialPrivacyPLSC-Draft.pdf [accessed 1 February 2013].

Buchanan, E. (2009) 'How do various notions of privacy influence decisions in qualitative Internet research? A response' in Markham, A. and Baym, N., eds, *Internet Inquiry: Dialogue among Researchers*, Thousand Oaks: SAGE, 88–92.

Chalil Madathil, K., Koikkara, R., Gramopadhye, A.K. and Greenstein, J.S. (2011) 'An empirical study of the usability of consenting systems: iPad, touchscreen and paper-based systems', *Proceedings of the Human Factors and Ergonomics Society Annual Meeting* September 2011, 55, 1813–17.

Elm, Malin Sveningsson (2009) 'How do various notions of privacy influence decisions in qualitative Internet research?' in Markham, A. and Baym, N., eds, *Internet Inquiry: Dialogue among Researchers*, Thousand Oaks: SAGE, 69–87.

Ess, C. and the Association of Internet Researchers (2002) *Ethical Decision-making and Internet Research*, available: http://aoir.org/reports/ethics.pdf [accessed 10 October 2013].

Grodzinsky, F. and Tavani, H. (2010) 'Applying the "contextual integrity" model of privacy to personal blogs in the blogosphere', *International Journal of Internet Research Ethics*, 3, available: http://ijire.net/issue_3.1/4_Grodzinsky_Tavani.pdf [accessed 26 November 2013].

Lewis, K., Kaufman, J., Gonzalez, M., Wimmer, A. and Chistakis, N. (2008) 'Taste, ties and time: a new social network dataset using Facebook', *Social Networks*, 30 (4), 330–42.

McKee, H. and Porter, J. (2009) *The Ethics of Internet Research: A Rhetorical, Case-Based Approach*, New York and Berlin: Peter Lang.

Markham, A. and Buchanan, E. (2012) *Ethical Decision-making and Internet Research v 2*, available: http://aoir.org/reports/ethics2.pdf [accessed 12 November 2013].

Munt, S.R., Bassett, E.H. and O'Riordan, K. (2002) 'Virtually belonging: risk, connectivity, and coming out on-line', *International Journal of Sexuality and Gender Studies*, 7 (2–3), 125–37.

Nissenbaum, H. (2011) 'A contextual approach to privacy online', *Daedalus*, 140 (4), 32–48.

Rosenberg, A. (2010) 'Virtual world research ethics and the public/private distinction', *International Journal of Internet Research Ethics*, 3, available: http://ijire.net/issue_3.1/3_rosenberg.pdf [accessed 26 November 2013].

Senft, T. (2008) *Camgirls: Celebrity and Community in the Age of Social Networks*, New York: Peter Lang.

Tagg, C. (2009) *A Corpus Analysis of SMS Text Messaging*, unpublished PhD, University of Birmingham.

Whiteman, N. (2010) 'Control and contingency: maintaining ethical stances in research', *International Journal of Internet Research Ethics*, 3, available: http://ijire. net/issue_3.1/2_whiteman.pdf [accessed 26 November 2013].

Whiteman, N. (2012) *Undoing Ethics: Rethinking Practice in Online Research*, New York: Springer.

Zimmer, M. (2010) '"But the data is already public": on the ethics of research in Facebook', *Ethics and Information Technology*, 12 (4), 313–25.

# Chapter 5

# Analysing discourse

## Qualitative approaches

## Outline of the chapter

In this chapter we cover:

- The nature of discourse.
- What kinds of questions qualitative research can answer.
- How to collect, select and analyse qualitative data.
- Different frameworks for discourse analysis, including conversation analysis, multimodal discourse analysis, critical discourse studies and computer-mediated discourse analysis.

## Introduction

In Chapter 3, we presented qualitative and quantitative research as two poles on a spectrum, which allows for many, often nuanced, variations in methodology. In this chapter, we will focus on the qualitative end of this spectrum: in other words, we will discuss the different kinds of questions we might ask about language use in social media from a qualitative perspective, look at how to collect and select data for qualitative studies, and introduce some different types of frameworks for analysis. Qualitative approaches are common in a wide variety of social science disciplines, and although they typically involve relatively small datasets and numbers of participants, the detailed, nuanced analysis of data they typically involve can provide considerable explanatory power.

Although qualitative analysis is not synonymous with discourse analysis, we will discuss the definitions, types and models of analysis used in relation to 'discourse' in some depth, not least because we (as authors) all draw on the concept to varying degrees in our own work. It has also been very influential in the development of linguistic analysis in the field of computer-mediated communication, particularly in the form of Susan Herring's CMDA paradigm, which we introduced in Chapter 2. In this chapter, we expand on our earlier introduction, and introduce two further approaches which draw attention to the importance of contextualising linguistic analysis: critical discourse analysis and multimodal discourse analysis. Each of these treats contextual factors in different ways (in terms of data collection), but all reflect the social and political meanings that accrue in online interactions.

## Discourse? Discuss!

Just like in Chapter 1, where we defined social media, and Chapter 2, where we defined language, in this chapter we have another elusive concept to define: discourse. This term has gone through various waves of definition and redefinition, and has fallen into and out of favour regularly in linguistics, and more broadly in the social sciences. Currently, there are three main ways in which the term discourse is used that are relevant to this book. These can be defined broadly as:

1   The unit of language above the level of the sentence (e.g. Stubbs 1983).
2   A particular way of seeing and representing the world (e.g. Fairclough 2003).
3   Language in use in its social context (e.g. Wodak and Meyer 2009).

The first is a rather formal definition, and fits better with the more structural understanding of language we outlined in Chapter 2. It suggests that we should be concerned with the higher-level features of language – not just the 'nuts and bolts' of small units of linguistic form and meaning (such as words, clauses or sentences), but whole texts and genres. Context in this understanding of discourse refers mostly to 'co-text', the other texts that surround the text we are interested in. The other two definitions move beyond the text and co-text, and suggest we need to consider the broader ideological and social context of interactions (what we described in Chapter 2 as "extra-situational context" and what in Chapters 6 and 7 are treated in ethnographic approaches under the broader label of 'culture'). Fairclough's definition is chiefly concerned with the ideological functions of language: texts are never neutral, and discourses (the count form "a discourse" or plural "discourses" is usually used for this understanding of the term) can be associated with particular ideological orientations. The ways of seeing the world that are identified and critiqued are often '-isms', such as racism, sexism and other forms of discrimination and domination. The final definition, exemplified by Wodak and Meyer's work, is concerned primarily with the social function of language: each utterance is a social action that influences and is influenced by utterances and other social actions that come before and follow. This final definition of discourse is also most compatible with the more progressive understanding of the role of language in communication outlined in Chapter 2. In this sense, the etymology of the word, which comes from the Latin *discurrere* meaning "to run back and forth", is a rather nice metaphor for what researchers do when engaging in discursive research

(Wodak 2006, p.595): they move between data and theory, between language and society, and between their own interpretations and those of others. In the remainder of this chapter, we will move back and forth between describing how to do qualitative and discourse-based research into language in social media, because of the large overlap between the two. A final point about discourse is that it is often considered to be multimodal. While verbal text (often written, but also spoken) has historically been the primary focus of discourse analysis, there is an important subset of research in this area that focuses on visual semiotic resources (e.g. Kress and Van Leeuwen 2001, 2006; Van Leeuwen 2008).

## Asking qualitative questions

One of the main ways in which research at the qualitative end of the spectrum differs from quantitative work is not only in the amount of data considered, but also the kinds of questions that it attempts to ask and answer about language. Discourse analysis of various kinds allows us to give detailed interpretations of what motivates particular linguistic (and social) practices in these contexts; in other words, to answer questions along the lines of "Why does X occur in context Y?" or "What effect does linguistic practice X have on social group Z?" For instance, qualitative research questions might look something like these:

Why did protestors tweet jokes during the Occupy Wall Street protests?
How does English–Arabic code-switching allow international students to negotiate their identities in Facebook chats?

These questions situate particular linguistic practices (joke-telling and chatting, respectively) within a broader social context (the Occupy protests and international education). But qualitative questions can of course also be concerned with more specific or 'micro' linguistic features. And even if questions do not include the word "why", they may still implicitly be concerned with interpreting reasons related to language practices, as in the following examples:

How do the Facebook friends of university students react to their use of non-standard spellings in status messages?
What stance markers do movie bloggers use to indicate their expertise?
Does the social function of intensifiers (*so*, *very*, *really*) in online chat by teenagers aged between 13 and 17 years vary by gender, and if so, how?

### Avoiding superficiality and over-generalisation

Researchers (e.g. Friedman 2012; Wodak 2008; Heigham and Croker 2009) have found that two of the biggest potential pitfalls of qualitative research are superficiality and over-generalisation. The former often occurs when researchers just describe linguistic features without any interpretation and without relating them to social context. The latter can occur when researchers go too far the other way: from a given set of observations of language, they make assumptions that go far beyond the scope of their data. One of the reasons these problems may occur is a misunderstanding of 'representativeness' in qualitative research. The principle that a social group can be represented by certain individuals is deeply enshrined in a number of social scientific traditions, particularly those that employ methods at the quantitative end of the spectrum (see Chapter 8 for more detail). For instance, a marketing survey of 1,000 people may try to recruit a sample of participants that proportionally matches the overall population with regard to variables such as age, gender, level of education, household income, etc. On this basis of the responses from the smaller, selected sample of partici-pants, the researchers will then make claims about the overall population. This has become significantly easier for market researchers, and to a certain extent academic researchers, through the use of social media, because often the required demographic information is already recorded by the social media platforms. It is feasible for large projects that involve qualitative methods to also follow this principle: for instance, if we wanted to explore attitudes towards language use by teenagers on Facebook, we could recruit ten focus groups, each consisting of a certain demographic group (e.g. a group of young teenagers, a group of older teenagers, a group of parents of teenagers who are themselves active social media users, etc.). The problem is that the amount of time, effort and money this would require usually puts it outside the scope of a single researcher working on a short-term project.

Even research that does not require direct involvement of human parti-cipants, for instance a study of news reporting on social media use by teenagers, may raise issues of representativeness. Researchers might want to ask themselves on how many texts one can conduct detailed, qualitative analysis in the time they have available to complete a project. For example, can you include both traditional print journalism and online-only sources in the project? Is it feasible to include video/audio reportage as well as written documentation? What about including reports from different ends of the political spectrum, i.e. news sources with explicit ideological orientations? Reportage from just one country, or several? Can user com-ments be included as well, and should this include only comments on the news site itself, or also comments on social media platforms? What about the time frame of the reports – will this be a diachronic study of changing attitudes, or a snapshot of a given point of time? It is easy to see how the amount of data needed to achieve 'representativeness' of all news sources could quickly spiral out of control. There are two ways of dealing with this problem, the first of which is to include elements of quantitative and qualitative methods in the research project. Mixed-method research is discussed more fully in Chapter 7 and Chapter 9. Second, the researcher can clearly and explicitly point out the limits on the validity of claims arising from analysis of a given data set. 'Limitations' in this context should not be seen as a fault of the research – rather, they are an essential feature of the research design that allows us to strengthen our claims by making them more specific. This is often done even at the stage of formulating the research questions: for instance, the research question about English–Arabic code-switching is already limited to a group of language users in a broad context, but could be made even more specific by specifying which kinds of international students, which kind of university and which kind of location limit the selection of participants and interactions in the study. A reformulated version of the research question might look something like this:

How does English–Arabic code-switching allow Egyptian students at a UK university to negotiate their identities in a Facebook chat with friends studying in Egypt?

There is a fine balance between including too much and too little information in a research question. At one extreme, if the researcher includes assumptions about the data that they have not yet found evidence for, this pre-empts other aspects of the research (for example, in the focus on particular features rather than others, or the choice of a particular type of analysis). On the other hand, if we make the question too vague, this may mean we cannot carry out the research that would allow us to answer it (see Chapter 3 for more general considerations around research design). By carefully framing questions, and choosing appropriate methods to investigate them, it should be possible to avoid both superficiality and over-generalisation. Furthermore, research questions can be refined and reframed as the research continues. In qualitative research, this often occurs when the researcher's interpretations are shared and discussed with participants (see Chapter 6 for how this applies to ethnographic approaches too). We describe some of the principles of data collection for qualitative/discursive research in the following section.

---

### Points for reflection

Are you more interested in what people do with language in social media, or in how and why they do it?

What are the practical limits on your research in terms of time, energy, resources, access to data?

## Collecting qualitative data

### Gathering versus eliciting

One of the first questions researchers should ask is whether their research questions can be best answered by gathering data that already exists (for instance, posts already made by an organisation to a social network site) or by eliciting data from participants who have been asked to take part in the study (for instance, representatives of an organisation). The latter could involve a number of different methods such as questionnaires, individual or group interviews, "think-aloud" protocols (where a participant talks about something they're doing while doing it) or even experiments (e.g. eye-tracking studies). As we have already suggested several times, there is no clear dividing line between qualitative and quantitative research, and many of these methods can be used in research at either end of the spectrum, or in mixed-method research. For instance, a questionnaire could include multiple-choice questions, which might be analysed quantitatively (see Chapter 9) but also open questions for which participants can write longer responses, which could then be subjected to qualitative analysis. These methods could also be combined with ethnographic research (see Chapters 6 and 7), for instance in a comparison of what newspapers say about teenagers' social media use (using text analysis of the articles) with ethnographic observations of a group of teenagers' actual practices. Discourse research often involves both gathered and elicited data (as is advocated for instance by Androutsopoulos 2011).

### How much data to collect

With both data gathering and eliciting methods, it is important that the dataset is suitable for the research questions and methods at hand, but also that it is feasible to collect, process and analyse it in the time available for the research project. For instance, for someone researching the question about movie bloggers above, it would be relatively easy to gather thousands of blog posts about movies from a variety of bloggers. But as this research question requires detailed textual and contextual analysis, collecting this much data may be a waste of effort, and it would be better to collect just ten. Figure 5.1 shows some of the main considerations which might determine how much data the researcher chooses to collect.

### Difficulty of collection

For elicited data, finding willing participants and getting their informed consent can be rather time-consuming (see Chapter 4). Data collection methods such as interviews, qualitative questionnaires or focus groups

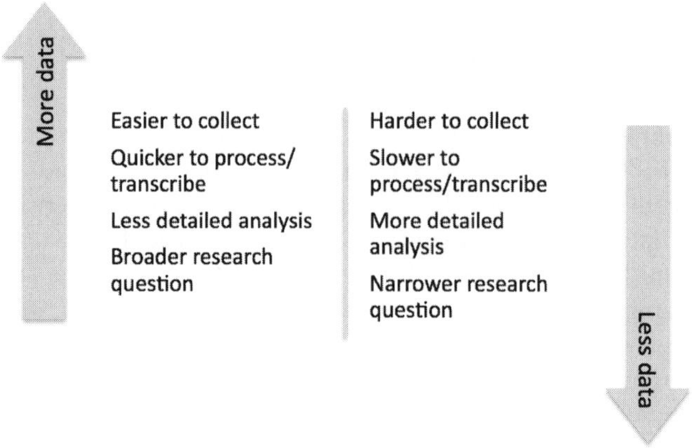

*Figure 5.1* Factors which influence how much data to collect.

often require a considerable investment of time by the participants. Further-more, researchers often examine the data in minute detail. As discussed in Chapter 4, for some kinds of research, particularly when contentious issues such as people's attitudes and beliefs, or their non-standard language use, are being examined, there are also ethical factors which might make the collection of data tricky; there is more potential to intrude into partici-pants' lives or make them feel uncomfortable. On the other hand, once participants have been recruited, they often love having the chance to talk about a topic that is important to them, and to participate in research that may further understanding or lead to change in some way. Gathered data can also pose challenges, for instance because social media texts are frequently changed, or even removed entirely, it can sometimes be hard to make sense of materials that in retrospect appear incomplete. For other types of social media data, texts may only be produced sporadically (e.g. blog posts). Some data may only be available to access at particular locations, or may require constant attention by the researcher (e.g. a fast-moving forum discussion).

### Transcription/processing

Some data may require transcription (e.g. YouTube videos, focus groups), or some other form of processing (e.g. tidying up web texts, adding metadata, or annotating screen captures as we return to in more detail in Chapters 7, 8 and 9). Again, the more of this work is required, the less data it is feasible to collect for a given project. Transcription, particularly if it has to be detailed (e.g. noting down intonational features, gestures in You-Tube videos or how typed corrections get made in chat), can be very time-consuming, sometimes up to an hour or more of transcription per minute of collected data! It is also important to note that transcription is not a neutral activity – the researcher's decisions about what features to transcribe and how they transcribe them have implications not only for how the data is presented, but also on what can be analysed at all (Ochs 1979).

### Type of analysis

Some methods are much more time-consuming than others. If the analysis involves manual coding (i.e. identifying features that belong in certain categories and marking them accordingly), or if you want to analyse multiple features/categories (e.g. looking for particular verbal features as well as visual elements), this will add to the time required (see below for some examples of different kinds of analysis).

### Breadth of research question

This is probably the most important dimension which influences the data collection. As already discussed, research questions should always be limited in some way, either through an explicit statement as part of the question, or by describing the limitations elsewhere. Without appropriate limitations, research questions become impossible to answer. The limitations have a direct bearing on the amount of data required: the narrower, more specific the research question, the less data will generally be required to answer it adequately.

### General principle

Taking all these points into consideration, we recommend adopting the following general principle to deal with research projects of different scales (i.e. amount of data) and scopes (i.e. how wide-reaching the research questions are):

Collect at least as much data as you need to answer your research question(s), but no more than you have time to collect, process and analyse.

Where appropriate, consider using mixed methods to help deal with large volumes of data, or to select subsets of your data for further analysis (see below), and to strengthen the validity and reliability (see Chapter 3) of your research. Depending on the methods used, you may find it useful to conduct a pilot study or initial investigation to check that your data collection and analysis works as intended. This is also a good way of checking how long the different stages of your research (collection, processing and analysis) will take.

**Points for reflection**

What kinds of claims would you like to make about your data and how much data would you need to support them?

Will it be easier to collect large amounts of data and then narrow them down, or to decide beforehand which specific data you want to collect?

In the case studies in this chapter, the two authors explain some of the challenges they encountered when collecting data for their qualitative research projects. Both Mariza Georgalou and Aoife Lenihan faced challenges relating to the constantly changing nature of social media interactions. For Mariza, this related to social events which took place during the time she was collecting data. For Aoife, the sudden disappearance of the forum she was studying put her research at risk. Both researchers had choices to make about how to select their material in the first place, and when to stop collecting data.

## Box 5.1 The discursive performance of self in social network sites: Greeks on Facebook

### Mariza Georgalou

My PhD thesis explored the construction of identities on Facebook. Embarking on detailed discourse analysis of both verbal and visual modalities, I identified the ways in which Greek Facebook users:

- located themselves in terms of place and time;
- shared their expertise and buttressed solidarity among colleagues and fellow students;
- communicated emotions, tastes, thoughts, opinions and assessments;
- controlled the flow of information on their walls to secure their privacy.

To gather my data, I combined systematic and longitudinal observation of Facebook profiles with direct (mediated and face-to-face) engagement with their creators. The latter were recruited via convenience sampling. Initially, they were sent a message in which I explained the purposes of my study, asking them to fill in an online questionnaire on how they experienced social media mechanics. Five respondents (two females and three males; mean age = 28) agreed to participate in a series of semi-structured interviews via email, instant messaging and/or Facebook messages. My multimodal dataset included survey information, interview material, Facebook profile information, Facebook wall posts (status updates, comments, links, photos), field notes, and informants' comments on my analysis.

Drawing from my own research experience on Facebook, here are some helpful rules of thumb.

*Prefer friends of friends as a first sampling resort.* My initial contact message for finding informants was randomly sent to more than 100 MySpace and Facebook users. What I received was only 33 replies and a general feeling of unwillingness to be interviewed. I got frustrated and wasted precious time. When I asked my own friends and relatives to forward my message to contacts of theirs, the situation was surprisingly reversed. "I'm ready for a new questionnaire whenever you need, ok?!" one of my participants wrote.

*Learn from your informants' social media practices.* In preparing his MA dissertation, one of my informants created a Facebook event to recruit participants for his survey, asking his Facebook friends to share the event to that purpose. It was fun clicking 'going' to that particular event. Indeed, this kind of promotion proved to be very effective for my informant's study as 190 people completed his questionnaire in just 24 hours. Had I utilised Facebook in a similarly innovative way, I could have instantly got access to more interviewees.

*Show people what you are doing with their data.* How to handle data on my subjects' walls from users who had not given their consent constituted a thorny issue. Just asking for their permission to use their comments was not enough. Sending them samples of textual analysis of their Facebook interactions gave them a clearer picture of my research and secured their approval.

*Be ready to reformulate your research plan.* I started my PhD in 2009. My research took an unexpected turn within the next years because of the Greek financial and political crisis, which dominated the lives, and concomitantly the content of Facebook posts, of the people I was studying. In the end, almost half of my data was about the crisis, but this gave me the opportunity to examine stance-taking in my thesis.

#advice: Social media = cardiograph of society + language. if its content diverts u from initial RQ, seize chance to explore new linguistic topics.

## Box 5.2 The interaction of language policy, minority languages and new media: a study of the Facebook Translations application

### Aoife Lenihan

This research examines both 'top-down' language policy in new media and also the increasingly 'bottom-up' language practices and covert policies in new media. It aspires to draw conclusions about how to situate and perhaps redefine language policy, with regard to minority languages, in light of the new media context. The field of study is the Facebook Translations application (app), which is an app Facebook developed to localise their website. This app is open to over 100 languages and enables Facebook users, 'translators', to submit translations which their peers, organised into communities according to the language they are translating, then vote on. The Translations app was longitudinally examined from January 2009 to October 2011, using virtual ethnographic methods.

The ever-changing nature of the new media context can lead to methodological issues over the course of a longitudinal ethnography. In September 2009, the Discussion Board of the Irish Translations app was unavailable without explanation. Due to the volume of Topics and Posts in the Discussion Board I had not previously taken screenshots or printed them, so at this point, the majority of the data appeared to be lost (as I had taken for granted the availability and accessibility of the Translations app). Thankfully, the Discussion Board was reopened a few weeks later with its previous content intact. After that, I ensured all data were collected in both paper and screenshot formats. Virtual ethnographers must remember the fluid, dynamic nature of their research field at all times.

The biggest challenge of this research was when to stop collecting data, this question being raised and considered at many points during the ethnography. I had hoped to finish data collection when the Irish Translations app had completed the translation process, which occurred in three steps. However, as the ethnography continued I had to wonder if the Irish version would ever be completed given the ever-evolving nature of the site and the new terminology/elements these changes brought that would need to be translated. Therefore when a 'new' Translations app was launched in October 2011 I saw it as a somewhat 'natural' end to the ethnography as elements of it had been removed and changed. In conclusion, sometimes you will have some ethnographic luck and have a somewhat natural end to the virtual ethnographic context, however, at other times, the researcher must use their ethnographic and contextual sensitivity to ascertain the best time to end the research.

My primary recommendation is that the researcher must acknowledge that no ethnography is a complete, perfect, all-encompassing ethnography. Every methodological decision made by the ethnographer impacts and limits the ethnographic account in some way. Like the primary method of data collection here, the screenshot, this ethnography is a snapshot of a period of Facebook and its Translations app considered using theoretical frameworks from language policy. The researcher's thoughts and findings come from and are specific to this context, over the time period of the research, as it was experienced.

#advice: New media is dynamic, don't take it for granted that your data will be online forever, backup no matter how many screenshots it takes!

## How to select data for qualitative research

Data collection is an important part of the research process, but for qualitative research, data selection is an equally important part. As suggested above, it may not be possible to analyse all the available data. Returning to the example of movie bloggers, we suggested it might make more sense to choose only ten bloggers out of the thousands available for detailed analysis. But how can a researcher decide which ten out of the thousands of potential participants to choose? First, the researcher has to decide at what stage to carry out the data selection, before or after collection. Some elements of the selection process will already have been decided by limiting the data collection to movie blogs, rather than blogs on other topics or entirely different social media texts. If it is relatively easy to collect a lot of data, it may make sense to collect more than is needed, and then do the selection afterwards. On the other hand, if it is harder (for instance, if each blog post required a considerable amount of processing to tidy it up for inclusion in the research project), it would make more sense to select more exactly the materials you want before you begin collection. Usually qualitative researchers do a mixture of pre- and post-selection. Pre-selection may for instance involve identifying a particular field of interest (e.g. movie-blogging), and language (e.g. Spanish, because this is the only language the researcher feels competent to analyse), and may be driven by the researcher's own interests or competencies. Even if these choices seem obvious or the only alternative, they should be documented and made transparent when the research process is described.

Again, one of the most important considerations for data selection is the breadth of the research question. For instance, if a project involved examining gender identities in movie blogging, this factor might also narrow the selection process – perhaps choosing only female bloggers if we are interested in femininities in the movie-blogging world. But if after that, the researcher is still left with too many blogs, an additional selection criterion may be useful – perhaps they could choose only blogs written in the past year, or choose one per year from the past ten years.

These are all examples of applying more text-external or contextual criteria to the process of selection; in other words, they are features that researchers cannot necessarily find out about just by looking at the text itself. However, it is also possible to select data using text-internal criteria: for instance, if we wanted to explore how movie bloggers express scepticism towards claims by representatives of the movie industry, we might reasonably look for a stance marker like *apparently* in the content of the texts. We could of course limit our data by selecting only those blogs that include this word, but that would not allow us to say anything about other ways of expressing scepticism, and would thus limit the strengths of the claims we could make about how scepticism is expressed. It would not make sense to claim that one of the main ways movie bloggers expressed scepticism was using the word *apparently* if this word was the basis of our data selection. This is not to say that text-internal criteria can never be used. For instance, in a study of English–Arabic code-switching, it would make sense to select only texts that include these two languages. As with qualitative and quantitative research, the criteria text-external and text-internal should be seen more as points on a spectrum rather than discrete categories.

Researchers sometimes fall into the trap of selecting only the data that support their argument, a practice also known colloquially as 'cherry-picking'. To avoid this, it is vital that research questions, data collection and selection, and the scope of claims made about the data all relate to each other. The following list shows some of the main criteria that can be used to select social media data for qualitative research.

- Platform: often research focuses on only one specific social media platform, e.g. Facebook, Twitter or Wikipedia.
- Time: a limited time period (e.g. a certain day, a certain year) or a certain amount of time before and after a key event (e.g. two days before and five days after).
- Number of utterances/texts or word length: for instance, the last 100 tweets from a particular account, or the last ten blog entries, or ca. 1,000 words of comments on a newspaper website. Selecting by exact word length can cause problems for qualitative analysts, because it can mean texts or utterances are cut in half, so if this criterion is used it is better to

use approximate figures if statistical comparison is not important (as it might be for quantitative analysis; see Chapter 9).

- Identity of author(s): for instance, gender, age, nationality, ethnicity, status within a particular community of practice, and so on.
- Popularity of text: for instance, number of 'likes' on a Facebook page or post, or how often a tweet has been retweeted.
- Self-selection by participants: data chosen as exemplary of a particular practice by participants themselves. This is common in ethnographic research (see Chapter 6).
- Language (variety): data that contain instances of a particular language or language variety, e.g. Spanish or Multicultural London English.
- Topic: what the text is about (e.g. movies): this can be difficult to determine, either because of vagueness in the text, or because of lack of contextual information.
- Presence (or absence) of a particular feature: for instance, word, syntactic structure, word class, type of argumentation, and so on.

Often researchers use these different data selection criteria in combination, but whatever criteria are chosen, it is extremely important to be transparent and to make these decisions clear in the write up of the research. In this way, accusations of cherry-picking can be easily refuted.

## The different flavours of discourse analysis

The general considerations discussed above are about qualitative research questions, data collection and selection, and are generally applicable to a wide range of qualitative social-science approaches. We move now to considering which specific methods and frameworks allow us to answer such questions, and analyse such data. Frameworks can emerge as recognised models (such as explanatory paradigms and categories) and practices (ways of analysing data) within particular schools of thought or fields of interest. The analytical frameworks developed in discourse analysis of offline interactions (such as Coulthard and Candlin 1985) or sociolinguistics (such as Labov 1972) might provide the starting point for making sense of the linguistic patterns found in interactions on social media genres such as blogs or social network sites. But often, as the following sections and chapters will show, these frameworks can raise as many questions about the language used in social media contexts as they help the researcher to answer. These frameworks are not static tools, but can be adapted, refined or rejected as they are tested in the process of researching how people use language in social media. In the following section, we give a broad overview of some of these frameworks, and give examples of particular studies that draw on them.

Qualitative research in linguistics is often interested in language users' opinions and experience of their language practices. This kind of work will often bring together rich and multilayered interpretations of this experience and often can incorporate direct interaction with participants. While some information about the users of social media can be obtained via social media metadata, more comprehensive, richer accounts may require ethnographic approaches to data collection. This section considers several important, and sometimes not mutually exclusive, overarching frameworks that can be used to explore the ways in which people interact with each other through social media texts and contexts.

### Discourse analysis

Discourse analysis is a varied technique that aims to understand the social meanings that are made in texts through close analysis of the language used. The analysis often comprises whole texts or genres, and may include multimodal features as well as the verbal text. One way of thinking about the methods typically employed in discourse analysis is that it "employs the tools of grammarians to identify the roles of wordings in passages of text, and employs the tools of social theorists to explain why they make the meanings they do" (Martin and Rose 2003, p.4). It affords the researcher rich insights into the patterns of meaning that unfold in texts. Discourse analysis will often incorporate information about the context of the text such as the "context of situation" (e.g. description of the social function of a particular genre, e.g. narrative genres in blogging) and the "context of culture" (e.g. blogging cultures), ideas drawn from Malinowski's (1923) ethnographic work on context. An example of close discourse analysis of social media is Page's (2012) work on narrative interaction in blogging communities where she investigates illness narratives in personal blogs as well as the relationship between editorial intervention and narrative coherence in an experimental wikinovel. Another is Myers' (2010) work on the discourse of blogs and wikis which uses close textual analysis to interpret how authors position themselves relative to others.

Collecting data for discourse analysis usually involves determining which texts are appropriate for close manual analysis by the researcher (e.g. determining the presence of particular linguistic phenomena such as passive verb constructions) in order to answer some question about both the language and its social function. Because of the intensive nature of discourse analysis, a relatively small sample of texts and relatively simple data collection methods such as 'cut and paste' of texts into .txt files may be appropriate for studies considering verbal language alone (which will not consider dimensions such as layout). Where more contextual information is to be considered (as we will see in the sections on critical discourse studies and multimodal analysis below) screen captures may be useful.

### Conversation analysis

Conversation analysts would argue strongly against including their approach as a subset of discourse analysis (Wooffitt 2005). Nevertheless, the concepts, tools and methods of analysis and transcription originally developed by Sacks, Schegloff, Jefferson and others have come to be widely used in many forms of discourse analysis. Conversation analysis (CA) is traditionally concerned with examining and identifying patterns in spontaneous speech. CA starts from the assumption that speech is highly ordered, even though it often does not resemble standard written grammar. The structures found in conversational interactions carry meaning, and are used to organise both the interaction and the relationships between the interlocutors. The main linguistic features that are important in traditional CA are (for a thorough overview, see Ten Have 2007 or Sidnell 2010):

- Turn-taking: who speaks when in a conversation, and how is the transition between speakers managed. For instance, a speaker may pause, or glance at their interlocutor, to indicate that they are willing to give up 'the floor' in a conversation.
- Sequential organisation: particular forms tend to be followed by a matching form, such as a greeting followed by a greeting in return, or a request for information followed by the information being supplied. In CA these are called adjacency pairs, and together with various other sequences they are seen as ways of managing the interaction.
- Repair: when something unexpected happens (e.g. difficulty hearing, or a misunderstanding), participants in a conversation try to repair what they have said or heard. This could for instance mean repeating the early part of an utterance, or checking whether they have been understood.

The early focus on the 'spoken-like' nature of many digitally mediated texts (see Chapter 2) meant that CA was seen as a useful method for analysis, particularly for instant messaging and other chat platforms. Herring (2013) includes CA as one of the methods suitable for studying interaction in digital texts (see Chapter 2 and below), and various scholars have sought to adapt and improve CA for social media. For instance, CA makes allowances for adjacency pairs that occur across several turns. But when applied to chat, so-called 'instant' messaging is often not instant, and long delays (days, weeks) may occur between turns. On the other hand, some platforms that are seen as less conversational (email, message boards) may be virtually instant, with 'conversations' pinging back and forth almost as quickly as the interlocutors can read (and write) the messages. Darics (2010) looks at the issues around what may be considered synchronous and asynchronous in work context in her study of a corporate chat platform (see also her Case Study in Chapter 1). A further difference to spoken conversations is that turns are managed in different ways – in instant messaging, it is usually possible for everyone to type at the same time, and messages appear in an ordered fashion on the screen. With speech, too many people speaking at the same time make it harder to understand any one individual – thus, floor-management in spoken conversation tends to be much more rigid, and any deviation from the norm (e.g. continually interrupting other speakers) may be regarded as impolite.

### Multimodal discourse analysis

Written text is often treated as 'monomodal', that is, language alone is assumed to convey meaning. However, given the different media in which it may be rendered (e.g. print in a book or on a screen) and the choices in layout (e.g font) that are made, this clearly is an imprecise portrayal and all written language is multimodal. More obviously multimodal texts are those that embed images, audio and video. Qualitative studies interested in exploring the multimodality of social media texts over a small range of instances may find 'quick-and-dirty' techniques such as screen captures adequate for collecting the data required. These studies may be concerned with exploring how particular instances of multimodal meaning work together in a given text in a particular context (see Jones 2005). Small multimodal corpora, usually specialised corpora, may also be used in qualitative discourse analysis and for some kinds of limited quantitative analyses (see Allwood 2008). Multimodal corpora can include prosodic, gestural and proxemic features (Knight 2011) occurring in a face-to-face interaction, or in the case of electronic discourse, 'static' texts such as web pages (including images and presentational dimensions such as layout) (see for example Bateman's (2008) annotation schema for static documents) as well as 'dynamic' texts such as video.

Social media often incorporates written messages alongside video and audio. Bateman (2008, p.265) suggests that when we attempt to analyse these kinds of texts, we need to "move from text-based data to *time-based data*" meaning that transcription and annotations need to be linked to "a particular temporally sequenced track as the 'reference' track and all other phenomena ... then related back to the elements of that reference track". Time-based data requires specially designed transcription and annotation tools (see Chapter 9). An important consideration is the format that the transcription software uses to output the transcribed text and whether or not this is compatible with the annotation system that will be used. For example the open source system 'Transcriber' (http://trans.sourceforge. net/en/presentation.php) allows the user to fairly seamlessly import the transcribed text into the video annotation system ELAN (http://tla.mpi.nl/ tools/tla-tools/elan/) so that the video may be annotated in parallel to the transcription. Such considerations are crucial to the workflow of a linguistic project (see for instance the different approaches used by Pihlaja 2013; Darics 2010; Georgalou 2010; Frobenius 2011).

Alongside the huge proliferation of video and audio on the web, there has been an almost equally impressive increase in the amount of content such as scripts or transcripts of TV and film, political broadcasts, song lyrics, and even searchable transcripts of web comics (http://www.ohnorobot.com/). These can be an invaluable resource and are sometimes the only feasible way of getting huge volumes of a particular kind of verbal data for quantitative or mixed-method analysis, but researchers interested in language in social media should approach them with caution. They are not necessarily core social media texts (see Chapter 1) but may still be of interest to researchers looking at social media data in conjunction with other data (e.g. comments on a political speech). But many are crowd-sourced, some are produced automatically (e.g. using voice-recognition software to transcribe news reports), and they may thus contain high error margins. Some may be scripts (i.e. produced before the spoken text was delivered) and not transcripts of the final spoken texts. Even if they are 'accurate' enough for everyday use, they may not contain the necessary detail for linguistic analysis (e.g. indications of pause length between utterances). Furthermore, they often do not contain the visual and contextual information required for multimodal analysis. Thus, they may serve as a starting point, but should almost always be checked and probably augmented if they are to be useful for discourse analysis of any kind.

### Critical discourse studies (CDS)

Like many of the frameworks introduced in this chapter, critical discourse studies should not be seen as a single method or even a coherent theory, but more of a general orientation to research and a set of assumptions about the nature of society and language. The following important principles are shared by different kinds of critical discourse studies and critical discourse analysis, but are not necessarily the basis of the other kinds of discourse analysis introduced in this chapter (adapted from Unger 2013, p.30):

- Discourse and society mutually affect and constitute each other; discourse is thus a form of social practice (see section on discourse above).
- Texts are meaningful units of analysis.
- Every text is accompanied by a context (see Chapter 2). It should not necessarily be assumed that a context's influence on a text can be directly established, but rather there is a complex relationship between the two, which must be carefully studied to validate assumptions.
- Ideologies, or "coherent and relatively stable sets of beliefs or values" (Wodak and Meyer 2009, p.9) are formed by repeated production and

reproduction of belief systems in texts, which are connected with each other in various ways, for example through specific practices. Once established, the ideologies then influence future texts and practices and are thus reinforced by repetition and recontextualisation. Most texts thus have an ideological dimension, which can again be more or less transparent in its linguistic realisation

- Hegemonies are pervasive, relatively stable systems of ideologies supported by institutional and even private social practices. They support the status quo, keeping the powerful in power and the powerless in their place.

- Social wrongs, which are often related to power imbalances, have a linguistic dimension. Partially through the use of language, certain groups within society are suppressed and hegemonies are maintained by more powerful groups. Sometimes language is used in a relatively transparent way for this purpose (e.g. the imperative form of a verb used in giving orders) while at other times the linguistic dimension is more obscure (e.g. the complete absence of a certain social actor from a text, see Van Leeuwen 2008).

- Discriminatory and marginalising social phenomena should not be seen in a purely objective, positivistic light, as an unchangeable status quo. Rather, they can be exposed and challenged, in some greater or lesser ways, by CDS research and by practical assistance given to marginalised groups by CDS researchers.

While other linguistic approaches may typically start with a question about language, CDS researchers typically take a question about or problem in society as a starting point, for instance the prevalence of hate-speech directed against women in certain social media platforms (such as the events described in Bennett-Smith 2013). For this reason, CDS research is not 'neutral' or 'objective', nor does it claim to be: rather, it is motivated by a desire for positive social change.

Once this starting point has been identified and formulated as a research question, CDS researchers then choose a suitable theoretical and methodological framework, as well as an appropriate set of data to allow this problem to be explored in detail. Most CDS research to date has drawn heavily on the theoretical frameworks of sociologists, philosophers and political scientists such as Foucault, Marx, Bourdieu, Althusser, Bakhtin and Habermas, but also on linguists such as Fowler and Halliday. More recently scholars have also drawn on ideas from feminist theory (such as Lazar and Kramarae 2011), media studies (such as Khosravinik 2010), and many other disciplines. Often, these frameworks are concerned with explaining power imbalances between different groups or individuals in society. The important thing is to choose a particular theoretical framework that has something to say about the social issue that is under investigation.

At the methodological level, researchers have drawn on methods such as detailed text analysis (e.g. text linguistics, De Beaugrande and Dressler 1981), systemic functional analysis (Van Leeuwen 2008), multimodal analysis (Jiwani and Richardson 2011), argumentation (Van Eemeren *et al.* 2011) and others. One of the things that makes CDS challenging for researchers interested in social media is that there has not been much work on social media using this approach so far. As with discourse analysis of social media in general, this is very much an emerging area. Some earlier work (like Mautner 2005) suggested the use of web corpora to support corpus-assisted discourse studies, but for the most part, this has not been taken up by mainstream CDS researchers to date. The general methodological steps recommended by CDS scholars can also be applied to social media, however. Here, we present the steps suggested in one kind of CDS, the discourse-historical approach (adapted from Wodak 2004, p.210).

1   Sample information about the co- and context of the text (social, political, historical, psychological, etc.). This includes:
   - the immediate, language or text-internal co-text – in other words the utterances or visual elements adjacent in space or time to the social media utterance we are interested in, for instance the comments on a news article;
   - the relationship between the utterances, texts and genres under investigation and others (intertextuality and interdiscursivity) – e.g. looking at links to a particular blog post and seeing how the post is reframed/described/critiqued;
   - the broader context of situation – for instance the typical practices found on a given social media platform and how these relate to the text under investigation, or the limits imposed by particular affordances like the 140-character limit on Twitter;
   - the broadest socio-political and historical contexts, which the discursive practices are embedded in and related to – this may include issues such as the role of censorship in a given society, or the ways in which governments react to dissenting practices that make use of social media.
2   Once the practices around a text have been established, sample more ethnographic information, establish interdiscursivity (texts on similar topics) and intertextuality (fragments of other texts included in the one under investigation, or vice versa).
3   From the problem under investigation, formulate precise research questions and explore neighbouring fields for explanatory theories and theoretical aspects.
4   Operationalise the research questions into linguistic categories.
5   Apply these categories systematically to the text while using theoretical approaches to interpret and explain the social meanings of particular linguistic choices.

6 Make an interpretation of the overall relationship between the text and society, while returning to the research questions and to the problem under investigation (this is sometimes called abductive reasoning).

At the end of this process, CDS researchers then decide whether there is something they can do about the linguistic and social problems they have identified and analysed: this is called prospective critique. For instance, you might approach a forum administrator with a suggested list of guidelines for communication in the forum. Or use your knowledge to support activist organisations campaigning for a particular cause. Or even just raise awareness about the problem amongst your own networks (see, for instance, Clarke's 2009 critical discourse study of forum discussions in teacher education).

### Computer-mediated discourse analysis (CMDA)

CMDA has already been introduced in Chapter 2. In this chapter, we return to it briefly in the context of other traditions of discourse analysis. As we have already suggested, the main proponent of CMDA, Susan Herring, does not see it as a single method, but rather as a methodological toolkit. Herring suggests using various forms of linguistic analysis methods and approaches (e.g. text analysis, conversation analysis, critical discourse analysis) which were designed to examine offline interactions (such as face-to-face conversations, or written interactions) can also be used to analyse different aspects and phenomena found in social media contexts. Much of the work on CMDA was carried out before the rise of social media, but recently there has been a growing interest in what Herring calls "Discourse 2.0" (2013, p.4), that is, discourse analysis of the social and participatory web. She also suggests a new term is needed to draw attention to the convergent nature of social media (see Chapter 1), with multimodal communication becoming more prominent, and different platforms becoming ever more densely networked (e.g. links to Flickr posted on Facebook, or tweets scrolling along the bottom of TV shows). One possible label she suggests for the study of these phenomena is "convergent media computer-mediated communication", though we will subsume this under the more general label CMDA.

One of the many contributions that CMDA can make to discourse and qualitative analysis generally is the more nuanced understanding that researchers have developed of specific genres found in digital media (see also Chapter 2). Researchers following approaches like CDS or multimodal discourse have sometimes struggled to apply more traditional notions of genre (e.g. "the newspaper editorial") to texts and utterances found on the web. Herring suggests there is some value in distinguishing between genres that are well-established in pre-social media web texts, those that show some continuities, and those that are new: she labels these familiar, reconfigured and emergent (Herring 2013). Herring's example of a familiar genre feature is the use of emoticons and non-standard orthographies in social media texts – practices that involve creating new norms of spelling and punctuation use are decades old. A reconfigured genre is for instance the status update. While these have existed in chat platforms for some time, the changing affordances of social media platforms have led to new forms of these short updates and caused particular syntactic changes to the language that typically occurs in these posts. Finally, examples of an emergent genre include the collaborative texts authored by the users of wiki platforms like Wikipedia. These are not found in any pre-web or early-web genres, and have developed their own norms and forms for interaction.

## Summary

In this chapter, we have explored the principles of data collection and selection for qualitative analysis, and outlined different forms of discourse analysis. We have positioned qualitative analysis as one end of a spectrum that includes quantitative and mixed-method research. We have discussed some of the key principles underlying the broad approach of discourse analysis and three more specific related approaches: (multimodal) discourse analysis, critical discourse studies and computer-mediated discourse analysis. In doing so, we have tried to show what might motivate a researcher to adopt one of these approaches, and what they can contribute to the study of social media. When the research seeks to answer questions about "why" or "how", or when it is not yet clear what can be measured, discursive research at the more qualitative end of the spectrum can be an extremely useful way of furthering knowledge about particular social media contexts.

## References

Allwood, J. (2008) 'Multimodal corpora', in Lüdeling, A. and Kytö, M., eds, *Corpus Linguistics: An International Handbook*, Berlin: Mouton de Gruyter, 207–25.

Androutsopoulos, J. (2011) 'From variation to heteroglossia in the study of computer-mediated discourse', in Thurlow, C. and Mroczek, K., eds, *Digital Discourse: Language in the New Media*, Oxford: Oxford University Press, 277–98.

Bateman, J. (2008) *Multimodality and Genre: A Foundation for the Systematic Analysis of Multimodal Documents*, Basingstoke: Palgrave Macmillan.

Bennett-Smith, M. (2013) 'Facebook vows to crack down on rape joke pages after successful protest, boycott', *The Huffington Post*, available: www.huffingtonpost.com/2013/05/29/facebook-rape-jokes-protest_n_3349319.html [accessed 29 October 2013].

Clarke, M. (2009) 'The discursive construction of interpersonal relations in an online community of practice', *Journal of Pragmatics*, 41 (11), 2333–44.

Coulthard, M. and Candlin, C.N. (1985) *An Introduction to Discourse Analysis*, London: Longman.

Darics, E. (2010) 'Politeness in computer-mediated discourse of a virtual team', *Journal of Politeness Research*, 6 (1), 129–50.

De Beaugrande, R. and Dressler, W.U. (1981) *Introduction to Text Linguistics*, London: Longman.

Fairclough, N. (2003) *Analysing Discourse: Textual Analysis for Social Research*, London: Routledge.

Friedman, D. (2012) 'How to collect and analyse qualitative data', in Mackey, A. and Gass, S.M., eds, *Research Methods in Second Language Acquisition: A Practical Guide*, Chichester: Wiley-Blackwell, 180–200.

Frobenius, M. (2011) 'Beginning a monologue: the opening sequence of video blogs', *Journal of Pragmatics*, 43 (3), 814–27.

Georgalou, M. (2010) '"Pathfinding" discourses of self in social network sites', in Taiwo, R., ed., *Handbook of Research on Discourse Behavior and Digital Communication: Language Structures and Social Interaction*, Hershey: IGI Global, 39–65.

Heigham, J. and Croker, R.A. (2009) *Qualitative Research in Applied Linguistics*, Basingstoke: Palgrave Macmillan.

Herring, S.C. (2013) 'Discourse in web 2.0: familiar, reconfigured, and emergent', in Tannen, D. and Trester, A.M., eds, *Discourse 2.0: Language and New Media*, Washington, DC: Georgetown University Press, 1–25.

Jiwani, Y. and Richardson, J.E. (2011) 'Discourse, ethnicity and racism', in Van Dijk, T., ed., *Discourse Studies: A Multidisciplinary Introduction*, London: Sage, 241–62.

Jones, R. (2005) '"You show me yours, I'll show you mine": the negotiation of shifts from textual to visual modes in computer mediated interaction among gay men', *Visual Communication*, 4 (1), 69–92.

Khosravinik, M. (2010) 'The representation of refugees, asylum seekers and immigrants in British newspapers: a critical discourse analysis', *Journal of Language and Politics*, 9 (1), 1–28.

Knight, D. (2011) *Multimodality and Active Listenership: A Corpus Approach*, London: Continuum International Publishing Group.

Kress, G. and Van Leeuwen, T. (2001) *Multimodal Discourse: The Modes and Media of Contemporary Communication*, London: Bloomsbury.

Kress, G. and Van Leeuwen, T. (2006) *Reading Images: The Grammar of Visual Design*, London: Routledge.

Labov, W. (1972) *Sociolinguistic Patterns*, Philadelphia: University of Pennsylvania Press.

Lazar, M. and Kramarae, C. (2011) 'Gender and power in discourse', in Van Dijk, T., ed., *Discourse Studies: A Multidisciplinary Introduction*, London: Sage, 217–40.

Malinowski, B. (1923) 'The problem of meaning in primitive languages', in Ogden, C.K. and Richards, I.A., eds, *The Meaning of Meaning*, London: Routledge and Kegan Paul, 296–336.

Martin, J.R. and Rose, D. (2003) *Working with Discourse: Meaning beyond the Clause*, London: Continuum.

Mautner, G. (2005) 'Time to get wired: using web-based corpora in Critical Discourse Analysis', *Discourse and Society*, 16 (6), 809–28.

Myers, G. (2010) *The Discourse of Blogs and Wikis*, London: Continuum.

Ochs, E. (1979) 'Transcription as theory', in Ochs, E. and Schieffelin, B., eds, *Developmental Pragmatics*, New York: Academic Press, 43–72.

Page, R. (2012) *Stories and Social Media: Identities and Interaction*, London: Routledge.

Pihlaja, S. (2013) 'Truck stops and fashion shows: a case study of the discursive construction of Evangelical Christian group identity on YouTube', in Herbert, D. and Gillespie, M., eds, *Social Media and Religious Change*, Berlin: De Gruyter, 165–84.

Sidnell, J. (2010) *Conversation Analysis: An Introduction*, Chichester: Wiley-Blackwell.

Stubbs, M. (1983) *Discourse Analysis: The Sociolinguistic Analysis of Natural Language* (Vol. 4), Chicago: University of Chicago Press.

Ten Have, P. (2007) *Doing Conversation Analysis*, London: Sage.

Unger, J.W. (2013) *The Discursive Construction of the Scots Language: Education, Politics and Everyday Life*, Amsterdam: John Benjamins.

Van Eemeren, F.H., Jackson, S. and Jacobs, S. (2011) 'Argumentation', in Van Dijk, T., ed., *Discourse Studies: A Multidisciplinary Introduction*, London: Sage, 85–106.

Van Leeuwen, T. (2008) *Discourse and Practice: New Tools for Critical Discourse Analysis*, Oxford: Oxford University Press.

Wodak, R. (2004) 'Critical discourse analysis', in Seale, C., Gobo, G., Gubrium, J.F. and Silverman, D., eds, *Qualitative Research Practice*, London: Sage, 197–213.

Wodak, R. (2006) 'Dilemmas of discourse', *Language in Society*, 35, 595–611.

Wodak, R. (2008) 'Introduction: discourse studies– important concepts and terms', in Wodak, R. and Krzyzanowski, M., eds, *Qualitative Discourse Analysis in the Social Sciences*, Basingstoke: Palgrave Macmillan, 1–29.

Wodak, R. and Meyer, M. (2009) 'Critical discourse analysis: history, agenda, theory and methodology', in Wodak, R. and Meyer, M., eds, *Methods of Critical Discourse Analysis*, 2nd edn, London: Sage, 1–33.

Wooffitt, R. (2005) *Conversation Analysis and Discourse Analysis: A Comparative and Critical Introduction*, London: Sage.

# Chapter 6

# What are ethnographic approaches?

## Outline of the chapter

In this chapter we cover:

- An introduction to ethnographic approaches.
- Common principles of ethnographic approaches.
- Examples of ethnographic studies of the Internet.
- An outline of the steps to take when undertaking a project using ethnographic methods.

## Introduction to ethnographic approaches

Ethnographic approaches to the study of language have a long history in language and linguistics research and are increasingly drawn upon when researching social media. They are concerned with how language is embedded in culture and they bring with them particular beliefs about what language is and how it can be studied (see also Chapter 2 on what might count as 'language'). This chapter introduces ethnographic approaches to researching language in social media. The chapter builds on the previous chapter which focused on analysing interaction in texts, moving on to the practices which those texts are located in. Ethnographic approaches provide a coherent way of thinking about language and the Internet and they encompass a set of methods united by some overarching principles. The plurality of "ethnographic approaches" in the title of this chapter has been deliberately chosen as there is a range of approaches where the word *ethnographic* is invoked. Studies carried out within this approach can range from carrying out a 'full ethnography' of a culture through to more circumscribed studies which draw upon some ethnographic principles. This can most easily be seen by first examining the roots of ethnography.

### A brief history of ethnographic approaches

Ethnography is a methodology which takes a broad cultural view of human life which is researched through detailed studies of people's lives. It was developed as a way of carrying out research in anthropology, long before the advent of computers or social media, in the nineteenth century. Its aim was for a researcher to understand an isolated and previously unknown culture which was based in a specific physical location. The idea was to study 'a culture', that is, everything about a culture. From this perspective, the culture being studied was seen as isolated and bounded, with the researcher positioned outside the culture, researching that culture as 'the other'.

To carry out a study, the researcher went out to a site, 'the field', and spent an extensive amount of time there immersed in the culture. Then the researcher left the research site and returned home to write 'an ethnography', based on their accumulated field notes. Historically there was little concern for describing the methodology that underpinned ethnographic research, and little advice given to the new researchers. Instead, the starting point has commonly been described simply as "hanging around". The main methodology has been participant observation, which is both observing and participating in the culture as a way of understanding it. In this way the researcher moves from their 'outsider' position, becomes part of the unknown culture and gains an 'insider's perspective'.

Of course there have been many developments in more than a century of ethnography, but it is in these roots of the approach that we can see many of the strengths and how it fits in well with understanding online cultures. At the same time there are potential problems when transferring a model of offline ethnographic practices to the online world in general and researching language in social media in particular. For instance, life online is not characterised by isolated, physically distinct spaces. Rather, it is commonly thought of as highly connected and interactive. Often the researcher is part of the online culture even before starting the research and is not an outsider to the culture. The researcher and the people being studied are not immersed in specific spaces to the exclusion of others, but rather tend to move from space to space and it is not clear that there is a distinct culture, or cultures in the online world (see also Chapter 1 on the blurred distinction between social media and other kinds of online platforms and sites). These are issues for all online research and we return to them later.

Within linguistics there has always been a strong strand of ethnographic work where linguists have studied the structure and uses of specific languages within a cultural framework, often grouped under the broader label of "Linguistic Anthropology" (Duranti 1997; Ahearn 2012) and continuing up to the more recent "Linguistic Ethnography" (Creese 2010). An ethnographic focus on language has also been important in developments in other areas of linguistics. There have been ethnographic studies within child language acquisition and within educational research, for instance, especially in classroom research. Increasingly researchers have drawn upon specific aspects of an ethnographic approach. Rather than doing a full ethnography associated with anthropology, other linguists contrast this with the possibility of taking an "ethnographic perspective" (as in Green and Bloome 1997). This more integrated model accepts that there is a wide range of approaches that are closer to or further from what might be thought of in traditional terms as a full scale 'ethnography' but which nevertheless reflect a common approach.

Within sociolinguistics there is a history of ethnographic studies of language strongly associated with the work of Dell Hymes in the 1970s (see Hymes 1974) who researched 'speech events'. Shirley Brice Heath's work (1983) examining 'literacy events' and the relation between language use at home and in school in different communities grew out of this tradition. This complements the work at the same time by the anthropologist Brian Street (1984) which contributed the notion of 'literacy practices'. These concepts form the basis of Literacy Studies, a rich socio-cultural approach to understanding reading and writing over the past 30 years which has been strongly influenced by ethnographic methods. This approach has examined literacy practices extensively in everyday life, as well as in educational and work contexts. The concepts and models developed from these studies in offline contexts can be particularly revealing for understanding language use in social media since the Internet and social media are created by acts of writing and there are distinct writing spaces where literacy practices are enacted (Barton and Lee 2013).

The chapter shows how the ethnographer's focus on social practices makes an important contribution when researching language in social media. The next section identifies common principles underlying ethnographic research and provides some examples which illustrate how these principles have been applied in particular studies. The chapter then moves on to show how ethnographic research shares common issues of methodology with all research, picking up on some of the issues raised in Chapter 3. The purpose of this chapter, then, is to provide a general backdrop to ethnographic approaches and their relevance for language use in social media contexts. In Chapter 7, we turn to the importance of writing in an ethnographic approach to social media, and look in detail at specific methods of ethnographic data collection and analysis. We are interested throughout in the role of language.

## Common principles of ethnographic approaches

The idea of 'ethnographic approaches' can best be put across by identifying the common methodology or general principles which such studies draw upon. As we discussed in Chapter 3, the notion of methodology is much broader than that of 'research methods' and relates more broadly to everything from the first formulation of the research, through to analysis and impact, and including the writing up of research, all of which is related to what the researchers are trying to find out. Attention to methodology in ethnographic research has grown in the past 20 years as the ethnographic approach has become well known beyond anthropology and seen as an important part of the social sciences. It is now a crucial component of discussions of qualitative research. To understand more about ethnographic approaches and when they are appropriate, we next identify some common principles underlying ethnographic approaches.

### Cultural context

One defining characteristic of an ethnographic approach to language and social media is that it is interested in locating particular instances of language use in their broader cultural context (which would include what we called the extra-situational context in Chapter 2). Understanding this cultural context involves making sense of specific activities (often including activities which take place in specific behavioural contexts), and in this way ethnographic studies are interpretative. The notion of culture is also extended to talk about the culture of particular professions and other groups within society which can have their own ways of acting and ways of using language. As this description implies, what counts as the 'culture' can be multilayered and sometimes quite subjective: in ethnographic approaches, it is common to accept that cultures can be embedded within cultures, accepting that there can be different perspectives on an event, and that participants can have different perceptions of it. Contemporary ethnography accepts this uncertainty, and it accepts that different people can have different understandings of the same situation.

However, to study a particular culture or aspect of a culture, a field site has to be identified. The boundaries of this field site need to be constrained so that a project is manageable. What constitutes a field site in networked, social media contexts is problematic, and in contrast to geographically-based field sites, may be 'ambient' in nature which means that drawing those boundaries around the site can sometimes be tricky. For example, undertaking a social media ethnography might involve exploring a particular practice (e.g. hashtagging practices) in a single 'context of situation' (Malinowski 1935, p.11) such as the hashtags used by a single group of participants in relation to a single event or across a very large network of online interactions. Deciding what counts as that single context, or where to end examining the network of interactions, can depend on a number of factors, such as your research question and the scope of your project.

So far we have emphasised how ethnographic approaches can be applied to the cultures and field sites that are constructed through the online sites of social media. This emphasis on online sites of interaction was probably important when social media research first started, to emphasise the newness and distinctiveness of this area. But increasingly we now try to take into account the ways in which the online interactions are also located in material, behavioural contexts. The person roaming a virtual world dressed as a chicken is also sitting on an uncomfortable seat, maybe peering at the screen of a PC, and can be multi-tasking, maybe using other devices such as a phone and a tablet as well as chatting to people physically nearby. The aspects of online and offline contexts are fused and it may be preferable not to address the online as a distinct space separable from the offline. In this way, often ethnographic research aims to understand more about the relationship between online and offline lives, online language practices and interactions, and how they are embedded in participants' everyday lived experiences.

### People's perspectives

The focus on lived experience means that it is important to see people's perspectives in any situation and so to provide an insider's view. It is necessary to see how participants make sense of an activity (including their language practices), what it means to them and how it fits in with the rest of their lives. This insider perspective is called an 'emic' perspective, as opposed to an external 'etic' perspective (in parallel with the distinction between phonemic and phonetic). Taking an 'emic' perspective leads to an interest in the sense-making and theorising of participants, and in turn how this is framed by the culture in which people are located. Thus ethnographic research can shift from an interest in how an individual makes sense of an activity to how a culture makes sense of it, to the interactions which people participate in, and to broader institutional structuring. So, a person's particular language choices when writing comments on a social media site could be located in broader cultural practices of language use.

The approach to analysing participants' practices is underpinned by the more general idea that 'people make sense', whether or not the researcher agrees with them, is offended by them, or thinks them to be wrong. The aim of ethnographic research is not to impose the researcher's perspectives and values on the members of the culture they are studying, but rather it is to accept that the world makes sense to people (sometimes in quite different ways) and the researcher's goal is to understand those different views as part of the research process. An important aspect of the ethical approach of ethnography is to respect and try to understand the perspectives of others, and not rush to evaluate them. There can be multiple perspectives from different participants in a situation and sometimes these can conflict with each other. An example of where multiple perspectives came to light through ethnographic research is shown in the case study by Heather Horst. Her case study raises issues about taking the perspectives of young people seriously in relation to their parents, and giving equal consideration to both perspectives. The case study is taken from a broader study. Its framework of interest-driven and friendship-driven genres of participation is chronicled in two books: Ito et al. (2009) and Ito et al. (2010).

## Box 6.1 Coming of age in Silicon Valley: research engagement dilemmas

### Heather A. Horst

This case study explores the encounter between the researcher, youths and their parents when trying to understand the meaning of social media use in young people's lives, particularly the significance of social media in identity formation and its role in "friendship-driven genres of participation". It draws upon a case study of 25 families in Silicon Valley, California, that constituted part of a broader study, the Digital Youth Project, of young people's engagements with new media carried out with over 800 youths in the United States.

At the time of research there were a myriad of media reports contributing to the moral panics around the social network site MySpace. When I first arranged to interview 17-year-old Ann, her mother called my cell phone to inquire about my motivations behind interviewing her daughter(s). During our initial conversation, Ann's mother stated, "The girls will probably tell you that they are mad at me". She was fearful that her daughters could be lured away or abducted by strange men. She continued to explain that she did not think the girls fully understood that the site was not private and for this reason she decided to take a hard line, forbidding them from accessing and maintaining a profile on MySpace.

When I finally interviewed Ann, she was quick to tell me that her parents had banned her from using MySpace multiple times. The first time her parents banned her use of MySpace, Ann decided to change a few things and tried to conceal her usage but her mother eventually discovered it. After deleting the profile, Ann broke down and created yet another new profile because she felt left out of her social world at school and also realised she missed a vehicle of expression, illustrated by the profile page she had carefully designed to match the colours and décor of her bedroom (an aesthetic Ann learned from her mother). While Ann's parents placed a great deal of pressure on their daughters to stay off MySpace, outside of her family, the pressure to have a MySpace profile was immense (her friends even created a new MySpace page for Ann). But after another story of a girl on MySpace going missing hit the media, Ann was left no choice but to delete her profile again.

While the Digital Youth Project was primarily focused upon documenting current practices, its broader agenda included taking the perspectives and contributions of youths seriously. Although at the time of research we did not know it, the findings from the project were later translated into the design and programming for after school spaces such as YOUMedia which provides teen learning spaces in Chicago public libraries and other efforts across the MacArthur Foundation's Digital Media and Learning initiative in the United States. As ethical and engaged researchers, we need more tools and strategies to facilitate productive conversations of the value of social media for Ann's identity formation and her parents' desires to protect the space for Ann to explore and express that identity.

### A focus on practices

As pointed out above, the key concept of ethnographic research as rooted in anthropology is the study of cultural practices. Linguistic anthropologists are interested in language practices, often spoken practices, and researchers in Literacy Studies focus on literacy practices. These approaches stress the idea that language can only be understood in the ways in which it is located in broader social practices: written interactions with textual contexts are inherently intertwined with extra-situational and behavioural contexts (see Chapter 2). The idea of 'practices' refers to the general cultural ways of using language: how people use language to get things done and what it means to them. The concept of practices then provides a way of bringing broader cultural and structural aspects into a specific situation. Practices can be seen from a theoretical standpoint as describing regularities and patterns which are abstracted from particular events. Texts are located in the practices of how they are made and how they are used and practices provide a way of bringing in the social world in which texts are located. As the interactions on social media sites are largely created by their users (for example in writing updates, posts, circulating materials, uploading images and so on), this focus on text-making practices can be revealing.

### The role of the researcher

In many areas of research, the researcher is seen as being outside of the research, almost as if the researcher is hovering above the research site with an all-seeing eye and therefore not influencing the data that they observe and collect for analysis. However, ethnographic approaches accept that the researcher is central, and that all views are partial and therefore the researcher is always positioned in some way in relation to the research. The researcher is not an outsider to the research site but a crucial part of it. In ethnographic research, it is important to acknowledge this and to make the researcher's role explicit.

This is especially true of online research, where often people are researching a site which particularly interests them and which they are enthusiastic about. And by participating they are taking up a role in relation to the topic of the research and to other participants. (This is analysed linguistically in terms of stance in Barton and Lee 2013.) As we saw in Chapter 4, establishing your position as a researcher in relation to the other participants in the study is an important decision which informs how you might manage the ethical considerations of your project, but in ethnographic research this has more extended implications. For example, one part of the research process is to ask how the other participants construe the researcher, for example as a fellow game player, as a teacher, as an outsider, since this is likely to affect their interactions with the researcher.

### Multi-method

While some approaches to ethnography emphasise key methods such as participant observation, in fact most ethnographic studies draw upon a range of methods which might include interviews, observations, collection of documents, analysing texts, taking photographs. Although these are largely qualitative methods, the ethnographer may also carry out small quantitative surveys and draw upon the results of large surveys. Within each of these methods there are many possibilities, so if a project will include the use of interviews, there can be different degrees of structure in different interviews, and there can be group interviews, focus groups, repeated interviews and much more. Ethnographic research typically ends up being multi-method research, so the focus on underlying principles is important. In fact, as we will see there is no single method which defines ethnographic approaches. The aim is to understand a culture and the role of language and this can be done in several ways. As with research methods more generally, the different ethnographic approaches are likely to highlight different aspects of the culture and to bring different insights. A straightforward example of mixing methods in a study is given in the case study by Carmen Lee, which comes from Lee (2007).

## Box 6.2 Researching text-making practices in instant messaging

### Carmen Lee

This case study is based on my research about how young people in Hong Kong deployed their multilingual, multiscriptual and multimodal resources when participating in Instant Messaging (IM). With a strong focus on the texts of IM, the study also viewed writing activities associated with IM as social practice, and aimed to address three key research questions:

- What are the characteristics of activities in IM?
- What are the text-making practices involved in IM?
- How do variations and conventions in text-making practices emerge in IM?

To answer these questions, the study generally took a mixed methods and multiple case study approach. Data were collected from 19 young people in Hong Kong, aged between 20 and 28. They were recruited through convenience sampling or snowballing, as it was difficult to collect private and personal chat histories from strangers.

Two sets of data collection methods were developed to respond to individual participants' preferences and needs. The first approach involved primarily face-to-face research methods, including the following phases:

1 *Initial observation*: the researcher went to the participant's home or student residence and sat behind them to take field notes as they were chatting with their friends online. This way, the researcher had access to the participants' private spaces of communication.
2 *Collection of chat logs*: the participant was asked to print out the chat history from phase (1).
3 *Face-to-face interview*: based on the researcher's field notes, a face-to-face interview was then conducted with the participant on the spot.
4 *Initial analysis*: the researcher analysed all the data collected from (1) to (3). This phase started with a discourse analysis of the chat texts. Linguistic features identified in texts then became themes for follow-up interviews.
5 *Follow-up interviews*: follow-up interviews were conducted either face-to-face or online. Keeping in touch with the informants helped track changes in their IM usage.

As the research progressed, an alternative data collection procedure was developed. In this approach, the participants were studied primarily through online methods. This was particularly suitable for researching people who the researcher did not know well or had only met electronically, or those who were not available for face-to-face interviews and observations.

1  *Electronic diary*: the participants were asked to keep a seven-day word-processed diary, in which they described their daily IM and online activities. They were also asked to copy-paste their chat logs onto this diary, which was then emailed to the researcher.
2  *Initial analysis*: the logbooks were analysed and coded for discourse features and meanings. Interview topics were identified from this analysis.
3  *Online interview*: follow-up interviews were conducted through IM.

While a close observation of the IM chat logs was important in understanding text-making practices, insights from qualitative data such as interviews and diaries allowed the researcher to delve into the participants' lives and understand how their text-making on IM might have been mediated by other existing online practices. Both within-case and across-case analyses were conducted to elicit details of individual practices as well as to identify emerging patterns of practices across participants.

### Responsive research

Ethnographic research is responsive. This means, for example, that different methods can be used with different participants in the research, so that photography, for instance, might be appropriate with one person but not with the next, or as in Lee's case study, that face-to-face methods of observation could be complemented by later, online methods of documentation. A responsive methodology is also less tied down at the beginning, so that the overall research questions for a project can be more fluid and can change and develop during the project. For instance, if working with two people as case studies, over time the research can go in different directions, so a series of interviews with different people might well follow quite separate paths. Decisions about direction have to be made during the research; they cannot necessarily be predicted in advance. As we point out in Chapter 3, documenting these research paths and the reasons for such decisions is an important part of the methodology. Responsive also means to be responsive to new spaces of activity (both physical and virtual). If the methodology is responsive, then as an overall methodology it can respond to the possibilities offered by the Internet; reflecting this, Hine refers to virtual ethnography as being "adaptive ethnography" (Hine 2000, p.154).

### Case studies

The overall study a researcher carries out can be seen as immersion in a detailed case study: the aim of an ethnographic study is to understand what is going on in a specific place at a specific time. Individual cases are used to identify themes about the nature of language and literacy. Over time, as more studies are carried out, common themes and repeated findings can be identified across the studies. This builds a powerful base of evidence. For example, James Gee studied his own participation in online gaming alongside his son's participation. In describing how his son interacted with other people and moved in and out of being a gamer alongside other online activities, Gee found these observations that went beyond single, isolated instances allowed him to reflect that the concept of being a member of a 'community of practice' did not work very well. The well established concept of communities of practice seemed to be too stable and unchanging to capture what was happening on gaming sites as observed from the longer, broader picture of interactions. Instead he found it more useful to talk in terms of people participating in more transient "affinity groups" (Gee 2003, 2005). Studies of literacy practices online and offline have referred to the significance of people acting as part of broader groups, whether they are identified as communities of practice, as affinity groups or in other ways. The term "affinity group" has thus become an important addition to the 'language of description' for understanding online activity and has been taken up by other researchers examining other domains of online activity.

### Developing theory

The example of the term "affinity group" shows how individual detailed studies can contribute to developing theory. Linguistics works with a set of interrelated concepts which are constantly being extended, refined and clarified. This is the language of description which the discipline works with and ethnographic studies can contribute to this language of description. It is applied to the object of study, in this case the language of social media. Partly as a result of changes in language use with new technologies, but also for other broader social reasons, the terminology is in flux and changing. Concepts in sociolinguistics such as 'superdiversity' and 'languaging' which challenge existing paradigms of linguistics are often clarified and pinned down by detailed ethnographic investigations. This is the approach taken by Jan Blommaert (2013) and colleagues in developing the concept of 'superdiversity', drawing on a wide range of ethnographic material, including work on multilingual text messaging in South Africa (Blommaert 2011) and a Chinese rapper's use of the Internet (Varis and Wang 2011).

In fact the constant change and fluidity of contemporary life is one of the reasons why an ethnographic approach is an important component of research in social media. This can be seen in many ways: people move across platforms effortlessly; they are often involved in many diverse activities at the same time; and they are often not working with fixed texts written by single authors. Research in this area needs to draw on existing methods to study this, but at the same time be open to new possibilities. It is because of the changes in practices, and the very existence of social media, that we need to be explicit about methodology.

To summarise, an ethnographic approach locates how individual people act within a broader cultural context. It examines language in its cultural context with a focus on practices. This involves highlighting people's perspectives, including that of the researchers' positioning. The research consists of responsive multi-method studies of particular cases and develops theory. Having provided this framework of principles we now turn to particular examples of research which have used ethnographic approaches to explore contemporary media.

## Ethnographic studies of the Internet

There have now been many ethnographic studies of the Internet, and even more which would not be described as 'full' ethnographies but which incorporate an ethnographic approach. In this section we describe a small number of studies to illustrate the variety of approaches and different methodologies that researchers have used thus far. Many terms have been used for undertaking this kind of work, including online ethnography, digital ethnography, netnography, virtual ethnography, cyber ethnography and connective ethnography. For an overview of ethnographic approaches to digital media, see Coleman (2010). All these studies are important for understanding the Internet and how it structures a new context for language use. At the same time they provide examples of an important methodology for linguistic studies. However, they do not necessarily have language as central to their concerns.

The first study to be described here is the research reported by Christine Hine in her book, *Virtual Ethnography* (Hine 2000). This has been foundational in providing an explicit methodology for online ethnographies and in clearly laying out the steps taken in her innovative study. The aim of the study was to explore what the Internet meant in people's lives at that time, including the relationship between online and offline activities. The topic Hine chose to study was the case of a British nanny in the United States who was accused of the murder of a child who was in her care. This case was a high-profile news story at the time.

Hine started out by examining and reflecting on her own participation in terms of how she had found out about the case. She then searched for and analysed websites covering the case. With a carefully composed email she then contacted 35 website authors; this was an important ethnographic step of 'entering the field'. Ten of these authors then participated in the study. Hine designed a personalised questionnaire for each person, relating to the issues she had observed on their particular websites. The questionnaires were then followed up individually in different ways with each participant using available technologies. There was "sustained interaction" with some of them over several weeks. To understand these people more, she also explored other traces of their lives on the Internet. This study was followed up by a focused study of newsgroups which discussed the case. She followed active newsgroups for one month and contacted people through a general request to each group. Finally, she carefully approached a key informant and had extensive email communication with him. After that there was a clear point of disengagement from data collection and a decision to leave the site. It is clear that the study was multi-method, it drew on the resources of the Internet available at that time, and methodological decisions were made in an iterative fashion as the project progressed. Analysis started from the beginning and informed the next stages of data collection and interaction with participants at each point. Hine wrote up the study in terms of key themes which emerged from the data. These included her observations of how the Internet affected the organisation of relationships in time and space, how identities were performed and the extent to which people perceived a boundary between online and offline activities.

This research was carried out in 1997, before the activities typically associated with social media genres had become mainstream (see Chapter 1). There was no dominant search engine but a range of small ones, and there was no Facebook and no Twitter. Whilst the study provides a glimpse into an earlier world of the Internet, the methodology remains relevant and up-to-date as a template for how ethnographic approaches can be applied to social media contexts. To summarise its key points: Hine's research was concerned with overall cultural issues; it focused on practices which could be examined in relation to particular online platforms and websites and was interested in people's perspectives; the role of the researcher was explicit from the beginning; and it was a multi-method and responsive study which aimed to develop theory. Hine uses the case of the teenage nurse as a 'telling case' which reveals how people used the Internet. This virtual ethnography differs from earlier ethnographies in that it is not located in a particular place, it is not a clearly bounded site (either in physical or virtual terms) and the researcher was not an outsider to the culture. While Hine's study did not focus on language itself, it helps us understand the context of language use online and the new practices people were participating in. Linguists, incidentally, would point to the important role of language in the practices described in the study. Another early virtual ethnography, which there is not space to pursue here, is a study of the impact of the Internet in Trinidad carried out by Daniel Miller and Don Slater (Miller and Slater 2000). These studies, along with other early ethnographic studies, have been reviewed by Leander (2008) as examples of "connective ethnographies" of new literacy practices.

A more recent study using different methods and which can be regarded as using ethnographic approaches to research social media without being a full ethnography is Ilana Gershon's study of how American college students used Facebook, mobile phones and other technologies when breaking up relationships (Gershon 2010). In a course on language and culture, Gershon had asked her students about rules for behaving on first dates. When she went on to ask them what counted as a "bad breakup", she was struck by how the students in her classes all talked about "mediated breakups", ones carried out through Facebook or messaging. To explore these issues about the role of media and media ideologies, she then moved on from in-class surveys and interviewed 72 students from across her university. They responded to a general email request to participate in the research and were interviewed individually face-to-face. To keep to the methodology, and not the interesting findings, note that there was no participant observation, and it would be very difficult for there to have been, and there was no online interaction in the data collection. Rather, the data was all retrospective accounts of people's practices given in recorded interviews. Nevertheless the study was about what the Internet meant to participants and the aim of the study was to develop understanding of the significance of social media, so it was ethnographic in approach.

A further example of an ethnographic approach which focused more exclusively on social media interactions is seen in the work of Barton and Lee (2013). A set of studies of language issues on the Flickr photo-sharing site began from the two authors' own participation on the site and their observations about the complexity of people's language choices on Flickr, leading to an initial aim to investigate multilingualism online. The first step in moving beyond their own experiences was to carry out an exploratory observation of the photo streams of 100 active Flickr users to get an overview of the distribution of languages on these sites. At the same time the researchers also explored Flickr more generally to identify the common writing spaces used by members. The next step was to take a closer look at the multilingual language practices of 30 individual users. Concentrating on multilingual people who used Chinese and English or Spanish and English, participants were invited to complete an online survey questionnaire which covered general questions about their Flickr practices, including their multimodal text-making practices. Participants were contacted through the private Flickr email system and there was a 50 per cent response rate. The 50 most recent photos of those who responded were then analysed in terms of their language choice, as shown primarily in the titles and descriptions of the pictures, in the tags used and in any comments. The survey was then followed up by a series of individual email interviews asking people about particular details of their actual use of language on Flickr. The email interviews allowed the researchers to pursue specific questions about the different media and interests that were important to the participants. The interview data was then coded and categorised according to emerging themes about language use. The analysis thus took into account the social media texts generated by the participants as well as their language practices, both as identified on the sites and as reported in interviews. This initial study (Lee and Barton 2011) then acted as a starting point for further studies of language online, including work on vernacular practices (Barton and Lee 2012) and on learning (Barton 2012).

Barton and Lee's research aimed to understand people's practices: how they made sense of Flickr and how they used it in their lives. The research used mixed methods as appropriate to the site being investigated. The researchers brought their own knowledge of and participation in Flickr into the research and remained in contact with several of the participants after the study was completed. Barton and Lee's research was framed theoretically by a literacy studies approach (as was Gee's study of video games discussed earlier), viewing practices as key. And like the other ethnographic approaches reviewed in this chapter, the research in this case also has contributed to the development of that theory, specifically by identifying new forms of multilingual encounters, by refining notions of identity in global contexts and by examining forms of everyday learning online.

## Undertaking a project or dissertation

### Taking a multi-method approach

Here we examine how a project or dissertation can be conducted using ethnographic approaches. From the examples of this chapter, it can be seen that each study used several methods and that often they were linked together in an order. Using different methods can form stages of the research where one method provides information to feed into the next method. We will just give an outline of some methods here and describe how they fit in with an ethnographic approach.

As well as reflecting on one's own practices and interviewing others, there are further sources of information online. Social media provide ample opportunities and ways for online users to write about themselves, thus allowing them to create and constantly update their own autobiographies. Many popular platforms, such as Facebook, are structured as a collection of user profiles. A profile starts out as a sketch of the basic information about someone, which can develop as they add to this either in more detail on their profile page or through the interactions they incorporate in other parts of their profile. For example, on a Facebook user profile, information can range from demographic details such as name, location, date of birth and education, right through to writing about one's personal philosophy and favourite movies. Another popular form of expressing the self online is writing short messages about our lives, especially feelings and activities, in social media. Many of these short messages, such as status updates on Facebook, are written in the form of short narratives serving a wide range of discourse functions. These can all be rich sources of data.

Other forms of data collection can involve taking photos or videos of people's activities and collecting the relevant documents being utilised. All existing pre-Internet research methods are enduring and carry over to the online world, but at the same time they are transformed by social media and the existence of the Internet and associated technologies. The range of methods can be seen as a set of tools, each appropriate to specific jobs in the research process. However, there is not a universal tool-box. Rather, to stretch the metaphor, there is the range of tools appropriate to and framed by different theories and approaches. For example, the idea of an interview appears in many approaches to research. Nevertheless what it is like and how it is carried out, and how the data from it is made sense of, can be quite different in different studies.

The methods of data collection and analysis which are used require attention to detail, and they draw on the underlying philosophy of examining particular instances in order to understand broader patterns. Whatever the starting point of the research project, often one wants to find out more about the site, the people or the practice being studied. The first activity is likely to be some sort of 'hanging around' which has its roots in the history of ethnographic approaches. (Incidentally, this has a parallel with the 'hanging out' activities of young people on social media sites identified by Mimi Ito and colleagues (2010) as a central step in how they use the Internet and learn from it.) Underlying this is the idea of having a 'sustained presence' and 'immersion' in the culture. Ethnographic research takes time. As hinted at above, one way of getting to an insider's perspective is through examining what already exists online through what is written in websites, blogs, micro-blogging and the many other spaces where people are 'writing the web'. This can lead to a need to interact with people and to ask specific questions, which may arise from their existing web presences, from what they have written or from what they are doing, that is from their texts or from their practices. This is where interviewing and other forms of interaction are crucial.

'Hanging out' is a form of observation and is the least intrusive form of research. It can be open-ended or it can be more focused observation, looking for particular things. As already stated, often people are already engaged in interactions with the social media platform or area which they are researching. With the Flickr study, David Barton and Carmen Lee were already participating in the site and as they shifted to start the research they changed their relation to Flickr. They changed their stance to that of researchers, for example by keeping records of what they did and what others did, by saving web pages, and by starting to write field notes as a way of reflecting on what was happening. Writing field notes is a basic way of record-keeping for the ethnographer.

The next steps to be taken in a study, and the methods that are chosen, are linked to the research questions you are addressing in your project, as discussed in Chapter 3. In fact, these questions act as threads which hold together the aims, the methods and the analyses in a particular project. Particular methods will provide particular sorts of data which will address particular research questions. As we have seen earlier, 'hanging out' is a specific form of observation. By taking part in what is going on in the sites in this way, researchers are in fact utilising a key methodology of ethno-graphic approaches, that of 'participant observation'. And as we have also seen in the examples of ethnographic research discussed earlier in this chapter, there are different ways of participating (in Gershon's study (2010), she was not 'hanging out' or participating in the practices she researched, for example), but in all cases, understanding the researcher's participation and relation to the topic being studied is always crucial, and it takes on a new meaning in online research. All this needs to be acknowledged, and the researcher's stance needs to be made explicit.

The next step in methods is interacting with people by interviewing them in some way. Interviewing as a methodology ranges from informal chatting to people through to more structured interviews. Ethnographers often refer to 'semi-structured interviews' as a mid-point between the almost unstructured conversations which might be carried out in oral history research, on the one hand, and the formal fully structured interviews of market research, on the other hand. With a semi-structured interview the researcher often has in mind a set of topics to be covered, an 'interview protocol', but the researcher is not particularly concerned with the order the questions are addressed or the specific form the questions take. The person being inter-viewed can take seeming digressions and tell stories and roam off-topic in ways which would not be possible in more structured interviewing. Often such digressions do lead to useful data and so rather than being discounted can be included in a project.

A powerful form of interviewing which can still be semi-structured is 'focused interviewing'. Focused interviewing uses a text or other artefact (such as a web page of social media profile constructed by the participant) as a focus for the interview discussion. This can be a powerful way of examining details of language use and provides a focus for discussion that can often lead to richer interviews than a more general set of question prompts can do. There can be individual interviews, group interviews and focus groups, and, again, the latter can often lead to rich discussions. Other variations in interviews can reflect the format used for interaction; inter-views can be conducted face-to-face and people physically co-present or they can be carried out at a distance using messaging, emailing, phoning or micro-blogging.

Small surveys can be regarded as closely related to interviews. Historically there has been a difference between interviewing, as speaking face-to-face, and surveys, as written, and carried out at a distance. The online world of course disrupts this distinction, where much communication is through writing and one can be face-to-face but distant. In a survey the same questions can be put to many people. A survey can be used at different times in the research. It can be used as a way of initially contacting people when 'entering the field'. Alternatively in the middle of research after interviews, a survey can be used to get a broader picture of individual experiences. Note that in using a survey, an ethnographer need not restrict themselves to qualitative research methods – it is fine to use quantitative methods and such surveys have often been used as part of ethnographic studies. We return to how surveys can be designed as a quantitative research tool in Chapter 8.

Using artefacts in interviews can be regarded as carrying out interventions and 'interfering' with everyday life. Ethnographers may be wary of interventions, the staple of the psychology experiment, as distorting the realities of life, but there are many forms of 'intervention' which can be revealing and increase understanding. Sitting next to someone and observing them using social media is invaluable and may be enhanced by asking them to talk through what they are doing; this technique of talking while doing is known as a speak-aloud protocol. Asking people to record their activities over a day or a week as a diary or a log can also be informative. Getting them to collect screenshots or to photograph their surroundings can provide new insights into people's literacy practices and language use. All these possibilities move in the direction of involving the participants in the research and the project can become a form of collaborative research. Involving participants in the methods of data collection is one step in broadening the possibilities of involving participants in all stages of the research process.

In all research, choosing the people or sites to study, i.e. sampling, is important (we also discuss samples for quantitative projects in Chapter 8). A sample relates to a 'population', the people the sample is thought to represent, but online this is a difficult concept. For instance, the population of all registered Flickr members or all registered Twitter members is not a useful concept as most people registered on such sites probably are not active. One way around this is to set parameters for a sample and select a smaller number of participants to be involved in the research. Thus in Barton and Lee's (2013) multilingualism study, the researchers deliberately chose active members of the platform as their sample, as have other studies. Although there may be small numbers involved, thinking about how to select the people studied in an ethnographic project (and indeed in any research project) is still important. The participants chosen as the 'sample' have always been chosen in some way. Often in ethnographic studies there are some 'key informants' who are focused on for the research, and again, their choice needs to be explained.

Students usually carry out individual projects but contemporary ethnographic research has shifted from approaches solely associated with lone scholars and individual interpretations, to including collaborative ethnography involving researchers working in a variety of ways with each other and with informants. Research does not have to be an individual effort, and collaboration changes the data collected, the analysis and writing. In particular, informants can be involved in data collection through keeping diaries and taking photos and in analysis in examining transcripts of interviews. There is a space for innovative methods to include ways for others to participate in the research. Using the platforms (such as Twitter or Facebook) which are being studied to aid the research process also provides exciting directions for online research (see for example, Maria Georgalou's case study in Chapter 5 on creating an event in Facebook as part of the research process). Student researchers are encouraged to be innovative, but at the same time it is often a good starting point to find an existing study and to begin by following their methods.

Mixing methods in social media research can also be a form of innovation. For instance, connections can be made which aim to link up discourse analysis with ethnographic approaches. In work moving beyond the text, discourse analysts such as Ruth Wodak and colleagues have developed a discourse-historical approach to critical discourse analysis (Wodak and Meyer 2009) where the researchers collect texts to develop an understanding of the context, as well as drawing upon their background knowledge. A strand of work which aims to bring together discourse analysis with ethnographic approaches is Androutsopoulos' "discourse-centred online ethnography" (DCOE) (2008). This approach has developed from his work studying German-based websites. One of his projects has looked into sociolinguistic styles and identity constructions on sites devoted to hip-hop culture. In carrying out discourse-centred online ethnography on these sites, Androutsopoulos started with systematic observation of the discourse of the sites, moving on to interviewing Internet actors to elicit insiders' perspectives. The discourse analysis led him to the need to interview. In these two studies, the discourse analysis starts out from the texts and then uses empirical methods to provide further information about the meaning and interpretation of the discourse analysis. In contrast to this, when working with both texts and practices, literacy studies research tends to start from practices and then from this work identifies salient texts for analysis (as in Barton and Lee 2013). Researchers are finding many ways to bring these approaches together. This is important for understanding language online where written language is constantly being reused and recontextualised, and where language moves between physical places and social media spaces. It can be revealing to locate ethnographic approaches in these broader research traditions. Often ethnographic methodologies include other qualitative approaches such as history, narrative analysis or grounded theory (see Merriam (2009, pp.21–37), who distinguishes these approaches clearly). It is also worth exploring the many websites devoted to methods and a growing number of ethnography apps which can be used for collecting and analysing data.

### Starting points for a research project

The studies summarised above are larger in scale than many projects which readers of this book might carry out. Nevertheless, the examples illustrate many issues of methodology which arise for a study of any size. As we pointed out in Chapter 3, the starting point for research can begin with a hunch, a 'problem', a worry. For Hine's work, it was an interest in what the Internet meant to people, for Gershon, it was how young people use technology when breaking up relationships, and for Barton and Lee it was questions about multilingualism and how people use their languages as resources on the Internet. A study may start from a language issue such as informality, politeness (or impoliteness), or language and gender issues. It can be driven by any area of linguistics including syntax, semantics or pragmatics. The 'problem' can be a social issue, such as unequal access, or issues of learning. In turn, these areas for concern can shape more specific research questions which are progressively revised as the project unfolds.

At the outset of this chapter, we pointed out that historically, ethnographers have laid great importance on 'entering the field', and the importance of situated observation in a physical place. One of the things which can be different when researching the online world (and social media in particular) is that the researcher can already appear to be quite knowledgeable when starting the research. However, getting to know a particular site in more detail can be an important first step in the research process. So a more detailed look at something one already knows, whether it is Twitter, Facebook, Flickr or a specialist website, is invaluable. These wider observations can be an important step by which the researcher needs to 'make the familiar strange' and realise that others may use the same platform in quite different ways (and so go beyond the limitations of their own use of the site). Alongside this, the systematic study of one's own involvement can be an important component of a study, as in Barton and Lee's Flickr study, or it can be the whole study, as in Davies and Merchant's 'auto-ethnographic' research of how academics use Flickr (2007). With studies of virtual worlds, the notion of entering the field and encountering a new culture may be closer to the original ethnographic intent. This is argued in Boellstorff's ethnography of Second Life (2008) and in a more general book on ethnographic methods for studying virtual worlds

(Boellstorff *et al.* 2012) but, as Gillen and Merchant carefully state, "for some users on some occasions, virtual spaces may constitute a distinct domain ... but in the final analysis, we would argue that interactions in virtual worlds are always related to the agency of human beings in material circumstances" (2013, p.24).

Ethnographic studies help us understand more about language in social media. They contribute in three ways: they can offer data, they can offer theory, and they can offer method. Starting with the data they provide, in a simple sense they can show us how people use language to get things done in online spaces and how they make sense of what they are doing. This can be data for the linguist, for example of language learning, of language change, or of sociolinguistic aspects such as gender, power relations and access. The outcomes of a study can be clear examples of how people use language in particular situations. But these are not merely individual illustrations. Such studies can provide a 'telling case' of language use more generally which can then complement a quantitative study. Ethnographic research can pull different approaches together; it can locate linguistic details in the broader picture and can make sense of individual statistics. This interpretation and 'sense-making' is a crucial aspect of ethnographic approaches. Ethnographic data can be used to challenge myths about social media and the Internet. In so doing, it can fulfil the important role for ethnographic data online and offline to provide a critique and challenge taken-for-granted assumptions about language and literacy practices.

While ethnographic studies provide data, alongside this there are contributions to theories about what language is and how it works. This can be seen most clearly in the development and clarification of terms which linguists use. In Gee's research, described earlier, the case was an individual person and their game-playing practices were described, but it was the concept of 'affinity groups' which was taken up from elsewhere and then applied to online gaming. The term has then been found to be of value more broadly. Overall the rise of social media has seen the need for new terms, such as 'context collapse', and the need to redefine existing notions such as 'audience'. These lead to changes in the language of description and are a contribution to theory. Ethnographic research can provide evidence on whether the concepts like 'digital divide' reflect reality and are useful. And it can provide perspectives which help clarify moral panics about the Internet such as whether it is good or bad for grammar and spelling, and for language use in general. As well as providing data and contributing to theory, ethnographic studies can also offer methods of research for others investigating situated practices. For instance, the ways of focusing on practices used here can be adopted as methods appropriate in the classroom at all levels of education. Examples of how this can be done are given in Chapter 7.

**Points for reflection**

How will you first make contact with potential informants, and do you have any concerns about this?

If you combine different methods, will they give you different sorts of data?

Are there ways in which your research can be responsive and take account of different contexts?

Are there different groups of participants in your study who might have different perspectives from each other?

## References

Ahearn, L. (2012) *Living Language: An Introduction to Linguistic Anthropology*, Oxford: Wiley-Blackwell.

Androutsopoulos, J. (2008) 'Potentials and limitations of discourse-centred online ethnography', *Language@Internet*, 5, article 8.

Barton, D. (2012) 'Participation, deliberate learning and discourses of learning online', *Language and Education*, 26 (2), 139–50.

Barton, D. and Lee, C. (2012) 'Redefining vernacular literacies in the age of Web 2.0', *Applied Linguistics*, 33 (3), 282–98.

Barton, D. and Lee, C. (2013) *Language Online: Investigating Digital Texts and Practices*, London: Routledge.

Blommaert, J. (2011) 'Supervernaculars and their dialects', *Working Papers in Language and Literacies*, 81, available: www.kcl.ac.uk/sspp/departments/education/research/ldc/index.aspx [accessed 19 November 2013].

Blommaert, J. (2013) *Ethnography, Superdiversity and Linguistic Landscapes: Chronicles of Complexity*, Bristol: Multilingual Matters.

Boellstorff, T. (2008) *Coming of Age in Second Life: An Anthropologist Explores the Virtually Human*, Princeton: Princeton University Press.

Boellstorff, T., Nardi, B., Pearce, C. and Taylor, T.L. (2012) *Ethnograpy and Virtual Worlds: A Handbook of Method*, Princeton: Princeton University Press.

Coleman, E.G. (2010) 'Ethnographic approaches to digital media', *Annual Review of Anthropology*, 39, 487–505.

Creese, A. (2010) 'Linguistic ethnography', in Litosseliti, L., ed., *Research Methods in Linguistics*, London: Continuum, 138–54.

Davies, J. and Merchant, G. (2007) 'Looking from the inside out: academic blogging as new literacy', in Knobel, M. and Lankshear, C., eds, *A New Literacies Sampler*, New York: Peter Lang, 167–98.

Duranti, A. (1997) *Linguistic Anthropology*, Cambridge: Cambridge University Press.

Gee, J.P. (2003) *What Video Games have to Teach Us about Learning and Literacy*, New York: Palgrave Macmillan.

Gee, J.P. (2005) 'Semiotic social spaces and affinity spaces: from *The Age of Mythology* to today's schools', in Barton, D. and Tusting, K., eds, *Beyond Communities of Practice: Language, Power and Social Context*, Cambridge: Cambridge University Press, 214–32.

Gershon, I. (2010) *The Breakup 2.0: Disconnecting Over New Media*, Ithaca, NY: Cornell University Press.

Gillen, J. and Merchant, G. (2013) 'From virtual histories to virtual literacies', in Merchant, G., Gillen, J., Marsh, J. and Davies, J., eds, *Virtual Literacies: Interactive Spaces for Children and Young People*, London: Routledge, 9–26.

Green, J.L. and Bloome, D. (1997) 'Ethnography and ethnographers of and in education: a situated perspective', in Flood, J., Heath, S.B. and Lapp, D., eds, *Handbook of Research on Teaching Literacy through the Communicative and Visual Arts*, New York: Macmillan, 181–202.

Heath, S.B. (1983) *Ways with Words*, Cambridge: Cambridge University Press.

Hine, C. (2000) *Virtual Ethnography*, London: Sage.

Hymes, D. (1974) *Foundations of Sociolinguistics: An Ethnographic Approach*, Philadelphia: University of Pennsylvania.

Ito, M., Horst, H., Bittanti, M., boyd, d., Herr-Stephenson, B., Lange, P., Pascoe, C. and Robinson, L. (2009) *Kids Living and Learning with New Media: Findings from the Digital Youth Project*, The John D. and Catherine T. MacArthur Foundation, available: http://digitalyouth.ischool.berkeley.edu/report [accessed 8 October 2013].

Ito, M., Baumer, S., Bittanti, M., boyd, d., Cody, R., Herr, B., Horst, H., Lange, P., Mahendran, D., Martinez, K., Pascoe, C., Perkel, D., Robinson, L., Sims, C. and Tripp, L. (2010) *Hanging Out, Messing Around, Geeking Out: Living and Learning with New Media*, Cambridge, MA: MIT Press.

Leander, K.M. (2008) 'Towards a connective ethnography of online/offline literacy networks', in Coiro, J., Knobel, M., Lankshear, C. and Leu, D.J., eds, *Handbook of Research on New Literacies*, New York: Lawrence Erlbaum, available: www.newliteracies.uconn.edu/pub_files/Handbook_of_Research_on_New_Literacies.pdf [accessed 19 November 2013].

Lee, C. (2007) 'Affordances and text-making practices in online instant messaging', *Written Communication*, 24 (3), 223–49.

Lee, C. and Barton, D. (2011) 'Constructing glocal identities through multilingual writing practices on Flickr.com', *International Multilingualism Research Journal*, 5 (1), 39–59.

Malinowski, B. (1935) *Coral Gardens and Their Magic: A Study of the Methods of Tilling the Soil and Agricultural Rites in the Trobiand Islands*, London: Allen and Unwin.

Merriam, S.B. (2009) *Qualitative Research: A Guide to Design and Implementation*, San Francisco: Jossey-Bass.

Miller, D. and Slater, D. (2000) *The Internet: An Ethnographic Approach*, Oxford: Berg.

Street, B. (1984) *Literacy in Theory and Practice*, Cambridge and New York: Cambridge University Press.

Varis, P. and Wang, X. (2011) 'Superdiversity on the Internet: a case from China', *Diversities*, 13, 71–83.

Wodak, R. and Meyer, M. (2009) *Methods of Critical Discourse Analysis*, 2nd edn, London: Sage.

# Chapter 7

# Carrying out a study of language practices in social media

---

## Outline of the chapter

In this chapter we cover:

- Using techno-linguistic biographies to research your own literacy practices.
- The steps in constructing a techno-linguistic biography.
- How to research the self.
- Identifying differences in language practices across time and space.
- Using published surveys to provide broader context.
- Ways of writing up ethnographic projects.

## Starting with the self: techno-linguistic biographies and researching one's own practices

I, David Barton, have been getting my university students at both under-graduate and postgraduate levels to research everyday literacy practices and, more than 20 years on, I am still doing it. There have been tremendous changes in their practices over this time. When I started to do this, the students submitted handwritten assignments and cut-and-paste meant cutting and pasting pieces of paper. They would produce a handwritten poster, often with photos glued onto it (as in www.literacy.lancs.ac.uk/studentprojects/ dating from 1999), whereas now they leave comments on a website and produce multimodal presentations based on Microsoft PowerPoint or Prezi, often including videos or sound clips. The approach of carrying out a detailed study of practices has been changing as well, and I now focus on researching how their literacy practices are embedded with their use of various technologies in different contexts and at different stages of their life. Often, this research begins with students examining their own literacy practices, in what I refer to as their *techno-biographies* or, where it is closely related to language use, their *techno-linguistic biographies*.

In this chapter we build on the general principles of the ethnographic approaches covered in Chapter 6 – namely, making the role of the researcher explicit, being responsive in the research process and building a case-by-case picture of broader patterns of language practices – by applying these to the concept of people's techno-linguistic biography, that is people's technology-related lives where language plays a central role. Techno-linguistic biographies are a type of techno-biography, in short, a life story in relation to technologies. Techno-linguistic biographies can be used as an important source of research data and provide a method for researching language and identity online. It is a participant-centred way of documenting change over time in social practices, especially as these relate to people's lived experiences with technology and their language use online. Researching the self and developing a techno-biography links in with narrative research (for more on narrative analysis as a research methodology in linguistics, see Gimenez 2010). It is also part of a growing methodology, that of researching oneself through an auto-ethnography, whereby the researcher makes explicit their position in the ethnographic research process, introduced in Chapter 6.

Of course, the narrator's account of their literacy practices online need not be restricted to social media as there is not a strict division between social media sites and other sites and, as we pointed out in Chapter 1, many platforms have incorporated elements of social media. Nevertheless, social media can be a significant point of demarcation for particular groups of participants in particular contexts. In the example which follows in this chapter, several university students said that they 'ring fence' certain kinds of social media and don't want lecturers involved in those interactive sites; similarly teachers may well not want students involved in their social media worlds. Indeed, in some contexts, teachers and students may be proscribed from including one another on their list of contacts (like Facebook Friend lists).

This chapter describes constructing a techno-linguistic biography in relation to university students. Nevertheless, this is an adaptable methodology and can work not just with university students at any level, but also with kindergarten children, teenagers, pre-service teachers and adult learners. As such, although we will describe how the students structured their research process, we think very much of the students as researchers. As you read the rest of this chapter, you might like to think about how techno-biographies could be used in your own research interests. The process has a set of steps which will be covered one-by-one. It can be used to explore commonalities between people, but at the same time it identifies how practices are situated and located in time and space and how everyone has an individual profile of literacy practices in their life story.

### Stage 1: researching the self

There are several possible ways of approaching the task of developing a techno-linguistic biography. In the module that I, David, teach along with my colleagues at the University of Lancaster, students can begin by documenting their *current practices* and I found it useful to suggest a set of questions which can act as prompts, such as: what are the sites you use most often, and what are the ones you have contributed to? The students are encouraged to be specific in their responses. It is important that the responses focus on *ways of participation*, realising that there are very different ways of participating in a site, so the framing questions try to probe the varying forms of participation, such as:

- Have you commented on news or products?
- Voted on the quality of service?
- Submitted a review or a wiki entry?
- Uploaded pictures or videos for comment?

Concepts discussed in Chapter 6 can also be introduced as part of the course content, such as discussing the usefulness of communities of practice and affinity groups in relation to different forms of participation. Identifying the mixture of person-oriented versus interest-driven activities can be revealing, as can discussion of the notion of social media sites and practices.

On the course which we will use as an example here, the students document their current practice in seminars by noting down and reflecting on their online activity. They then discuss their own practices with fellow students and they get to see similarities and differences with their classmates: "I thought I was the only one with five email accounts", one student commented when realising how similar his practices were to those of his fellow students. What the students say changes from year to year, and all such studies are reflecting practices in a certain place at a certain time. It is important to note that this quote is taken from a group of undergraduates majoring in English Language or in Linguistics at a UK university in November 2012. The other kinds of practices students in this class mentioned included talk about integrating iPads with other technology in their lives, or getting to use Twitter more, and some were tiring of Facebook. They discussed how online social media seamlessly co-ordinated their offline lives. They reflected on the different ways they watched TV programmes, increasingly on a laptop, and using catch-up services to watch programmes at different times of the day.

A related activity that can be used to investigate their current practices is to get students to think in terms of 'A day in the life' where they go chronologically through a recent day. Here they consider questions such as:

Thinking of yesterday, what technologies did you first deal with when you woke up, how did it continue during the day?

This kind of activity, which invites a clearly narrative account grounded in specific times and places, is often an effective prompt which brings to light everyday practices which otherwise go unnoticed. It is possible to do this in groups using visual resources such as making story boards.

Having established their current practices, we then turn to constructing the students' biographies in which they are encouraged to examine changes in their literacy practices over time, perhaps noting how they are similar to or different from when they first carried them out. These accounts are similar to episodes in a *life history*, for example prompted by questions like:

- When did you first use a mouse?
- Send a text message?
- Search Wikipedia?
- Start using Facebook?

These first encounters can be very different for particular students. For instance, they report contrasting family attitudes to having a mobile phone when they were young. Some were allowed to have one from an early age in primary school as an issue of safety, whilst others were forbidden to have one until they were older. On the other hand, they discovered similarities across the student group. Most of the British students recalled shifting from MySpace to Facebook around the same time, even though they had lived in different parts of the country. Another starting point can be the phones, computers and other technologies they have had access to over time. As well as documenting first usage, the students also identified *transitions*, asking: did you change your practices of keeping people's addresses, arranging to meet friends, using maps, etc.? Reflecting on transitions can be useful as a way of heightening awareness of current practices which may have become naturalised in the students' present experiences. The temporal contexts for these starting points and transitions in practices can be documented by plotting the life histories on a digital timeline, making use of online timeline creation software such as tiki-toki, dipity or timeglider.

The techno-biography provides a background for examining in more detail the linguistic choices made in social media. Investigating language choices is best done in relation to particular examples of language use, such as a specific discussion on Twitter or a set of comments in relation to a YouTube video, a book, a movie, a hotel or restaurant. Such data can be the focus of a linguistic analysis starting with general issues such as language choice, genre, intertextuality, cohesion and coherence before moving to a closer look at the language. The direction linguistic analysis goes in depends on the research questions and the data. For example, the role of participants and how they position themselves can be examined more closely by looking at pronouns, sentence types, passivisation and nominalisations. A broader look at stance can include politeness, hedging, informality and non-standard language use. Analysis of discussions and arguments can examine the warrants used to support claims. In these ways the biography becomes a techno-linguistic biography.

Students are asked to focus on 'everyday life', which is a loose concept. In fact they begin to look more broadly and to contrast different *domains of life* which have different practices, such as religion, sports and politics. Possible questions to pose include:

- Are there differences in your everyday life, your student life, and in any work life?
- Are there other domains?
- Do these domains differ in what is possible, what is encouraged and what is prohibited?

In particular education and everyday life can be seen as different domains often with quite different uses of language. Systematic comparisons can be made between 'in-school' and 'out-of-school' digital practices. Quite often the students recalled that their home computers were more up-to-date than ones available at school and they had better access and better networks of support in their everyday lives. Nevertheless, they also remembered the frustrations of sharing equipment at home when they were younger and their access being supervised and limited. Ordinary jobs they had, such as working in bars and restaurants, also revealed the distinctiveness and complexities of digital workplace language and literacy practices, such as in relation to the technologies involved in ordering, stock checking and paying bills. Some students also reported being asked to leave positive comments on the sites of the companies they worked for. Others referred to dilemmas of how to be polite in online workplace communication and how their own use of social media was regulated whilst at work.

To summarise this first stage of investigation, a list of possible questions which can act as starting points for a techno-linguistic biography is given in Box 7.1.

## Box 7.1 Possible questions and approaches for a techno-linguistic biography

*Current practices*: what are the sites you use most often, and what are the ones you have contributed to?

*Participation*: have you commented on news or products? Voted on the quality of service? Submitted a review or a wiki entry? Uploaded pictures or videos for comment?

*A day in the life*: think of yesterday, what technologies did you first deal with when you woke up, how did it continue during the day?

*Life history and digital timelines*: when did you first use a mouse? Send a text message? Search Wikipedia? Start using Facebook? What phones have you owned and how have you used them differently?

*Transitions*: did you change your practices of keeping people's addresses, arranging to meet friends, using maps, etc.?

*Language choice*: what languages and genres do you use? Where are choices made about informality and politeness? Where are non-standard forms and digital devices such as emoticons used?

*Domains of life*: are there differences in your everyday life, your student life, and in any work life? Other domains, such as religion, sports, politics?

*Cross-generational comparisons*: differences across generations, parents, grandparents, children; differences across cultures, friends from other countries; gender differences, prohibitions.

### Stage 2: differences across time and space

The second step, the next week in the course, is for students to interview other people who differ from them in age, gender or culture. In this way, they can explore differences across time and place. This moves the research outwards in both content and methodology. Students move beyond their own experiences and they can compare themselves with others. The questions and approaches of Box 7.1 can also be used as starting points for researching other people. Students need to be encouraged to carry out open-ended interviews and to get people to talk and think about the questions. If they have already been trained to use interviews as part of their research methodology, often they have been trained in market research type interviews with strict interview protocols and precise questions wanting short, easily codable, one-word answers. Here they need the opposite: they need open-ended questions which encourage their interviewees to talk and to reflect on their practices. They need to think of the interviews more in terms of oral history than market research. To see examples of oral history narratives with a similar focus on literacy practices it is worth looking at Cynthia Selfe's digital archive of literacy narratives (http://daln.osu.edu).

Students who have used techno-biographies in their research have always found it interesting to interview people who differ from themselves. In the most recent course where this was carried out, they had a great deal to report. Often the students held age-related stereotypes: for instance, to them 'older people' meant anyone over 35 years, and as one of them put it "landlines are for grandparents". Some felt that older people were out of touch, whilst others marvelled at the practices of grandparents researching family history online or being part of specialist networks. They also praised the online sophistication of their younger siblings, thus demonstrating that everyone, whatever their age, seems to regard anyone younger than themselves as being a 'digital native'. Looking across cultures, we unravelled the different platforms used by students from China (like Weibo and WeChat) and how they used both Chinese and Western sites for social networking, micro-blogging, following news, searching and buying.

There are possibilities for many comparisons when using interviews to examine the literacy practices of other people. Cross-generational investigations included perspectives gained from interviewing parents, grandparents and children and comparing their practices with the students' own practices. Differences across cultures were investigated through discussions with friends from other countries, and some students also explored gender differences. As we pointed out in Chapter 6, interviews can be carried out in different media, and here students used interviews in face-to-face settings or online using Skype or other conferencing tools. Any of the practices identified in stage one of the techno-biography can become a point of difference which can then be explored in stage two. Some student practices seem specific to their roles as students and lively discussions have been had between students and their teachers, with both sides expressing surprise at the others' online practices. Some examples of techno-linguistic biographies can be found in Barton and Lee (2013, pp.70–82) and Lee (2014). The techno-linguistic biography of a student in Hong Kong, detailing her use of different languages online and offline, is shown in Box 7.2. This has been adapted from Barton and Lee (2013, pp.77–8). The biography was written by the researcher after an interview with the student. The student initially filled in an online questionnaire. Then there was a screen recording session which was carried out before the interview between the student and the researcher.

## Box 7.2 One student's techno-linguistic biography

Yan was a second-year History major at the Chinese University of Hong Kong. She had been born in mainland China and moved to Hong Kong with her parents when she was around ten. Before arriving in Hong Kong, Yan spoke mostly Hakka, a southern Chinese dialect, at home with her parents and school friends, though also knew Cantonese. As soon as she moved to Hong Kong, her family all switched to Cantonese even at home. Yan specifically told us how surprised she was about the 'sudden' switch of language at home.

Her first memory of computer use was computer gaming around 2003. She remembered this year vividly because it was the year when the SARS pandemic attacked Hong Kong. Schools were suspended for months. She had to stay at home most of the time so playing games on the computer seemed to be the best activity to kill time. Her first real "online" experience was actually a school assignment in which she was asked to send five emails to her Chinese teacher as a kind of self-reflection task. Since then, she started communicating with teachers and friends regularly via email, in standard written Chinese. She used to be an active blogger. On her blog, she wrote longer pieces of narrative, reflecting upon life and so on. At the same time, her younger sister also introduced her to the world of Instant Messaging by signing her up on ICQ, which was the most popular IM programme in Hong Kong before MSN took over. In Yan's view, IM was reserved for private and interpersonal interaction with close friends and family. On IM, she would still insist on writing in standard Chinese, even if her chat partners wrote in English. Now as a university student, she felt that she used IM less often than when she was a secondary school student. Facebook has become a major social network site on which she frequently posts her feelings and everyday activities.

She considered Chinese, mostly standard written Chinese, mixed with Cantonese writing, as her main written language on all these platforms. She said this was partly due to her mainland Chinese background, but the major reason behind her preference for Chinese was that she had very little exposure to English ever since she started university. As her major subjects are taught in Mandarin Chinese, she did not see the need to use English regularly. Yan also affectively attached herself to Chinese. She insisted that on her blog she had to write in standard written Chinese. She related this to her school subjects:

> I usually blog about in-depth feelings and I want to use a serious language to express myself.

Despite her personal attachment to Chinese, Yan felt that she had to brush up her English for more practical reasons. She had never had any proper English education before she arrived in Hong Kong, where she received formal English lessons in school. She had always felt that she was lagging behind. This had not bothered her too much until on one occasion, she was unable to answer questions at a scholarship interview where she was required to speak English throughout. Since then, she thought she should equip herself better. One thing that she thought would help was to listen to English songs regularly on YouTube. Yan saw that as a good way of exposing herself to the English language. At other times, Chinese still remained as her primary language online. Yan's knowledge of Hakka dialect also gave rise to creativity in her texting activities. From time to time, she would write and receive text messages written in Hakka with her friends back home in mainland China. However, Hakka itself is not a written language – at least there is no standardised written form. So Yan and her friends playfully invented a system for Hakka by using similar sounding characters in standard Chinese. At first she found some of those 'stylised' Hakka messages sent by her friends incomprehensible, but she gradually enjoyed the process of exchanging and decoding them.

---

**Points for reflection**

What have been some of Yan's different literacy practices online?
How did she learn to participate in new practices?
What are some examples of how she uses different languages to express her identity online?
What feelings (affect) does she express about different languages?
How are Yan's literacy practices similar to or different from your own?

---

### Stage 3: the broader context: using published surveys

As we noted in Chapter 6, ethnographic approaches are often multi-method and can integrate in-depth analysis of individual texts and instances with larger, contextualising results which may be quantitative in nature. Hence the third step in researching one's own language practices is to examine the results of large-scale surveys like the PEW reports in the United States and the Ofcom reports and those published by Oxford Internet studies in the UK. In this way, the individual perspectives recorded in particular techno-biographies of the student's own experiences and those of their friends and families are contextualised in broader patterns of national and international life. In all these steps, the students as researchers are encouraged to find both similarities with others, and differences which surprise them. The statistics of Internet usage by age, for instance, can situate what they have discovered in earlier weeks and challenge any previously held stereotypes of practices (based on age, gender and so on). They may also see documented trends about issues of access which they may not have thought about before, and they read statistics which challenge previous assumptions, such as that 'Everyone has a smart phone'. Each week the students thus revisit their own practices and over time they reveal more details of practices which had become naturalised and which initially they had not thought of as being relevant.

### The value of a techno-biographic approach

By investigating their own and others' techno-biographies, students can encounter and use different methodologies. In the first stage, mini auto-ethnographies or techno-biographies help develop attention to ethno-graphic detail. The interviews carried out in the second stage provide examples of experiences beyond their own and incorporate a range of other participant perspectives. Thirdly, the large surveys carried out by others can be used to add further layers of context and wider social and cultural perspectives. These methodologies can complement each other and provide different ways of seeing the world. Each kind of methodology and the data that is collected can also allow the researcher to explore different kinds of generalisations. Here biographical work shifts to being ethnographic when it makes broader statements about culture – in this case about the nature of language and social media. Throughout this ethnographic process, the concept of practices remains central, where 'skills' and 'habits' are located in this broader concept. This contributes to developing the language of description used to describe the social world and how uses of technology fit into people's lives.

The accumulation of field notes and reflective observations typical of ethnographic research runs alongside the three stages of investigating techno-biographies. In the case of the module we describe here, students also make a posting on the course website each week. This is often 'unnoticed' writing and over the ten-week term it can build up to more than 4,000 words written by each student. This regular form of writing is a useful practice to integrate in all research, particularly with an ethnographic approach. By doing all this, students also become more reflexive about their practices and about their learning. This knowledge feeds into the rest of the course where they learn about other aspects of language and media as well as about research methodology. The pedagogic example we have used here illustrates the ethnographic principle of valuing participants' perspectives and not assuming that we, as researchers, have a complete understanding of our own or other people's use of language and literacy practices in social media (and other online contexts). The experience of researching literacy practices in this way brings to light the ways in which everyone's practices are constantly changing; that is precisely why we, as teachers, need to ask students about their practices, a topic where they are the experts. We need to learn about what they know and what they do.

## Data analysis

So far we have discussed the stages of planning research and collecting data. Having collected the data, often using several methods, the next step is to make sense of it and to look for patterns in it. This is the stage of the data analysis. Each method of data collection used has its purpose, in turn related to the research questions; each also provides different sorts of data. There may be field notes, interview transcripts, documents, photographs, screenshots, diaries, survey results and more. And do not forget, there are also 'head notes', the memories and sense-making in the researcher's head which are never written down or recorded, but still help shape the analysis (Sanjek 1990). Taken together, these forms of data constitute the materials which contribute to the analysis. However, amongst this array of different materials it can be challenging to know which elements might be the most important, and how to prioritise the process of analysis. As a first decision, it is probably useful to make one of the methods key and to see the other forms of data as fitting in with it. For instance, in studying an activity on Twitter, there may have been in-depth interviews with a small number of participants. Transcripts of these interviews could become the central form of data and other data from interviews or diaries then related to it. In Barton and Lee's (2013) Flickr study discussed in the previous chapter, the analysis of people's photo sites was central and information from interviews and analysis of the comments were always related back to the Flickr user's photo site.

There are different ways of actually carrying out the analysis. For smaller projects it will usually be done manually. For a longer project, such as a dissertation, it is often valuable to use some form of computer assisted qualitative data analysis software (CAQDAS) such as Atlas-Ti or Nvivo. These packages help the researcher organise the data and they provide an explicit set of steps in analysis. Whether doing the analysis completely manually or with the support of software, the first step of analysis is an obvious sounding step: to read and re-read the transcripts. The aim is to identify and develop themes in the data. The original research questions will suggest existing themes that the researcher will look out for as a starting point for their annotation of the material. At the same time, there will be 'emergent themes' which arise in the data and only become apparent once the researcher begins to work through the data she or he has collected. For example, Barton and Lee's Flickr study set out to study multilingualism and the initial themes related to language choice. As the data was analysed other themes related to learning, to being reflexive and to other topics emerged.

There is a set of simple steps to follow to get to the themes. Firstly annotate the transcripts, making notes about anything which seems relevant: this is referred to as 'memoing'. There is a constant process of selecting, of highlighting what seems to be significant in the data. The next stage is 'coding', saying that different instances are examples of a common phenomenon: there can be pre-existing codes and emergent codes. This process of annotation helps the researcher to identify patterns of similarity and difference within the data and this is done by a process of linking and sorting the annotated data (that is, connecting the annotated links that are similar and grouping them together in categories of different kinds). CAQDAS software can be very helpful in carrying out these procedures. In this process of annotation and sorting, there is a constant going back and forth between what the researcher already knows and is asking and what they find they want to know as they move through the process of analysis. In turn, the process of analysis also involves moving between data and theory. This cycle is part of the recursive nature of research and illustrates clearly the ways in which ethnographic approaches are explicitly responsive (rather than starting out with a single, predetermined question that remains unchanged during the course of the research).

Often, the overall research project is a case study but also within a study, particular people, events or sites can be treated as individual cases. In a study of a small number of people it often makes sense to treat them initially as separate cases, so getting to understand what the individual people are doing in their literacy practices and language use before the researcher starts to look across people at how their practices and perceptions might be similar or different to others in the sample. It is useful for the researcher to first read and code the data on one person, making a summary of the relevant themes that come to the fore in relation to that individual, and so helping the researcher to understand their practices. The researcher can then move on to the next individual participant's materials collected for the project and follow the same process, completing this for each person in the project in turn. Then, taking each theme separately, the researcher can look across all their annotations gathered from the participants as a whole to understand more about the themes. This can be imagined as a grid, where understanding the individual cases is referred to as doing the vertical analysis; then looking across the individual people for themes which are common is the horizontal analysis (as in Barton and Hamilton 1998/2012, pp.69–70). In Barton and Lee's research on Flickr, each person interviewed was initially treated as a separate case and after this there were comparisons across all the participants.

At this point, other forms of data can be brought into the analysis, such as information in field notes or informant diaries, juxtaposing what they say in interviews with what they are observed to do. In this process of analysis, it is useful for the researcher to find ways of standing back from their data and of having some distance from the interpretations they might begin to formulate. Here the contribution of other participants in the study can be very useful. In collaborative ethnography, there can be others to challenge your data and interpretations. Even in an individual study to share data and interpretations with others is fundamental, and it is worth finding ways of doing this with colleagues and co-workers.

## Ways of writing

The next stage of the research is the writing and there are ways of writing which are specific to ethnographic approaches. What gets written at the end of a full ethnographic project is referred to as 'an ethnography' (see Aoife Lenihan's case study in Chapter 5 for an example of this). Whilst a small project will not result in 'an ethnography', ethnographic approaches also see writing as a crucial stage of the research process (not as a separate product that happens after the analysis has taken place). Much sense-making and interpretation take place during the act of writing about the research and in ethnographic approaches, researchers are always encouraged to start writing early on in the research process. More generally, by writing you find out what you want to say and perhaps what you don't yet know and need to find out more about. In ethnographic approaches, writing up a project can initially be structured as a narrative, a story of the research. A chronological narrative is the most basic and accessible form of writing about the research, but the writing also can get beyond this and be structured as themes which analyse the literacy practices and language use which emerge from the data (and so do not just describe how the researchers went about collecting their materials). The research questions can structure the writing and provide threads across describing what was done, how it was analysed and what sense was made of it. Often the analysis and discussion can be structured around individual cases or specific themes.

In writing up qualitative research, there is a need to be explicit about the choices the researcher has made in the process of designing and executing a project. This helps address some of the issues of validity common to all research. For example one needs to make clear how a site was chosen, how a person was chosen to be interviewed, how much data one has and in what form. Choices are made throughout the research and these choices of direction taken and of directions not taken can be documented. All these enable a reader to make the judgements of how a particular study relates to other cases. Writing also needs to be explicit about the role of the researcher and to bring the researcher into the narrative in a reflexive way. In this chapter, we have shown how students can research literacy practices and language use in social media starting with their own practices, and how they can develop this into realistic projects and dissertations. In the next chapter we turn to the questions and methods that are used to gather data for quantitative research projects.

## References

Barton, D. and Hamilton, M. (1998/2012) *Local Literacies: Reading and Writing In One Community*, London and New York: Routledge.

Barton, D. and Lee, C. (2013) *Language Online: Investigating Digital Texts and Practices*, London and New York: Routledge.

Gimenez, J. (2010) 'Narrative analysis in linguistic research', in Litosseliti, L., ed., *Research Methods in Linguistics*, London: Continuum, 198–216.

Lee, C. (2014) 'Language choice and self-presentation in social media: the case of university students in Hong Kong', in Seargeant, P. and Tagg, C., eds, *The Language of Social Media*, Basingstoke: Palgrave Macmillan.

Sanjek, R., ed. (1990) *Fieldnotes: The Making of Anthropology*, Ithaca, NY: Cornell University Press.

# Chapter 8

# Collecting social media materials for quantitative projects

## Outline of the chapter

In this chapter we cover:

- Quantitative research questions.
- Types of variables.
- Samples and representativeness.
- Quantitative tools for eliciting data.
- Collecting data for a corpus linguistics project.
- Understanding metadata.
- The features of social streaming data.
- How to scrape social streaming data.

## Quantitative research questions

As we've stressed throughout this book, we believe in the value of multi-method approaches for analysing the language used in social media contexts. In Chapter 3, we presented a range of methods that can be used either separately or in combination when planning and executing a research project. While the discourse analytic and ethnographic approaches covered in Chapters 5, 6 and 7 most readily align with qualitative aspects of the research design, in the present chapter, we focus on the principles and practices for collecting data that would be used when a research project includes a quantitative element. In simple terms, quantitative research methods are those that involve counting or measuring particular phenomena (such as people, texts or language features). Providing quantitative accounts of the material you are studying might be important, even if a research project is primarily qualitative in nature. Quantitative information can be useful to contextualise close analysis of individual texts in relation to factors, such as how many people were involved in the interaction, how much material was included in the data collection, whether the data was collected at a single point in time, or collected periodically. But for research with a strongly quantitative focus in terms of the analysis required, including the work in linguistic subfields such as corpus linguistics, computational linguistics or certain types of sociolinguistic projects (especially those within the tradition of what is called variationist sociolinguistics), planning how to collect the data requires particular consideration of the quantity and types of material required for the research.

The kind of data needed for a research project depends a great deal on the aims of the project and the kinds of questions the researcher is trying to answer. Questions which are framed from a quantitative perspective usually involve some kind of measurement and often imply some kind of comparison. Some questions might seek to describe the frequency of linguistic features as they appear in social media forms. For example:

How often do viewers include different types of initialisms in their messages when they live-tweet their responses to given television programmes?

Are temporal adverbs associated with the present moment (like *now*) more likely to occur in blogs or social network sites?

Or they might compare the frequency with which particular groups of people use particular linguistic forms:

How does the use of intensifiers (*so*, *very*, *really*) vary in frequency between the Facebook wall posts written by men and written by women?

Other quantitative questions might compare attitudes towards language use or perceptions of social media use, for example:

What are the most frequent reasons people give for joining a social network site?

Some of these questions may investigate the influence of particular factors on the use of language in social media contexts. For example:

How does the length of time a person spends interacting on a social network site relate to their use of site-specific jargon?

Are women or men more likely to be the target of insults in YouTube comments?

As these examples suggest, and just like qualitative examples, quantitative research questions can vary from being very broad to very specific. Compare the relative breadth of the following set of questions:

Do women blog more often than do men?

How do women and men blog about their experiences of being diagnosed with cancer?

How do Latino-American women and men use evaluative language when they blog about being diagnosed with lung cancer?

The first question sets up a comparison based on the participants' gender (a binary comparison that might be criticised for all kinds of reasons). The second question narrows the type of blog that the research considers, while the third question narrows the groups of women and men who are compared, and introduces the linguistic feature under scrutiny (though "evaluative language" is still a somewhat vague term which could include a range of phenomena), and a more specific type of illness.

Formulating a research question requires an in-depth understanding of the properties and scale of the domain in which you might want to collect data. There is no definitive set of steps for formulating a quantitative research question in linguistics given the multitude of possible areas of inquiry, but some general principles apply. At the most basic level, the nature of the research question determines the kind of data that will then be collected. This is sometimes described in terms of research validity. Dörnyei (2007) describes the two aspects of research validity as the extent to which the results of a project can be generalised to a wider group (external validity) and the extent to which the research design is coherent (internal validity). The question of internal validity can be thought of as making sure you collect data that is consistent with the parameters (and only the parameters) set out in a research question. For example, if a project asked, "To what extent do teenagers use the same slang terms in Twitter and Facebook?" and only collected material from one of those sites (only Twitter or only Facebook), then the data would not help the researcher to carry out the comparative analysis the question required. Likewise, if researchers wanted to find out the most frequent reason that caused people to leave a particular social media site, it would not be very helpful to survey people who were still members of the site. The relative breadth or narrowness of the research question also determines the amount and kinds of data that a researcher needs to collect and in turn the kinds of analysis and claims that they are able to make later. The question of how representative a set of data might be has a specific meaning in statistics (and which we touch on below in the section on constructing a sample), but for now, it is most important to note the relationship between the parameters that a researcher sets in framing a research question and the kind of data they will then need to collect.

The internal validity of a research project also depends on the researcher making sure that the results are not influenced by additional factors outside the parameters of the research question. Controlling the influence of one factor rather than another can sometimes be complicated because of the multifaceted nature of people's identity and interactions. Participants have different aspects to their identities (age, gender, nationality, political affiliation, occupation, membership of different sites), interactions take place in different sites, at different times, accessed from different platforms and for different purposes, and language use can draw on multiple semiotic resources (words, sound, image, layout, gesture), in varying combinations and draw on multiple elements of the language systems at the same time. Isolating which of those multiple factors and features are being investigated is an important step in controlling the data collection process. For example, if you wanted to examine the language used on a social media site by a particular group (say, men), you might want to refine the selection criteria so that you gather or elicit material from only a certain group of men (of a certain age and nationality, or who speak a particular language, or have used the site for a particular length of time). Of course, a person's demographic or site-specific characteristics are not always clear from the profile information they publish on a social media site, and they might not wish for a researcher to use certain categories to describe them: those choices about categorising participants can sometimes be important depending on the kind of research project and approach. As we saw in Chapters 6 and 7, participants' perspectives on their identities are crucial to how the collection and analysis of data might proceed, and might change over time and across different sites. Nonetheless, for a quantitative approach that begins with pre-defined categories, controlling the variables in your project might be an important step in collecting data that enables you to answer your research questions satisfactorily.

A more subtle distinction can arise between collecting data about people's perceived use of language and their actual language use on social media sites. If the project aimed to compare how often different kinds of naming practices were used in Twitter by a group of people, asking people to answer a questionnaire about naming practices will not show the researcher how often people actually use different naming options in Twitter, it will collect data about how people self-report their language use. To find out about actual naming practices, you would need to observe a set of Twitter posts. Of course, self-reports of language practices are interesting in their own right (especially in the context of techno-autobiographies with a linguistic focus as described in Chapter 7), but they may not reveal the same patterns of behaviour that a researcher would observe when they examine actual language practices from the same people. In sociolinguistics, there have been important studies which documented how different groups of people tended to either over-exaggerate or downplay their tendency to use particular linguistic forms when interviewed, depending on the relative meanings associated with the form (Labov 1966 and Trudgill 1974). The same principles can also be at work when we investigate how people use language in social media contexts.

A second basic issue to consider when formulating a quantitative research method is whether or not the feature you are interested in can be counted or measured. How you count and compare particular phenomena as part of a quantitative analysis is a more complex question, and is considered in Chapter 9. But at the outset, it can be useful to think about the nature of the feature you want to analyse (your unit of observation) and how you might quantify it (unit of analysis). For example, some features seem relatively easy to quantify, such as how often a particular choice of word occurs. Other linguistic phenomena are harder to pin down, for example evaluative meanings are often constructed in a variety of means, some of which might appear as phrases (e.g. "I can't believe how difficult the task was"), some of which are words (e.g. the intensifier *really*), others are related to punctuation (like exclamation marks or non-standard spellings used for expression, such as *yayyyyy*) or paralinguistic features such as prosody or gesture. But these different aspects of language use often work in combination and the overall combined meaning is hard to reduce to single items that can be counted. The interpretation of evaluative meaning is also highly subjective and dependent on context: one person's opinion of evaluation can be different to someone else's, and determined by the surrounding text and additional factors like cultural values. Finally, some of the multimodal features that are so important in social media interactions (image, layout, icons, audio-visual resources) do not always have clearly defined units of analysis or map on to existing linguistic units.

## Questions and variables

Research questions with a quantitative element often investigate variation that can be measured. The underpinning interest in variation necessarily implies a point of comparison and an attempt to map the relationship between one feature or factor and another. These kinds of relationships can be a simple comparison (do emoticons or exclamation marks occur more often in Facebook wall posts?), or they can trace correlations (does the gender of the blog post author correlate with the gender of the blog post commenters?), or they can imply a cause and effect (are apologies posted in Twitter perceived as more or less sincere than apologies posted in mainstream news?), or they might investigate change over time (how did the hashtag #barackobama get used before, during and after the American elections in 2008?). Both within sociolinguistics and within statistics, the features and factors that are compared are referred to as different types of variables.

Within the tradition of variationist sociolinguistics, variables are distinguished according to whether they refer to the linguistic features that are being investigated (the linguistic variable) or the factors which relate to the contexts in which the linguistic feature might be used (for example, who, where, when and for what purpose the language is used). These contextual factors are sometimes called *speaker variables* (if they describe the characteristics of the people) or *social variables* or *contextual variables*. Some of the examples of research questions given earlier illustrate the difference between the linguistic and social variables (see Table 8.1).

In experimental studies, the relationship between factors can also be described in terms of cause and effect and described as dependent and independent variables. Imagine a project where the researcher wanted to

*Table 8.1* Examples of linguistic and social variables

| Question | Linguistic variables | Social/contextual variables |
|---|---|---|
| Are temporal adverbs associated with the present moment more likely to occur in blogs or social network sites? | Temporal adverbs | Type of social media site (blogs or social network sites) |
| How does the length of time a person spends interacting on a social network site relate to their use of site-specific jargon? | Site-specific jargon | Length of time spent interacting on a social network site |
| What are the differences in how women of different age groups interpret the use of emoticons in online chat? | Meaning of emoticons | Age |

find out whether a person's online anonymity influenced the amount of insults they posted to a social network site. The research question could be posed as, "How does the frequency of insults vary according to the anonymity of site members?" There are two factors (or variables) being compared in this question: the amount of insults generated and whether the site members choose an anonymous form of identity or not. The way data might be collected to answer the question might involve comparing the behaviour of site members who use anonymous representation and those site members who represent their identity through other choices (such as using a name or photograph that identified them). The independent variable is the factor which the researcher manipulates (here the anonymity of the site members) as a means of testing the possible causes of the language use. The dependent variable is the outcome or the effect (here, the frequency of the insults). The quantity of the dependent variable depends on the influence of the independent variable. One way to express this relation is to rephrase the question in a way that makes clear the dependency relationship, such as: "To what extent does the frequency of insults *depend on* the anonymity of the site members?" The difference between the dependent and independent variables can be illustrated with examples from the research questions given earlier (see Table 8.2).

Within statistics, there is a further set of subcategories applied to variables which distinguish between the kinds of measurements a researcher might want to make in their analyses. The different types of categorical variables include dichotomous variables, where a participant in a survey or questionnaire has only two choices of response. For example, if you asked a person if they owned a mobile phone, they could only answer "yes" or

*Table 8.2* Examples of independent and dependent variables

| Question | Independent variable(s) | Dependent variable |
| --- | --- | --- |
| How does the length of time a person spends interacting on a social network site influence their use of site-specific jargon? | Length of time spent interacting on a social network site | Use of site-specific jargon |
| Does gender or anonymity most affect the amount of insults posted by a site member to YouTube? | Anonymity of site member<br>Gender of site member | Amount of insults |
| Are apologies perceived as more sincere when posted to Twitter than when published in the mainstream news? | Medium of publication (Twitter or mainstream news) | Perceived sincerity of the apology |

"no". Nominal variables describe responses which are presented as a series of non-numerical categories. For example, a question such as, "What devices do you use to access social media content?" might offer a number of responses, such as a smart phone, a PC, a laptop, a tablet, a game console and so on. Lastly, categorical variables can be ordinal, meaning that they are factors that can be scaled. A well known example of an ordinal variable is a Likert scale. A Likert scale (named after its creator, Rensis Likert) can be used to grade responses to questions on a numerical scale that indicates intensity of response, where the end points of the scale (usually of five or seven points) indicate the least and the most points of intensity. Likert scales are useful because they allow responses to be neutral, as well as in agreement or disagreement with a statement.

There has been a growing body of research in the arts, humanities and social sciences that have employed quantitative methods to explore a range of contextual variables and their role as dependent variables in influencing the creation and interactions found on social media sites. Given that social media sites very often automatically capture contextual information such as the time and the place of the interaction, these variables have been given fresh emphasis along with well recognised speaker variables such as a person's age or gender as indicated through the information stored in their profiles on particular sites (though as we noted in Chapter 3, this kind of information is not always the same as the characteristics the same person might claim for his or her identity in other online or offline contexts).

- Geographic location – often geo-tagged social media texts are used studies that wish to make claims about the location-based properties of these texts. Sometimes the focus will be on location-based prediction (e.g. Kinsella et al. 2011).
- Time – temporal data is readily available in social streaming texts and is used to complement other forms of data such as location with a variety of aims (e.g. Hargittai and Litt 2011 provide a longitudinal analysis using survey data; Altman and Portilla 2012 examine the evolution of language in Twitter).
- Gender – identifying and predicting the gender of social media participants is a growing area of interest (Burger et al. 2011; Deitrick et al. 2012), and there are studies of the gender of @mentions in Twitter in relation to news stories (Armstrong and Gao 2010) and in relation to hashtags (Cunha et al. 2012). Multimodal studies are also beginning to appear looking at how gender is performed in social media images (Rose et al. 2012).
- Age – Studies of this variable may consider, for example, the effect of age and gender on blogging (Argamon et al. 2007; Rustagi et al. 2009; Schler et al. 2006).
- Community – since social media services function to establish networked relationships, many studies seek to explore the properties of the social network. For example they may explore the way in which information spreads through a network (Galuba et al. 2010; Kwak et al. 2010) and how key users 'influence' others within the network (Cha et al. 2010).

Most of this work has been undertaken outside the realm of linguistics. However, some studies do consider complementary linguistic variables such as:

- Language variety – this usually is inferred from the content of the social media text, although metadata about language is sometimes available. Some work is beginning to appear on dialectal variation (e.g. study of regional variation in slang (Eisenstein et al. 2010)).
- Community (based on language features not just links between users) – some studies attempt to automate classifying users into communities based on specific language features (e.g. based on noun phrases (Haythornthwaite and Gruzd 2007)).

No doubt more studies in the variation of social media language will continue to emerge long after this book is published, which address a range of research questions. You might like to evaluate the research questions and methods for gathering data in these (and other studies) along with your own project design by using the reflective questions in the list below.

ection

ariables are compared in your research question?
the linguistic features or language practices you want

narrow is your research question?
lata will you need to collect to answer it?
How might you need to control the variables in your project?

## Sampling and representativeness

Having established your research question and identified the variables you want to investigate and how you want to measure them, you are some way to deciding what kinds of material you need to gather for analysis. These choices will determine whether you can gather existing materials together for content analysis (and so compile either a dataset or a large-scale collection of materials in a corpus) or whether you will need to elicit responses from participants (for example through a survey or in an experiment). Regardless of the choice of tool you use, there will be criteria you need to apply when selecting your material in terms of the choice of texts, contexts and participants, and in terms of how much material you might want to collect. It is worth saying again at this point that although the focus of this chapter is on the principles and issues relating to quantitative approaches, very often quantitative approaches can be combined with other kinds of analysis, and that, just as in the qualitative approaches covered in Chapters 5, 6 and 7, documenting the criteria used to collect your data for a quantitative project is an important part of the research process to be included in writing up.

When approaching the process of selecting data, it may be useful to think about the types and amount of texts we are collecting along a "continuum" of discourse data (Bednarek 2009). We may be interested in rich analysis of only a handful of texts or statistical analyses of large volumes of data. In addition we may wish to combine both of these approaches in a single study. For example, Baker (2006) advocates a "two-pronged" approach to analysis, combining the qualitative insights of close discourse of small volumes of texts with the quantitative analysis made possible by using a corpus. Extending this kind of approach, Bednarek (2009) suggests a "three-pronged" method to corpus-based discourse analysis. This approach incorporates close manual analysis of single texts with manual, or partially-automated, small-scale corpus-based analysis that might complement quantitative work, often highly automated, using large-scale million word corpora (Figure 8.1). For example, I might be interested in certain kinds of evaluative language that are used in blogging. In order to study evaluative meanings in blog posts I might begin with close discourse analysis of a single post, considering

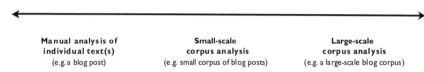

| Manual analysis of individual text(s) (e.g. a blog post) | Small-scale corpus analysis (e.g. small corpus of blog posts) | Large-scale corpus analysis (e.g. a large-scale blog corpus) |

*Figure 8.1* A continuum of discourse data. Adapted from Bednarek (2009, p.19).

how meanings are being made in a particular text type, for instance, analysing how evaluation functions in a post in a food review blog. I might complement this work by considering a range of blog posts collected as a small corpus of food review blog posts (assembled according to particular selection criteria). In addition I might like to compare how the language of food review blogging compares with general blogging by comparing them with a much larger set containing a representative sample of posts from a large volume of different kinds of blogs.

An important methodological concern is sampling, that is, determining the scope and criteria for collecting texts. Because it is impossible to examine all the possible language uses of all possible kinds of social media sites by all possible people, the researcher has to limit their choice of material in some way. In statistics, the ideal, generalised data a researcher might want to investigate (such as blogs written by men about mental health) is called the population and the actual set of materials that the researcher selects for analysis (the particular set of blog posts written by a particular set of blog authors) is called the sample. In the case of social media interactions, the sample can consist of texts, or of participants (e.g. survey respondents) or both, depending on the contextual variables being examined.

If a project is working within strictly quantitative methods with the aim of generalising the results of the research, then it may be important that the sample of selected material is representative, that is, that it matches the general characteristics of the population of interest. Imagine that a researcher wanted to examine the evaluative language used by women and men when they talk about a critical illness, like cancer. The researcher might start by finding out what kinds of cancers get blogged about most frequently and then select their data accordingly (for example, if more blogs were written about brain cancer than lung cancer, then the researcher might want to account for this difference in how many blogs of which type they collect). In other quantitative approaches, it might be more important to balance the size of each data sample proportionately, so for example if you were comparing the frequency of naming choices in Facebook and Twitter, you would want to collect equal numbers of posts from equal numbers of participants from each site.

The desire to produce quantitative findings that can be generalised can also determine the criteria used to decide how much data should be collected (how many participants, posts or survey responses and so on). The practicalities of carrying out a small-scale student term paper often mean that the researcher is working within constraints of time, budget and availability for recruiting participants. But this does not mean that sample size should be disregarded as a luxury available only to more advanced researchers. If the analysis will involve statistical tests, then it is important to make sure you collect enough data required for the particular test. It is easier to collect too much data and then select a subset for analysis later than not collect enough and have to go back to the participants or texts you are sampling from to gather more material afterwards. You should build in a 'safety margin' for collecting enough data to allow for the parts of the sample which might not be used in the final analysis (such as participants who drop out of a study, or who only partially complete a questionnaire; blogs or Twitter accounts that cease to be maintained actively over time, and so on).

The question of how much to collect depends not only on the extent to which you want to generalise from your findings (more is better) but also on the number of variables you are testing (the more variables you are testing, the more material you need). Dörnyei (2007, p.99) provides some approximate 'rule of thumb' measures, suggesting that for research that is attempting to correlate one factor with another, at least 30 participants or examples should be included, and for experiments, at least 15 participants per group. There are also mathematical formulae that will calculate the precise quantities that are suggested for projects that involve multiple variables, and we refer you to specialist quantitative methods handbooks for more details on how to apply these to your project design (see Rasinger 2008).

---

### Points for reflection

What is the population and the sample that you intend to study in your project?

What factors might require you to build in a 'safety margin' for your data collection?

How will you balance the number of participants and texts in your sample?

---

## Quantitative tools for eliciting data

Once you have identified the variables in your project and formulated your research question, and decided how many participants or examples you need to gather you then need to consider which tools might be best to collect the material you will analyse. There is a broad distinction between quantitative tools that can be used to elicit information (that is, to generate new material for analysis) and the processes used to gather existing material together (in a dataset or corpus). In the remainder of this chapter we cover two well-known tools for eliciting quantitative data (surveys and experiments) and close by considering the factors which are important for designing and gathering material for a social media corpus. The factors which underpin the design of surveys, experiments and corpora were well-established prior to the advent of social media genres, so the outlines presented here will refer you to existing, more detailed textbooks on the subject at various points. However, the characteristics of social media which enable rapid, collaborative interactions with potential large audiences mean that these tools can be adapted and adopted with new emphasis for research about the language used on social media sites.

## Surveys

Using a survey in the form of a questionnaire to be completed by the participants can be an efficient way of gathering large amounts of data in a relatively short amount of time. This is especially true when the process of gathering the survey responses can be handled through an online mechanism and distributed to a large audience through social media sites (such as a Facebook Friend list or a Twitter Follower list), and then re-distributed to further audiences as the survey is posted on again by the respondents to their own Friend or Follower list in a snowball effect. However, being able to elicit large amounts of material is only useful if the material can be used to answer the research questions set by a project. The design of a questionnaire is thus crucial: you need to make sure that you ask questions that will prompt responses useful to your project. It might seem very simple to make this observation, but working out how to frame and phrase survey questions effectively takes some thought and it is always essential to do some sort of piloting.

There are several factors that are important when preparing survey questions. First, different types of questions can be selected depending on how you want to quantify your results. Closed questions can be used if you want to measure dichotomous responses, such as "Are you a member of Twitter?" which can be answered with either an affirmative or negative response. Other questions can be used to gather graduated responses, which might be more useful if you are trying to elicit self-reported accounts of behaviour or opinions about a topic. With these questions, multiple choice or rank ordered responses might be useful which employ ordinal or non-numerical options. For example, you might ask participants to rank which kinds of social media sites they find most useful for accessing information about current events, or to indicate from a list of options which tools they use for accessing social media sites. Second, just as in face-to-face contexts, the way in which a survey question is phrased can make a great deal of difference to the way in which people answer it. Questions need to be worded in simple, unambiguous language, and to avoid jargon that may not be understood by the people answering the questions. The wording of questions should try to avoid presupposing a particular answer or using language that might be clearly evaluative (for example, compare the difference in asking, "What do you hate about the Facebook timeline?" and a more neutrally worded, "How would you describe the effects of the Facebook timeline?") Questions should only require one response: complex or multiple questions with only one response option make it difficult to process the responses. Finally, open-ended questions can be included in a survey (though strictly speaking they generate material that is more suited to qualitative analysis rather than a purely quantitative approach). These open-ended questions can be of different kinds: used to elicit responses to specific questions, or as a follow-up clarification. For example, it might provide a space for respondents to explain why they had ranked their choices in a particular order, or to provide further context about an answer given previously.

Surveys can be administered in a variety of formats: participants can be given paper copies of the survey and asked to complete them in writing, researchers can ask the participants questions and then fill in the answers on their behalf (either face-to-face or by telephone), or online survey templates can be used, which enable the participants to type in their answers to an online form set up by the researcher (and which then allow the researcher to export the responses in an electronic format of some kind). Different social media contexts can expand the range of survey tools too: the rating tools available (such as the 'like' button in sites like Facebook) can be used to create simple polls, and more bespoke polling tools have been created as apps that work with other social media sites like Twitter to allow participants to respond to questions or presentations in real time. Other kinds of contextual data automatically generated from devices like smart phones and streamed into social media services (such as location data in the form of GPS information, live-streamed video content from mobile camcorders or details generated from check-ins) can also be used in quantitative surveys that might wish to correlate participants' language or responses with their geographical location. However, as with surveys which are carried out in offline contexts, the wording of the question and the formats provided for responses will determine the data that is generated (even if this is in a form that is readily automated).

### Experiments and quasi-experiments

Unlike surveys where the researcher observes relations between linguistic and contextual variables, in experiments or quasi-experiments, the researcher alters one (or more) independent variables in order to test its effect on the dependent variable. It is often quite difficult to create experiments where the influence of additional variables can be eliminated from the research adequately (see Dörnyei 2007; Rasinger 2008). For example, imagine that you wanted to test whether using a social network site influenced the slang terms that were adopted when students joined a college course. Before they joined the college course, you might ask them to list all the slang terms they knew and then once they had joined the course ask them to repeat the test. But how could the researcher be sure that it was using the social network site that caused the change in slang terms reported by the students after they had joined the college course? It might be possible that students would just acquire new slang terms anyway, without using the site to interact with their peers. One way in which researchers can try to ensure that the influence of a particular variable on a given group is the cause of the observed effect is to compare the group who has been manipulated in some way with another comparable group who has not been manipulated: a control group. In the (fabricated) example given here, a control group of students (matched in terms of number and demographic character with the test group) who did not use the social network should also be tested to see whether their knowledge of slang terms also changed as they entered college, and if so, whether they changed to the same extent as their site-using counterparts.

Group 1: students who do not use the social network site tested for their knowledge of slang terms before joining college.

Group 2: students who use the social network site tested for their knowledge of slang terms before joining college.

Group 1: students who do not use the social network site tested for their knowledge of slang terms after joining college.

Group 2: students who use the social network site tested for their knowledge of slang terms after joining college.

Quasi-experimental research can use simulated scenarios to test participants' perceptions of language use, or their anticipated responses. For example, Schultz et al. (2011) presented respondents with fictional apologies made by a company but with one version posted to Twitter whilst another was posted to a blog. The research then examined the effect of the social media context (Twitter or blog) on the participants' perceptions of the apology's sincerity. The ability to create simulations in certain social media contexts such as virtual worlds would seem to lend itself to quasi-experimental research, but there are also many unknown and contentious issues related to research design in these contexts (such as being sure about the demographic characteristics of the participants, and how far the observer's paradox might operate in these contexts). In the last part of this chapter, we shift our attention from the tools used to elicit data for a quantitative project, to some of the technical processes involved in gathering existing texts that can be used for a particular subfield of language study: corpus linguistics.

## Collecting data for a quantitative project using corpus linguistics

A *corpus* is a technical term used within the field known as Corpus Linguistics to refer to "a collection of pieces of language text in electronic form, selected according to external criteria to represent, as far as possible, a language or language variety as a source of data for linguistic research" (Sinclair 2005). Corpus Linguistics was made possible as an academic discipline with the advent of computer processing technology[1] that allowed researchers to search for words and textual patterns in large volumes of digitised text. A social media corpus is a corpus that includes texts collected from social media services such as WeChat, Twitter and Facebook. The included texts may be verbal content encoded in plain text format (e.g. the written content of a micro-blog post). The texts may also incorporate multimodal resources such as images and video which require metadata in order to be processed and analysed in a quantitative project.

Due to the careful design principles that need to be applied when building a corpus, it is "not simply a collection of texts" (Biber *et al.* 1998, p.246). A corpus is only as useful as the rigour of its selectional constraints (the parameters used to decide which material to include) and the relevance of these selection criteria to the research question at hand. When building a corpus a researcher will take into account issues of representativeness (the extent to which the corpus can be said to generalise a particular variety or dimension of language given the variation possible in a linguistic sample) and balance (the range of genres, text types or linguistic features included in the corpus) (Sinclair 2005). For example, is a corpus of blog posts representative of the communicative patterns found in journalism blogging, or does the sampling of the texts (how many and what kind of text) mean that some text types are more frequent than others in the corpus? If you want to make claims about blogging within journalism, how many texts would you need to analyse? What range of blogs would you need to gather these texts from and how many different electronic sources would you need to consider? Applying Sinclair's (2005) suggestion of some important corpus design factors (shown in italics below) to the domain of social media corpora, we might consider:

- *Mode* – social media involve a range of semiotic modes (e.g. spoken and written modes in YouTube videos and their attendant comments/video responses).
- *Text type* – social media encompass a variety of text types and genres (e.g. blog posts, comments which include genres such as observations, anecdotes, etc.).
- *Domain* – social media are used across multiple domains, for example specialist or academic domains (e.g. live-tweeting[2] a conference) and popular domains (e.g. live-tweeting TV).

- *Language(s)/language varieties* – most social media are cross-cultural with a variety of languages present.
- *Location* – since social media are enacted online the entire concept of place becomes problematic.
- *Date* – time is crucial to social media and social media services usually encompass forms of streaming data (see explanation later in this chapter).

An important distinction that is commonly made when classifying corpora is the difference between a specialised corpus that aims to study a particular type of text (e.g. restaurant reviews in 'food blogs') and a general corpus intended to span a representative sample of language across a range of text types (e.g. a reference corpus such as The British National Corpus or the Corpus of Contemporary American English). There are many other ways we might classify corpora, but given the significant role of time in social media, issues surrounding the development of traditional diachronic corpora (corpora that include texts produced over a particular time period used to study language change) are of particular relevance. Some examples of the types of corpora which include social media texts are listed in Table 8.3, along with examples of published papers (where available) which show how these corpora have been used.

## Is the web a corpus?

Just as the World Wide Web (which is effectively an unprocessed collection of hypertext documents linked together in various ways) should not be thought of as a corpus[3] "because its dimensions are unknown and constantly changing, and because it has not been designed from a linguistic perspective" (Sinclair 2005) we should not think of the data made available by social media services

*Table 8.3* Examples of different sorts of social media corpora

| Type of corpus | Example | Studies using the corpus |
| --- | --- | --- |
| Specialised | Various hashtag corpora | Page (2012) |
| Reference | HERMES Twitter Corpus | Zappavigna (2012) |
| | Birmingham Blog Corpus | Kehoe and Gee (2012) |
| | Cambridge and Nottingham e-Language Corpus | Knight et al. (2014) |
| | Corpus of Global Web-based English | |
| Diachronic | Twitter Stratified Random Sample SRS | None available at time of writing |

as corpora. Collections of social media texts evolve as people add, modify and delete content and the linguist needs to approach this naturally-occurring text with the same careful gaze used in other data collection contexts. Searching with a search engine provided by a social networking service (e.g. Twitter's search interface) is not the same thing as searching a corpus. The algorithms used by these search functions are generally not available for public inspection, and thus we do not have adequate information about their parameters or which texts have been included to determine whether the search results map to what might have been returned using a corpus designed according to particular selection criteria. Nevertheless, just as online discourse has proven to be useful to linguists working in many areas, including lexicography, syntax, semantics and translation (Volk 2002) and corpora derived from Computer Mediated Communication (CMC) begin to appear, social media corpora will eventually gain traction.

Researchers usually build their own social media corpora since CMC is a semiotic mode that remains under-represented in most available traditional corpora. However, very large web-based billion-word corpora are beginning to emerge, such as the 25 billion word USENET corpus (2005–9) (Shaoul and Westbury 2010), a corpus consisting of public USENET postings collected between October 2005 and January 2010, and the Birmingham Blog Corpus (http://wse1.webcorp.org.uk/blogs/), consisting of approximately 629 million words of blog texts extracted from the web. In addition the field of Computational Linguistics has generated many very large Twitter corpora, particularly in the area of sentiment analysis (e.g. Bollen *et al.* 2011). An example of a corpus incorporating data from a range of social media types is the Cambridge and Nottingham eLanguage Corpus (CANELC), designed to form part of the Cambridge International Corpus. This corpus is a one million word collection of electronic communication including emails, tweets, blogs, text messages, post in electronic fora and chat room communication. Depending on the nature of the corpus and the institution within which it was created, access will either be free or via paid subscription (e.g. the USENET corpus (2005–9) is currently available as a Public Data Set on Amazon Web Services). The page hosting a corpus will usually provide links to researcher projects that have used the corpus and this can be a useful way to find relevant literature and people who are likely to be interested in the work that you are doing.

## Understanding metadata

Metadata is information about information. It usually describes something about the content of digital media, such as how it was created, its display, or its context. There are different kinds of metadata that can be created by an individual or automatically generated by software. For instance, a digital image might incorporate three forms of metadata: *technical metadata*, including information about the technical specification of the image captured by a camera, such as the ISO speed at which the image was taken, *descriptive metadata* such as keywords about the image assigned by the content-creator, and *administrative metadata* such as licensing information (Photometadata. org 2011). Social media services make use of a large range of metadata that can be mined by third parties. For example a service may attach information about the time and location at which particular content was created. An example of a linguistic study that has made use of such metadata is research into lexical variation using a geo-tagged Twitter corpus[4] that found that many slang terms such as *af* (as fuck) and *hella* (very) "have strong regional biases, suggesting that slang may depend on geography more than standard English does" (Eisenstein *et al.* 2010, p.1285). Other work adopting this kind of approach includes Brice Russ' study of dialect variation. In his case study, he describes the processes he used to exploit the geo-tagging metadata in a social media study of dialectology.

## Box 8.1 Twitalectology: examining large-scale regional variation through online geo-tagged corpora

### Brice Russ

Dialectology is a key component of sociolinguistic study; studying regional variation can often provide valuable insights into other social aspects of language, and discussing dialects can be a useful tool in building general interest in linguistics. Mapping dialects on a broad scale, however, has traditionally required surveying large, geographically scattered populations in a process that can take years of time and significant effort.

Twitalectology seeks to examine whether regional variation in some linguistic items can be studied and analysed using data from Twitter. If so, data from these variables could be collected in a matter of weeks or months without elicitation or supervision, making it significantly easier to conduct dialectological studies. Selecting linguistic variables which were suitable for Twitalectology was a challenging process. Twitter, being a textual medium, cannot accurately represent phonetic or phonological variation in most instances, so I limited my first round of experimentation to lexical and morphosyntactic variables. I also wanted to use variables which exhibited variation across a significant part of the continental United States, and to incorporate both well-studied regional variables and variables which had not yet been thoroughly nationally surveyed.

After examining data from the Harvard Survey of North American Dialects and other linguistic surveys, I decided on three variables: soft drink terms (specifically, *soda* versus *pop* versus *coke*), the usage of *hella* as an intensifier (in contrast with, for example, *very*), and the *needs* X-*ed* construction, as seen in phrases such as *The car needs washed*. Using a Python script which sent requests to the Twitter API (application programming interface), I constructed a corpus of tweets which contained a token of at least one of the desired linguistic variants, as well as the self-reported location of the account posting each tweet.

Certain terms in the corpus, however, may not refer uniquely to the desired variant; a tweet about *pop*, for example, could be talking about *Pop Tarts*, *pop music*, or other non-soda-related terms. To disambiguate these word-senses, I used collocations: series of words which, when juxtaposed, can refer to a unique concept. For soft drinks, for example, I removed all tweets that did not contain the collocations *drink* X or *drinking* X (e.g. *drinking pop*); those which remained were almost categorical examples of the desired linguistic variable. I then calculated the frequency of each linguistic variant on a city-by-city level and plotted the results on Google Maps; an example of this work can be found at www.briceruss.com and in Chapter 9 of this book.

Because corpus-based approaches to computer-mediated discourse require insights from a variety of linguistic fields, many of which are new and cutting-edge, I recommend that any prospective researchers not be afraid to ask others for help. Twitalectology would not be possible without the contributions and advice of many colleagues. I'd also note that a little programming knowledge can go a long way; I'm definitely not a computational linguist by nature, but I found that the scripting skills I did know went a long way towards helping me explore and analyse the large datasets that this project entailed.

#advice: Corpora created using data from social media can be useful and easy to collect, but don't trust them blindly.

Metadata can often appear in 'unfriendly' forms that appear difficult to make sense of. Some of the metadata that were collected in the process of building the HERMES corpus are summarised in Table 8.4. Although difficult to read, these automated examples of metadata can be very useful in a research project, for example the geo-tag, as we have seen in the studies on dialect variation mentioned earlier in this chapter, can be used to filter posts based on the location where they were produced. Location information of this kind will not always be available as this kind of feature is typically 'opt-in' due to the privacy concerns of social media users. This may also be the case with other forms of metadata such as information about gender. When designing your study you will need to consider whether the dimensions that you are interested in exploring correspond to the kinds of features that are tracked in a particular social media service's metadata. For example, some

Table 8.4 Examples of metadata about a post and a user account

| Type of metadata | Tag | Description |
|---|---|---|
| About the post | created_at | Coordinated Universal Time (UTC) timestamp for tweet creation |
| | in_reply_to_screen_name | Display name for the user that replied |
| | Geo | Geotag (location information) |
| | Source | Application used to tweet |
| | in_reply_to_status_id | Unique id for the user that replied |
| | Lang | language |
| | time_zone | The user's time zone |
| About the user's account | statuses_count | Number of posts the user has made |
| | profile_image_url | The URL of the user's avatar file |
| | utc_offset | Time between user's time zone and UTC time |

proprietary archiving systems will provide this kind of metadata in formats that can be exported for further analysis. If you are not using one of these systems to archive material, then you may need to consider whether you have the resources to create bespoke archiving tools to extract the information you need.

Aside from the metadata recorded by social media services about the context of a social media text, another important kind of social media metadata is created when users themselves produce tags to classify their own content. These might be labels assigned to blog posts or hashtags used in micro-blog posts. A broader definition of what we might term 'social metadata' includes "information about a resource resulting from user contributions and online activity—such as tagging, comments, reviews, images, videos, ratings, recommendations—that helps people find, understand, or evaluate the content" (Smith-Yoshimura and Shein 2011, p.10). The kind of collaborative tagging evolving with community use in social media is often referred to as a practice of folksonomy (Vander Wal 2007), or social tagging. This community-based metadata is very different to the top-down hierarchical approaches developed by subject classification in libraries. Whereas document classification involves experts, social tagging engages communities of general users. For example, it is used heavily on photo-sharing sites, such as Flickr, where it often functions as a cooperative form of verbal indexing involving a bottom-up approach to the kind of classification previously achieved by reference librarians (see Barton and Lee (2012) for an exploration of Flickr and the changing literacy practices involved in social tagging). An example of a linguistic study that leverages the insight into the 'topic' of texts afforded by collaborative metadata is work by Kehoe and Gee (2012), who in their work used Delicious tags and corpus linguistic methods to aid how researchers might go about determining textual 'aboutness'. Unfortunately since different social media services will store and present this kind of information in different ways there generally is not one elegant solution for isolating this phenomena so that it can be used in a research project.

## Social-streaming data

In order to build a social media corpus we need to understand the particular properties of the data we are collecting. Social media aims to allow people to connect with each other seamlessly during their daily lives. Thus most services will incorporate some form of 'streaming' capability whereby a user can broadcast a chronologically organised 'feed' of information (e.g. status updates, blog posts and vlogs) that can be delivered to other users in near real-time, depending on how other parties choose to consume their social media feeds.[5] This capability is sometimes referred to more generally as the 'real-time web'. Users are able to subscribe to feeds of their associates' status updates and multimedia content (e.g. photos and video). Often these updates are shared via a mobile device at the time an event occurs or an observation is made. The advantage that social streams of this kind offer to the researcher is the hope of automated data collection using technologies to access and store the data (which, as we will see in the following section of this chapter, can be achieved if the site makes its Application Programming Interface (API) available, as do Twitter and Wikipedia).

Streaming data does, however, pose some challenges for researchers, particularly those interested in exploring structural patterns, such as the 'conversational' interactions between users that can occur on social media. These include considerations such as:

- What is a useful time frame for a 'snapshot' of the unfolding social stream that you will capture? What will this time frame reveal? What are its limitations? How will the time frame skew the kinds of language you might find in your sample (e.g. increased frequency of sport-related lexis during international sporting events like the Olympics)?
- What kind of connections between user accounts or between unfolding instances of language use (e.g. a micro-blog post or a wiki edit) do you want to capture, keeping in mind that you may end up needing to track many-to-many relationships?

- How will you keep track of relationships between embedded and externally referenced multimedia (e.g. pictures referenced in a micro-blog post)?
- How will you cope with the changing nature of the technology underlying streaming data when it changes and causes collection tools to become redundant? (E.g. updates to the Twitter Application Programming Interface (API) have 'broken' many tools developed to work with the first version.)

As we suggested earlier in this chapter, social-streaming discourse is highly temporally bound, since its real-time production has increased the capacity of contextual variables to skew the data: people will often post about events as they happen and about topics that are on their mind at a particular time, often in reaction to shared situations. The time and duration of sampling from a social stream impacts on the representativeness and balance of language retrieved.

Alongside these abstract concerns is the practical problem of sampling in a principled way the vast amount of streaming data generated by social media services and the technical skills required to do this. Generally some basic programming and text processing skills are required to work with streaming data since most social media services will not release a tool with an interface that allows people to easily detect, sample and extract their data. Those services are instead likely to expect developers and researchers to interact with an Application Programming Interface (API). This is because the people working with social-streaming data are usually third-party developers with high-level programming skills who are using it as input into software applications that they are building. An API is the language that software tools use to communicate with a social media service's back-end database. If the API is public, developers can use it to write custom applications that interface with the service's data feeds, allowing them to 'scrape' its data feeds, in other words to download selected types of data. We deal with this process in the next section. If you do not possess basic programming skills it will usually be necessary to collaborate with someone with the appropriate technical background or investigate the range of paid data collection services that have emerged to meet demand for social media data in areas such as marketing. As Brice Russ points out, analysing the language of social media can often turn out to be a collaborative endeavour across the boundaries of different disciplines.

### Scraping social-streaming data

Social media scraping is a form of the more general technique known as web scraping, the process by which data is automatically collected from the websites using custom software. Collecting data from social media services usually involves working with the particular service's Application

Programming Interface (API). For example, the Twitter API is used by many third-party developers to create applications that deploy this streaming data in a range of ways, from simply allowing a user to track different kinds of phenomena that they may be interested in, to complex data visualisation and social media analytics. Social media data of this kind is often used in web 'mash-ups', combining the functionality from two or more sources (such as data made available by an open API) to create a new service that meets some particular, novel need. For example, Twittervision (Twittervision. com) is a web mash-up that combines Twitter feeds with Google Maps to create a display of tweets unfolding in real time on a map.

There is a range of custom software tools available to assist with scraping data from different resources, the details of which are not important here as they rapidly become obsolete. The best way to find information about where current resources might be found is to search developer message boards where you will find developers and research working on social media scraping software (e.g. the Twitter Development Talk Google Group). We should keep in mind that there is no universal solution due to the frequency with which social data changes. These tools need to keep up with the evolving nature of web services and the particularities of different APIs. What will remain more stable, however, is the general principle that, however streaming data is collected, it must meet the kind of selection criteria for building corpora that were introduced earlier in this chapter, inflected as they are by some difficult questions regarding how time units affect dimensions such as representativeness and balance.

Often linguists will need to create their own software (or hire a developer) in order to undertake the kind of scraping required for a particular research project. For example, in order to build the Hermes corpus, I (Michele) used a simple script that repetitively downloaded tweets using the Twitter API as this was the simplest solution at the time given the limited custom software available. The general method used to build the Hermes corpus (Zappavigna 2012, p.24) was:

1. Use a script to interact with the Twitter API and download all the unfiltered tweets from Twitter across a particular time-window or until a certain quantity is captured (keeping in mind that, in step 4, non-English tweets will be removed, reducing the overall number of tweets).
2. Separate the content of the tweets from other metadata, depending on how they will be imported/processed by the particular concordance software to be used with the corpus.
3. Convert any entity sequence, such as escaped characters,[6] into their native form.
4. Filter the text so that it contains only English tweets (or tweets from the particular language of interest). This step is not an exact science as current language filtering technologies are not 100 per cent accurate.

Another significant issue is the form that the scraped data will take once it has been captured. This again depends on the research design. If variables found in the metadata as well as the content of the social feed will be analysed (e.g. location data plus the content of a micro-blog post) then the material may need to be stored in a database, however often this solution does not scale well for large amounts of data which may require custom-designed scripts for processing. The reason why these technologies may be required is that calculating multiple relationships between large numbers of variables in large volumes of data can require a lot of computing power. If, however, more traditional text analysis using, for example, a concordancing system will be undertaken on only the textual content of a social media text (i.e. the linguistic patterns in, for example, a micro-blog post without the attendant metadata) then it may best be stored as plain text. However, this is not necessarily a simple option since getting the data into plain text format may require stripping it of superfluous information as well as processing the kinds of peculiarities that arise from differences in encoding formats (which we will discuss later in Chapter 9). In summary, a linguist thus has the following options in terms of data collection when using a social media corpus: use an existing corpus, modify that corpus in some way, or build a new corpus. Some questions that you might like to ask yourself when planning a quantitative research project are summarised in the following list.

---

### Points for reflection

Is there an existing corpus of that type of text which is already available and accessible that you might use for your analysis?

If you need to build a specialised corpus of some kind, is this restricted to material from a particular site?

Does the site you want to study have an API which allows automated text extraction?

What automated tools or services are available that can be used to gather material from the site you are interested in?

What contextual factors are important in your study and are they available as a form of metadata that can be collected automatically?

What format will the 'scraped' data be provided in? Will you need to adapt this to accommodate the size of the files, or to enable analysis using other automated tools (such as concordancing software or visualisation models)?

---

The process of selecting a particular text type and compiling a corpus for analysis is described in Andrew Kehoe's case study of building the Birmingham Blog Corpus, with which we conclude this chapter.

## Box 8.2 Using reader comments to help determine the topic of blog posts

### Andrew Kehoe

In order to index the web and make it easier for people to find the information they need, it is essential to determine what online texts are about. In the early days, web texts were often classified manually in topic hierarchies like Yahoo. With the growth of the web and recent explosion of social media, it has become increasingly important to develop effective techniques for determining topics automatically. Our focus was on blogs. We wanted to determine whether reader comments on a blog post would provide us with information about the topic of that post which could not be determined by looking at the post alone.

Our approach was a corpus linguistic one, compiling large amounts of data and using statistical analyses to extract the 'key' topic-related words from each post and set of comments. To achieve this, we needed a large collection of blog data, and this case study focuses on how we compiled the *Birmingham Blog Corpus (BBC)*. In doing this, we faced two main challenges. The first was in finding a source of blog data large enough to contain posts on a wide range of topics and to allow us to draw meaningful conclusions from our analyses. The second was in separating the reader comments from the blog posts which, given the required corpus size, would need to be achieved with minimal human input.

With these requirements in mind, we turned to the blog-hosting sites Blogger and WordPress. These sites are vast – Google returns more hits from Blogger (over 840 million) than it does for all *.edu* and *.gov* sites combined – and cover a diverse range of topics, from technology to tennis and politics to parenting. However, despite this apparent heterogeneity, we found that each hosting platform has a limited number of text formatting conventions (e.g. Blogger comments begin with the tag < *dd class* = "*comment-body*" > or similar). This is ideal in corpus compilation as it makes the removal of 'boilerplate' (advertisements, headers, menus) and the separation of comments from posts much more straightforward. Another advantage of blogs over general web data is that accurate publication dates are recorded. We were careful to preserve these in our corpus to assist users interested in language change across time.

To collect our data, we started with the lists of 'trending' blogs made available on each hosting site: 'Blogs of Note' on Blogger and 'Freshly Pressed' on WordPress. We wrote Perl scripts to download each post from each featured blog, together with its associated comments. From this initial dataset we extracted all links to other blogs, whether these were in a post, in a comment, or in a 'blogroll' (list of recommended blogs). New blogs were then added to the crawling queue, widening our coverage beyond the initial 'trending' list. This automated process continued for a month, during which time we processed 222,245 posts, totalling 95 million running words of text. In addition, we downloaded 86 million words of associated comments, revealing a wealth of linguistic knowledge which we could utilise to improve document indexing.

The Birmingham Blog Corpus is available to search at www.webcorp.org.uk/blogs.

#advice: Have clear requirements, understand the data, preserve info that may be useful later (to you or others), share your results and your data.

## Notes

1 Corpora, however, have been used to study language as early as the thirteenth century when monks painstakingly compiled manual concordances of the Christian Bible, and non-digital corpora were used during the 1950s in work on English grammar (O'Donnell, in press).
2 Live-tweeting refers to the practice where users will post real-time reactions to or descriptions of events or media such as public gatherings or television programmes.
3 Nevertheless, there is a body of research interested in finding ways to process web data so that it may be made useful to corpus linguists and more closely approximate the rigours of traditional corpora (Baroni and Bernardini 2006; Hundt et al. 2007; Kilgarriff and Grefenstette 2003).
4 There are also studies that use geo-tagged corpora to create models used to predict the location of tweets based on the language patterns in the post (Kinsella et al. 2011).
5 Many users adopt tools, such as a feed reader, to aggregate multiple web feeds into a single view, meaning that they do not have to visit sources individually for current information.
6 An escape character e.g. \ (a single backslash) signals that the character (or sometimes the sequence) following it is not an operator (a symbol interpreted by the computer as 'syntax' for a program) or some other special case.

## References

Altman, E. and Portilla, Y. (2012) Geo-linguistic Fingerprint and the Evolution of Languages in Twitter, paper presented at the Proceedings of the 2012 IEEE/ACM International Conference on Advances in Social Networks Analysis and Mining (ASONAM) 2012, 26–29 August 2012, Kadir Has University, Istanbul, Turkey, available: http://hal.inria.fr/docs/00/69/06/08/PDF/c6.pdf [accessed 12 November 2013].

Argamon, S., Koppel, M., Pennebaker, J. and Schler, J. (2007) 'Mining the blogosphere: age, gender, and the varieties of self-expression', *First Monday*, 12 (9), available: http://firstmonday.org/ojs/index.php/fm/article/view/2003/1878 [accessed 26 November 2013].

Armstrong, C.L. and Gao, F. (2010) 'Gender, Twitter and news content', *Journalism Studies*, 12 (4), 490–505.

Baker, P. (2006) *Using Corpora in Discourse Analysis*, London and New York: Continuum.

Baroni, M. and Bernardini, S., eds (2006) *Wacky! Working Papers on the Web as Corpus*, Bologna: GEDIT. Available: http://wackybook.sslmit.unibo.it/ [accessed 12 November 2013].

Barton, D. and Lee, C.K. (2012) 'Redefining vernacular literacies in the age of web 2.0', *Applied Linguistics*, 33 (3), 282–98.

Bednarek, M. (2009) 'Corpora and discourse: a three-pronged approach to analyzing linguistic data', in Haugh, M., Burridge, K., Mulder, J. and Peters, P., eds, *Selected Proceedings of the 2008 HCSNet Workshop on Designing the Australian*, available: www.lingref.com/cpp/ausnc/2008/paper2283.pdf [accessed 26 November 2013].

Biber, D., Conrad, S. and Randi, R. (1998) *Corpus Linguistics: Investigating Language Structure and Use*, London: Cambridge University Press.

Bollen, J., Mao, H. and Xiao-Jun, Z. (2011) 'Twitter mood predicts the stock market', *Journal of Computational Science*, 2 (1), 1–8.

Burger, J.D., Henderson, J., Kim, G. and Zarrella, G. (2011) 'Discriminating gender on Twitter', *Proceedings of the Conference on Empirical Methods in Natural Language Processing*, Edinburgh, United Kingdom.

Cha, M., Haddadi, H., Benevenuto, F. and Gummadi, K.P. (2010) 'Measuring user influence in Twitter: the million follower fallacy', Washington, DC, 23–26 May 2010. California: The AAAI Press. Available: www.aaai.org/Library/ICWSM/icwsm10contents.php [accessed 21 May 2011].

Cunha, E., Magno, G., Almeida, V., Andr, M. and Benevenuto, F. (2012) 'A gender based study of tagging behavior in Twitter', *Proceedings of the 23rd ACM Conference on Hypertext and Social Media*, Milwaukee, Wisconsin, USA: ACM, 323–24.

Deitrick, W., Miller, Z., Valyou, B., Dickinson, B., Munson, T., Hu, W. and Cusani, R. (2012) 'Gender identification on Twitter using the modified balanced winnow', *Communications and Network*, 4 (3), 189–95.

Dörnyei, Z. (2007) *Research Methods in Applied Linguistics*, Oxford: Oxford University Press.

Eisenstein, J., O'Connor, B., Smith, N.A. and Xing, E.P. (2010) 'A latent variable model for geographic lexical variation', *Proceedings of the Conference on Empirical Methods in Natural Language Processing*, 1277–87, available: www.cs.cmu.edu/~nasmith/papers/eisenstein+oconnor+smith+xing.emnlp10.pdf [accessed 26 November 2013].

Galuba, W., Aberer, K., Chakraborty, D., Despotovic, Z. and Kellerer, W. (2010) 'Outtweeting the twitterers-predicting information cascades in microblogs', paper presented at the 3rd Workshop on Online Social Networks (WOSN 2010).

Hargittai, E. and Litt, E. (2011) 'The tweet smell of celebrity success: explaining Twitter adoption among a diverse group of young adults', *New Media and Society*, 13 (5), 824–42.

The Harvard Survey of North American Dialects, available: www4.uwm.edu/FLL/ linguistics/dialect/ [accessed 12 November 2013].

Haythornthwaite, C. and Gruzd, A. (2007) 'A noun phrase analysis tool for mining online community conversations', in Steinfield, C., Pentland, B., Ackerman, M. and Contractor, N., eds, *Communities and Technologies*, London: Springer, 67–86.

Hundt, M., Nesselhauf, N. and Biewer, C. (2007) *Corpus Linguistics and the Web*, Amsterdam: Rodopi.

Kehoe, A. and Gee, M. (2012) 'Reader comments as an aboutness indicator in online texts: introducing the Birmingham Blog Corpus', in Oksefjell Ebeling, S., Ebeling, J. and Hasselgård, H., eds, *Studies in Variation, Contacts and Change in English Volume 12: Aspects of Corpus Linguistics: Compilation, Annotation, Analysis*, University of Helsinki e-journal.

Kilgarriff, A. and Grefenstette, G. (2003) 'Introduction to the special issue on the web as corpus', *Computational Linguistics*, 29 (3), 333–47.

Kinsella, S., Murdock, V. and O'Hare, N. (2011) '"I'm eating a sandwich in Glasgow": modeling locations with tweets', *Proceedings of the 3rd International Workshop on Search and Mining User-generated Contents*, Glasgow, Scotland, UK.

Knight, D., Adolphs, S. and Carter, R. (2014) 'CANELC – The Cambridge and Nottingham eLanguage Corpus', *Corpora* 9 (1). In Press.

Kwak, H., Lee, C., Park, H. and Moon, S. (2010) 'What is Twitter, a social network or a news media?' *The 19th World-Wide Web (WWW) Conference*, 26–30 April, Raleigh, North Carolina.

Labov, W. (1966) *The Social Stratification of English in New York City*, Washington, DC: Center for Applied Linguistics.

Lexicalist, available: www.lexicalist.com/ [accessed 12 November 2013].

O'Donnell, M. (in press) 'Between man and machine: the changing face of corpus annotation software', in Yan, F.and Webster, J.J., eds, *Developing Systemic Functional Linguistics*, London: Equinox.

Page, R. (2012) 'The linguistics of self-branding and micro-celebrity in Twitter: the role of hashtags', *Discourse and Communication*, 6 (2), 181–201.

Photometadata.org (2011) Classes of metadata, available: www.photometadata.org/ node/46 [accessed 12 February 2014].

Rasinger, S. (2008) *Quantitative Research in Linguistics: An Introduction*, London: Continuum.

Rose, J., Mackey-Kallis, S., Shyles, L., Barry, K., Biagini, D., Hart, C. and Jack, L. (2012) 'Face it: the impact of gender on social media images', *Communication Quarterly*, 60 (5), 588–607.

Rustagi, M., Prasath, R., Goswami, S. and Sarkar, S. (2009) 'Learning age and gender of blogger from stylistic variation', *Pattern Recognition and Machine Intelligence*, 205–12.

Schler, J., Koppel, M., Argamon, S. and Pennebaker, J. (2006) 'Effects of age and gender on blogging', paper presented at the AAAI Spring Symposium on Computational Approaches for Analyzing Weblogs.

Schultz, F., Utz, S. and Göritz, A. (2011) 'Is the medium the message? Perceptions of and reactions to crisis communciation via Twitter, blogs and traditional media', *Public Relations*, 37, 20–7.

Shaoul, C. and Westbury, C. (2010) A USENET corpus (2005–9), available: www. psych.ualberta.ca/~westburylab/downloads/usenetcorpus.download.html [accessed 17 March 2011].

Sinclair, J. (2005) 'Corpus and text – basic principles', in Wynne, M., ed., *Developing Linguistic Corpora: A Guide to Good Practice*, Oxford: Oxbow Books, 1–16, available: http://ahds.ac.uk/linguistic-corpora/ [accessed 12 November 2013].

Smith-Yoshimura, K. and Shein, C. (2011) *Social Metadata for Libraries, Archives and Museums Part 1: Site Reviews*, Dublin, Ohio: OCLC. Available: www.oclc.org/research/publications/library/2011/2011–02.pdf [accessed 12 November 2013].

Trudgill, P.J. (1974) *The Social Differentiation of English in Norwich*, Cambridge: Cambridge University Press.

Vander Wal, T. (2007) Folksonomy Coinage and Definition, available: http://vanderwal.net/folksonomy.html [accessed 12 November 2013].

Volk, M. (2002) 'Using the web as corpus for linguistic research', *Tähendusepüüdja. Catcher of the Meaning. A Festschrift for Professor Haldur Õim*, Publications of the Department of General Linguistics 3, University of Tartu, available: www.halskov.net/files/Volk_Web_as_Corpus.pdf [accessed 26 November 2013].

Zappavigna, M. (2012) *Discourse of Twitter and Social Media: How we use Language to Create Affiliation on the Web*, London: Continuum.

# Chapter 9

# Working with social media data

## Quantitative perspectives

## Outline of the chapter

In this chapter we cover:

- Choosing how to organise your material.
- Moving beyond raw frequency in calculating results.
- The challenges of concordancing social media texts.
- Annotating social media corpora.
- Analysing social media texts using concordancing software.
- Visualisation tools and social networks.
- Examples of social media text visualisations.

## Choosing how to organise your material

Once the materials needed for a research project have been collected, as discussed in Chapter 8, you are ready to organise and then analyse the data. There are some practical concerns that are important to consider at the initial stages of preparing to analyse social media texts from a quantitative perspective. Some of these relate to the size of the datasets that the project includes. Especially if the dataset is large, then it might not be practical for the researcher to sift and search through this material by hand: using some kind of computerised infrastructure can be useful. For example, as we saw in Chapter 7, preparing and storing the collected materials in a package like NVivo or Atlas-ti can enable the researcher to annotate the data with analytical labels (based on the linguistic and contextual, dependent and independent variables). This process can not only be useful for identifying themes that emerge from the data; additionally the software can also count and sort those themes to help the researcher identify the relative prominence of the patterns in the data. Other alternative packages can include using software like a Microsoft Excel spreadsheet to collate and then code examples, or you might choose to prepare material with bespoke statistical packages like SPSS or the open source package R. Once the researcher has stored their material in a suitable format (for example, choosing the file format required by the software), then they can begin to analyse the materials. The first step is to annotate the data. This might include labelling parts of the data to indicate that a particular linguistic feature is present (or not), or indicating some of the features of the contextual variable (such as the demographic characteristics of the participant, the type of text, number of people involved in an interaction and so on).

A specialised form of analysis which uses particular forms of computing infrastructure belongs to the methods of corpus linguistics. Most of this chapter will consider the practical and analytical concerns that are involved in preparing material for use in conjunction with concordancing software. Those practical concerns include factors that need to be considered when you are compiling and annotating social media materials. After this we describe some basic steps that can be used in corpus linguistics to examine social media texts, moving from simple searches which identify the frequency of individual words in a text, to more complex forms of analysis which compare frequencies across different corpora. We end the chapter by giving some examples of how quantitative forms of analysis might lend themselves to automated forms of representation as visualisation. Before we move on to these more specialised concerns, we begin with some general principles about quantitative analysis that also apply to working with smaller sets of data.

## Quantifying features: beyond raw frequency

In Chapter 8, we discussed the importance of collecting data to answer quantitative research questions, by making sure that the variables in the question matched the materials that were collected in type and proportion. However, even if the researcher has specified certain elements of the data collection with quantitative analysis in mind, there can be further factors about the relative size and balance of the data to take into account once analysis begins. This is true whether the scale of the quantitative analysis is relatively small, or is large enough that it requires analysis with the help of automated software like concordancing software. Imagine that the researcher was interested in comparing the intensifiers that were used by women and men when they posted Facebook updates (this was part of a project that I, Ruth, carried out). The participants for the project were selected based on parameters of gender and age, using a snowballing technique to recruit participants who were outside my immediate set of contacts on Facebook. Informed consent was negotiated with each of the participants, until I had recruited ten women and ten men in each of five age groups (15–18 years of age, 19–21 years of age, 22–29 years of age, 30–39 years of age and 40–49 years of age). I then examined the ten most recent posts that the person had published on their timeline at a given point in time (July 2008 and then again in October 2010). But what I had not accounted for in my data collection was that the women and men in different age groups would write posts that varied in word length. In fact, in 2008, the total number of words in the posts written by men was 3,627 while the total number of words written by women in their updates was 3,220. In 2010, a different pattern occurred, the total number of words written by men in their updates was 4,146 and the total number of words written by women in their updates was 4,407.

We could make some simple calculations from quantifying the size of the data samples, such as generating the average number of words per update, and we could go on to separate out the total word length so that the pattern according to age and gender was clearer. It might also be important to examine the word length of posts written by individual updaters so that the variation in the length of the post within each category becomes clearer (rather than just looking at aggregated scores). But just comparing the total or average word length for the posts does not indicate how important the difference in word length of posts is or whether it could be treated as significant: to assess that, statistical tests would need to be applied. And finally, just looking at the word length does not tell us anything about the linguistic feature that the project set out to examine. However, establishing the size of the dataset in terms of word length is important, especially if the linguistic variable you intend to examine matches the grammatical unit of a word (as opposed to a phrase, clause or other kind of unit).

Knowing the size of your dataset is important, because the raw frequencies of particular items can be a misleading comparison if the different sets of your data are different sizes. Imagine a more polarised (and fabricated) example. Say we wanted to examine the intensifier *so* and found eight examples in ten posts written by women and three examples in ten posts written by men, but that the total word length of the women's posts was 120 and the word length of the men's posts was 45. The figures from this imaginary sample could be summarised as in Table 9.1.

If we took the raw frequency of the intensifier (three and eight), or the frequency of the intensifier per post (0.3 and 0.8 per post respectively for men and women), then it would seem that women use *so* more often than do men. But this comparison is misleading as the word length for the posts written by women and men are different. If the frequencies of the intensifiers are calculated as a percentage of the words in each part of the dataset, it

*Table 9.1* An example of raw frequency in relation to word length

| Gender | Frequency of So | Number of posts | Total word length |
|--------|-----------------|-----------------|-------------------|
| Male   | 3               | 10              | 45                |
| Female | 8               | 10              | 120               |

turns out that women and men (in this example) use the same proportion of intensifiers. You can do this calculation for yourself to check: (8/120*100) and (3/45*100) both result in 6.67 per cent. In this case, the difference in word length across elements of the dataset could be offset by converting the raw frequencies to a percentage of the occurrences per number of words. But other kinds of calculations might be appropriate if your linguistic variable exists in units above the level of the word, or if your dataset is so large that percentages are not the most sensible way of making unevenly sized data samples comparable. The possibilities and problems that arise when you might want to use a very large set of materials (like a corpus) are dealt with in the remainder of this chapter.

## The challenges of concordancing social media texts: making your materials searchable

Chapter 8 introduced the concept of a *corpus* and considered the key issues that arise when building social media corpora. Here we move the focus to using a corpus to undertake linguistic analyses. Corpora are usually analysed using software packages to carry out the counting, sorting and presentation of language features. Some social media corpora contain bespoke search interfaces (as does the Birmingham Blog Corpus and the Twitter Stratified Random Sample). But other software can be used with a range of corpora, which can be more useful if you are using specialised corpora that you have developed for your own project. Commonly used concordancing systems include the propriety software, Wordsmith Tools (hereafter Wordsmith) Scott (2008), Wmatrix (Rayson 2009) and the freeware program, Antconc (Anthony 2005). Each of the software can be used to create a concordance, that is, an indexed list which collates all the instances of a searched for word or phrase within the chosen materials. Of course, concordances are nothing new: concordances have been created in previous centuries to enable searches across lengthy print texts, such as the Bible. The concordances created using software similarly collate (and quantify) words and phrases, often presenting the results in search windows that contain the concordanced lines in a vertical list with the search term (the keyword) positioned centrally in its textual context. Figure 9.1 shows a concordance for the search term *sorry* within a selection of Twitter posts, produced by using Antconc (Anthony 2005).

Before being able to search a social media corpus using this kind of software, you need to ensure that the materials in the corpus are in a format that means they can be analysed. Some problems arise when we need to process large volumes of these social media texts since they have some peculiarities that make them challenging to process for quantitative analysis. Sometimes there are textual features that need to be accounted for or manually cleaned-up before the data can be analysed. Researchers

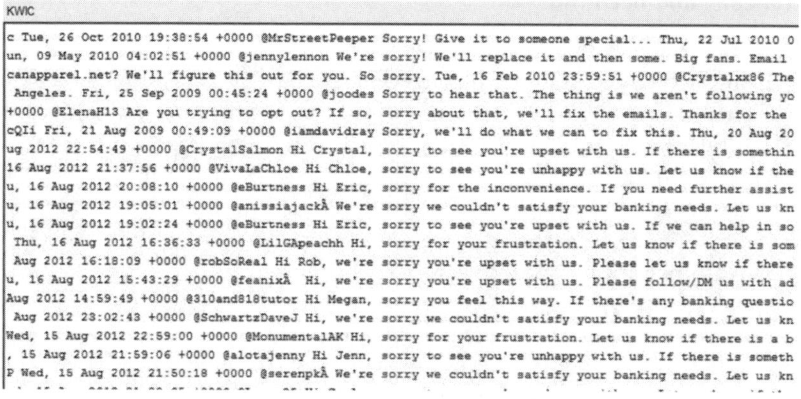

KWIC

```
c Tue, 26 Oct 2010 19:38:54 +0000 @MrStreetPeeper Sorry! Give it to someone special... Thu, 22 Jul 2010 0
un, 09 May 2010 04:02:51 +0000 @jennylennon We're sorry! We'll replace it and then some. Big fans. Email
canapparel.net? We'll figure this out for you. So sorry. Tue, 16 Feb 2010 23:59:51 +0000 @Crystalxx86 The
Angeles. Fri, 25 Sep 2009 00:45:24 +0000 @joodes Sorry to hear that. The thing is we aren't following yo
+0000 @ElenaH13 Are you trying to opt out? If so, sorry about that, we'll fix the emails. Thanks for the
cQIi Fri, 21 Aug 2009 00:49:09 +0000 @iamdavidray Sorry, we'll do what we can to fix this. Thu, 20 Aug 20
ug 2012 22:54:49 +0000 @CrystalSalmon Hi Crystal, sorry to see you're upset with us. If there is somethin
16 Aug 2012 21:37:56 +0000 @VivaLaChloe Hi Chloe, sorry to see you're unhappy with us. Let us know if the
u, 16 Aug 2012 20:08:10 +0000 @eBurtness Hi Eric, sorry for the inconvenience. If you need further assist
u, 16 Aug 2012 19:05:01 +0000 @anissiajackÃ We're sorry we couldn't satisfy your banking needs. Let us kn
u, 16 Aug 2012 19:02:24 +0000 @eBurtness Hi Eric, sorry to see you're upset with us. If we can help in so
 Thu, 16 Aug 2012 16:36:33 +0000 @LilGApeachh Hi, sorry for your frustration. Let us know if there is som
 Aug 2012 16:18:09 +0000 @robSoReal Hi Rob, we're sorry you're upset with us. Please let us know if there
u, 16 Aug 2012 15:43:29 +0000 @feanixÃ Hi, we're sorry you're upset with us. Please follow/DM us with ad
Aug 2012 14:59:49 +0000 @310and818tutor Hi Megan, sorry you feel this way. If there's any banking questio
 Aug 2012 23:02:43 +0000 @SchwartzDaveJ Hi, we're sorry we couldn't satisfy your banking needs. Let us kn
Wed, 15 Aug 2012 22:59:00 +0000 @MonumentalAK Hi, sorry for your frustration. Let us know if there is a b
, 15 Aug 2012 21:59:06 +0000 @alotajenny Hi Jenn, sorry to see you're unhappy with us. If there is someth
P Wed, 15 Aug 2012 21:50:18 +0000 @serenpkÃ We're sorry we couldn't satisfy your banking needs. Let us kn
```

*Figure 9.1* Screenshot of a concordance of the search term *sorry* using Antconc (Anthony 2005).

compiling a social media corpus might need to be particularly aware of the following factors.

### Non-standard orthography

Microposts typically contain non-standard orthography of different kinds. These variously creative uses of spelling, punctuation and other typographic resources can cause problems for the tools for corpus search and annotation, which were developed with standard orthography and "traditional" text genres in mind (Beißwenger and Storrer 2008, p.303). Typical problems can include the unconventional use of punctuation which compresses lexical words into a single graphological unit, as shown in bold font in the following example.

> I'm glad 2 read **this.I** haven't got many things 2 show in **youtube.I** put ur name just 4 curiosity and u **appeared!I** love twitter

Because the software will read *this.I*, *youtube.I* and *appeared!I* each as single words, this can cause problems for counting the lexical words in a corpus accurately.

Other examples of non-standard orthography include the many spelling variations that occur in social media sites. The spelling variations can make it difficult to search for all the examples of a particular word you might be interested in tracing through a particular corpus. Some variations have become conventionalised over time (such as *ur* for *your* in the example above), but other variations can be more idiosyncratic and therefore more difficult to identify. Some more recent concordancing software has been designed to take account of these spelling variations (see Tagg *et al.* 2013), but not all packages do.

### Emoticons and hashtags

The non-verbal resources (like emoticons and hashtags as shown in the examples below) which have emerged from computer-mediated communication and social media sites in particular, can pose further problems for concordancing software. Depending on the settings used by your concordancing software, some of the characters used in emoticons will not be considered 'valid' letters for that system and so will be filtered out of the concordance. They may also be interpreted by the software as marking word breaks or may have other special meanings to the system.

> Oh no! Be good to see you back properly next week :-))) I'm great thanks, very H-A-P-P-Y!! Glad it's nearly the weekend too Xxx
>
> I miss kindergarten when the only drama there was, was losing your crayon. #OhJustLikeMe

For instance, Wordsmith uses the hash character # to represent, as a group, all numbers that occur in the corpus. This is to avoid polluting the word frequency list with phenomena that interfere with interpretation of lexis. In addition, Wordsmith does not treat the hash character itself as a valid letter and responds as if it were punctuation. Similar effects may be seen with other kinds of characters and symbols found in social media texts. The researcher may need to adjust the settings of the software in order to be able to search and sift through their corpus to identify and analyse these non-verbal resources used in social media communication.

### Abridged posts

Because of the character-constraints imposed in micro-blogging, some users will attempt to circumvent these limitations by using a web service to extend their message (such as longertweets.com). These services allow the user to present an abridged version of the tweet in their stream, usually with a link to the full, longer post. The result is that some posts will appear in an abridged form in the corpus. Alternatively, the post may contain punctuation indicating that it continues in a subsequent post in the stream. Depending on the strategy used to extend the tweet, the elaborating tweet may not be captured when the corpus is constructed. However, these types of tweets are relatively uncommon and may be filtered out of the corpus if the analyst can identify regular syntactic patterns with which they can be identified and removed.

### Automated and rebroadcast posts

Spam has unfortunately infiltrated social media meaning that unwanted posts can be present in a corpus. These, and other various kinds of non-human, automatically-generated posts generated may be present in the corpus materials that may not conform to the researcher's selection criteria. For instance some services will generate automatic Twitter updates such as:

I favorited a YouTube video ~ Vocal training http://youtu.be/ S9hruS0ET18?a

These kinds of posts are relatively easy to identify in a corpus since they will occur multiple times with unexpected similarity. For example all instances of the post above contained the non-standard punctuation "~", giving us a clue that they were not manually produced.

If your corpus contains micro-blogging posts then it will also incorporate rebroadcast material such as retweets. The status of these tweets in your study is an important theoretical question. For example, in my (Ruth's) study of celebrities and their use of Twitter, I excluded retweets as I was most interested in the language being used by the celebrities (not in the people whose tweets were being forwarded by the celebrities). However, if I had wanted to study what kinds of topics were typically in forwarded messages, then including the retweets would have been vital. Depending on the intended use of the corpus, a researcher may consider some or all of these tweets as 'noise' and decide to:

- filter out all instances of repetition;
- filter out any tweets that seem to be spam;
- filter out retweeted tweets;
- filter out any automated, non-human tweets.

The decisions that are made in this respect will clearly have an impact upon the size of the corpus, and consequently on the quantitative analyses that involved calculations based on frequency.

Questions to ask yourself if you want to use linguistic concordances in your project are summarised in the following points for reflection.

---

**Points for reflection**

Can the social media data you intend to analyse be compiled as a searchable concordance (e.g. if the data is multimodal how will images and layout be archived and annotated)?

Which concordance software will be used (either proprietary or open source)?

How will you get the social media data into a format the concordance software will accept in light of features such as non-standard orthography, emoticons, hashtags, abridged posts, automated and rebroadcast material?

## Annotating social media corpora

Having built a corpus and refined the format of the materials, what kinds of linguistic features and patterns might we search for? An important factor determining the kinds of features that can be found in a corpus is how it has been annotated. Corpus annotation involves adding a layer of linguistic information to a corpus so that the researcher can search for recurring patterns. There are many different kinds of annotation that can be undertaken depending on the research question. A very common form of annotation is part of speech (POS) tagging. POS tagging can be employed to aid word sense disambiguation tasks that may be helpful for some kinds of discourse analysis. For example, perhaps the researcher might be interested in exploring emotional language in a micro-blogging corpus and wish to know how *like* functions in its evaluative sense. An unannotated corpus such as HERMES (Zappavigna 2012) will return results such as those in the following examples.

> @User.the whole concave look is gone cause its **like** almost the same length._. hahahaha
> RT @IDoThat2: RT if you sit there smiling **like** an idiot when you think of a happy memory. #idothat2
> @User I **like** the Ditty Bops! Never heard of them before, very cute x why does it have to be **like** this coba?
> ALWAYS ON THE RADIO RANTING, HE DON'T UNDERSTAND OUR PRESIDENT,. NO A PERSON **LIKE** U NEVER CAN. EVER. U SEE, ASS KISSER joe scarboro-
> Its seems **like** forever since they dated. lol

As these examples suggest, in order to isolate the instances where *like* is functioning as a verb (e.g. "I really **like** it!") we would need to disambiguate these from instances where it is used as a softener (e.g. "It was, **like**, so great!") or as a comparative (e.g. "It looks more **like** a dog than a cat."). In order to automatically retrieve only the desired instances, a POS tagger can be used so that the search function will only return particular kinds of items (e.g. all instances where *like* functions as a verb). The tags shown in bold in following examples would distinguish instances where *like* functions as a verb (VBP) from instances where it functions as preposition (IN), for example:

> @User I *like* /**VBP** the Ditty Bops! Never heard of them before, very cute x
> RT @IDoThat2: RT if you sit there smiling *like* /**IN** an idiot when you think of a happy memory. #idothat2

Unfortunately, many POS taggers are not trained to work with social media texts and so do not cope well with properties of social media texts such as non-standard orthography. However, an example of a POS tagger that has recently been developed to work with Twitter data is the Twitter POS tagger[1] (Gimpel *et al.* 2011). This POS tagger was trained on manually annotated tweets. Features[2] that are specific to Twitter (and online discourse in general) which this tagger aims to annotate automatically include:

- Hashtags (#): indicates topic/category for tweet.
- At-mentions (@): indicates another user as a recipient of a tweet.
- Discourse markers (~): indications of continuation of a message across multiple tweets.
- Links (U): URL or email addresses.
- Emoticons (E): typographic conventions indicating emotion or involvement.

Other concordancing programmes which include POS taggers include WMatrix (Rayson 2009), and there are a range of tools are available to support corpus annotation. Some tools focus on supporting relatively low volume manual annotation, while other tools focus on higher volume, partially automated analyses. An example of a tool supporting corpus-based discourse analysis of small corpora is the UAM Corpus Tool (www.wagsoft. com/CorpusTool/) (O'Donnell 2008). This tool allows the researcher to annotate a text using a schema which they define in the form of a network of choices. As we mentioned in Chapter 5, tools for multimodal annotation are also beginning to be developed such as UAM Image Tool (www.wagsoft. com/ImageTool/) and the relatively established, ELAN, used for video annotation (http://tla.mpi.nl/tools/tla-tools/elan/) (Wittenburg *et al.* 2006). These tools can be combined with quantitative as well as qualitative approaches. For a useful overview of the current state of corpus annotation tools see O'Donnell (in press).

In summary, annotating social media data involves:

- Deciding what features and patterns are important as the search terms in your corpus and whether part of speech tagging might be needed.
- Considering what kinds of manual and automatic annotation are possible for the corpus.
- Evaluating what you might do with the product of the annotation (e.g. statistical processing) and weighing up if it is worth the intensive effort.

## Analysing social media texts using concordancing software

Having made your corpus searchable, you are now ready to begin analysing the materials. Many different kinds of analysis can be done using concordancing software. Here we introduce three frequently used kinds of analysis: frequency, keyness and collocations.

analysis that can be carried out using concordancing software
ie frequency of words within the collected materials: corpus
en interested in establishing the regular patterns or norms
w.thin a particular set of materials. To start with, the researcher might be
interested in the frequency of individual words, or may want to create a list
of the words contained in the materials (for example, in decreasing order of
frequency). Table 9.2 shows us the ten most frequent words in the
Birmingham Blog Corpus and in the HERMES Twitter Corpus.

There are certain features we might notice from these frequency lists. For
example, we might notice that there is quite a lot of overlap between the
words which occur on both lists: (*the, to, a, of, and, in, I*) all occur in both
lists, and the top two words (*the* and *to*) are exactly the same. We might
conclude from this that perhaps the language of blogs and micro-blogs is
broadly similar to each other. However, we might also question how useful
this information actually is. For example, the Birmingham Blog Corpus and
HERMES are different sized corpora (628,558,282 words and 100,281,967
words, respectively), so the raw frequencies in the table are not comparable
for individual items. Instead, the frequencies will either need to be expressed
as a percentage of the dataset as a whole or to be normalised (which in
corpus linguistics often adjusts these to a relative frequency of occurrences
per million words (see McEnery and Hardie 2012)). Some software will
make this calculation for you; other software may require you to make this
calculation for yourself (which can be done relatively easily in a package
like Microsoft Excel).

We might also notice that there are some differences between the words
included on each list, such as the inclusion of the pronoun *you* and the
abbreviation *http* in the top ten items for the HERMES corpus, but not in

Table 9.2 Top ten word frequencies in Birmingham Blog Corpus and HERMES Twitter Corpus

| Rank | Birmingham Blog Corpus | | | HERMES Twitter Corpus | | |
| | Word | Raw frequency | % | Word | Raw frequency | % |
|---|---|---|---|---|---|---|
| 1 | THE | 24,986,273 | 3.98 | THE | 3,358,659 | 3.15 |
| 2 | TO | 15,523,666 | 2.47 | TO | 2,379,223 | 2.23 |
| 3 | AND | 13,226,449 | 2.10 | I | 2,236,470 | 2.10 |
| 4 | A | 13,169,504 | 2.10 | A | 1,674,654 | 1.57 |
| 5 | OF | 11,541,388 | 1.84 | HTTP | 1,631,187 | 1.53 |
| 6 | I | 9,736,364 | 1.55 | AND | 1,545,943 | 1.45 |
| 7 | IN | 8,442,980 | 1.34 | OF | 1,217,398 | 1.14 |
| 8 | IS | 6,700,706 | 1.07 | YOU | 1,194,631 | 1.12 |
| 9 | THAT | 6,635,605 | 1.06 | IS | 1,120,058 | 1.05 |
| 10 | FOR | 5,829,087 | 0.93 | IN | 1,118,227 | 1.05 |

the Birmingham Blog Corpus, but, on the whole, this does not give a very full picture of the variation between the language which occurs commonly in these two corpora from social media. Nor do these frequency lists on their own allow the researcher to see if these frequencies are typical of blogs and micro-blogs as distinct genres, or if the frequencies are simply common to English language use more generally. To get a clearer picture of how to interpret these frequencies, the researcher needs to search further. One option is to compare the frequency of the words with existing corpora drawn from offline examples of language such as the British National Corpus or the Concordance of Contemporary American English (COCA). Compared with offline language corpora, the researcher might see that a similar range of grammatical words are amongst the most frequently occurring items. (The most frequent items on the COCA word list are *the*, *be*, *and*, *of*, *a*, *in*, *to*, *have*, *to* and *it*.) This comparison tells us that the frequency of the definite article, *the*, is not particularly distinctive as a characteristic of blogging or micro-blogging, but the occurrence of the personal pronouns *I* and *you*, and the URL prefix *http* are more so. Perhaps this might suggest the interactional dimension of Twitter posts and its importance as a site for sharing linked material. However, once again, the frequency list alone is only the first step in the analysis: the researcher might want to find out more accurately whether or not the variation between one set of frequencies is meaningful or not.

### Keyword lists

If the researcher wants to find out which features are statistically significant when comparing corpora, then sometimes a small corpus will be compared with a second corpus to determine which items in the smaller corpus are determined to be 'key', that is, which features occur at higher frequency than the pattern represented in the reference corpus. This kind of work is referred to as keyword analysis. Baker (2010, p.104) defines a keyword as "a word which occurs statistically more frequently in one file or corpus, when compared against another comparable or reference corpus". For instance I might have built a specialised corpus of blog posts about climate change and wish to compare how climate change is represented in this corpus with a second, specialised corpus of traditional news media texts about climate change. I could then compare the differences between the blogs and traditional news media by comparing the two sets. Or, if the researcher wanted to see if the frequency of a particular word is typical of their corpus in particular, or of language use more widely, they could compare a specialised corpus with a larger, reference corpus. An example of this would be comparing the frequency of a specialised set of Twitter posts (say of posts made by a set of celebrities) with a corpus of Twitter language more generally (such as the HERMES Twitter corpus). As Julia Gillen's case study shows, a comparison of keyness can help the researcher see what was genuinely distinctive about the language use in the context she was studying: Second Life.

## Box 9.1 Investigating language use in a virtual world

### Julia Gillen

It is sometimes thought that the language used in new media, especially by young people, is of impoverished quality and that topics are trivial. It may be assumed that only everyday language is used, or, conversely, that dialogues are full of jargon. Furthermore, the quantity of written language used in many virtual worlds is sometimes also overlooked.

I investigated the language used in the Schome Park Programme pilot, led by Peter Twining at the Open University. This pilot, designed to investigate radically different models of education, received funding in 2007 from the National Academy for Gifted and Talented Youth and used a protected environment within Teen Second Life.[3]

In order to investigate the students' use of written language in the project, I conducted a corpus linguistic analysis of a large, randomised sample of the students' turns in chat logs, collected with fully informed consent. I used WordSmith as the concordancing software, and compared my specialised corpus of Second Life Student Chat with the reference corpus of BNC Baby, a four-million word cut-down version of the British National Corpus. This samples diverse genres, including newspaper articles, correspondence and everyday conversation by adults. My aim was to find out which lexical items were distinctive to the interactions "in-world", as we referred to the 3D simulated environment of the Schome Park Programme.

Significant findings included the following:

- Students' turns were characterised by considerable interrogation and inquiry, with a preponderance of question words such as *how* and *what*.
- Orienting in space and time was evidenced through the high frequency of words such as *time*, *here*, *there*, *now*, etc.
- There are various indications of positive relationship building and collaborative activities – *yes* was a keyword but *no* was not. *Haha* and *LOL* indicated shared humour. *Help* and *thanks* reflected an environment where assistance was asked for and readily given. Indeed politeness is prevalent with *please* also common.

- A few genre-specific terms – such as *schomer*, *RL* and *IM* – featured with high keyness, indicating the role of these specialised, 'in group' to suggest familiarity within the discourse community.
- *Thing, things, make* and *stuff* indicated activities around the construction of 'objects' and 'scripts'. These words appear often in the frequency list and in comparison with language overall. The use of such simple terms in complex and abstract domains of communication, such as laboratories, has been found in other studies.
- *Meeting* and *library* appear more often than they do in the overall language corpus, which is not unremarkable given that the reference corpus is adult and contains a considerable amount of text in formal genres.

#advice: It is not difficult to learn how to carry out a simple lexical analysis with corpus linguistics tools. It can be fruitful in investigating a specific discourse community, probing behind common assumptions.

Sometimes the keyword lists can show the researcher findings that they did not anticipate at the outset. For example, I (Ruth) built a specialised Twitter corpus gathered between 2010 and 2012 which gathered publicly available posts from celebrity, 'ordinary' and corporate accounts. By running a keyword test on different sections of the corpus, I was able to see that the addressed messages posted by corporate accounts were quite different in the relative frequency of the vocabulary choices. Words like *hi, thanks, sorry, please* occurred in the top ten keywords for addressed messages, suggesting that these interactions (as compared with other kinds of posts like general broadcasts or retweets) favoured a kind of institutionalised customer care talk not used in other kinds of Twitter interactions or by other groups of Twitter users. The data was not collected with the intention to explore customer care talk (such as greeting or apologising): it was only by using the search tools to examine frequency patterns that this distinctive use of language was brought to light. Even once the keywords had been isolated, the research was incomplete. It did not tell me how those customer care terms were used in context. To examine the function of those apologies, I needed to combine concordance searches with other, manual, qualitative analysis of particular posts.

### Collocation

One of the advantages of using concordancing software is that it allows researchers to examine large stretches of text. This can be combined productively with a more qualitative kind of textual analysis where the researcher can bring close focus to particular parts of the corpus and begin to examine the patterns that emerge in more detail. One way to do this is to trace the collocational patterns that are found in the data. Collocation refers to the co-occurrence of words in patterns that are regularly repeated and statistically significant. This principle of co-occurrence is familiar from language use in both offline and online contexts: the adjective *blonde* can be said to collocate with hair in a way that the synonym *yellow* does not (you might like to think of other examples of hair colours that have strong collocational patterns). Corpus analysis software can be a helpful way to approach collocations, because the software can sort selected words not only in terms of their frequency, but also organise examples where the selected words occur according to their textual contexts (the words which co-occur to the left or the right of the word). Sometimes this can reveal patterns that might not appear obvious without this large-scale process of sifting and sorting. For example, when I (Ruth) was comparing the temporal adverbs that occurred in the Twitter corpus collected to compare celebrity, corporate and ordinary Twitter use, I found that adverbs which emphasised the present moment (*today, tonight, now*) occurred more often than references to points of time in the past like (*yesterday*). However, when the keywords were examined in context, the results suggested that the celebrities and ordinary Twitter members used *today, tonight* and *now* in different ways. For example, the phrase *the show* collocated with the temporal adverbs for celebrities:

> Mannequin's going **into the show tonight** for the first time. I'm really excited for everyone to see it!–Britney
>
> I always love having Kid Inventors **on the show and today** is no exception. http://su.pr/23ZYZ0

However, it did not collocate with these adverbs for the ordinary Twitter members, as in the next example.

> Taking a break from coding **today**, need a break from all those letters and numbers. Instead I am spreadsheeting. Oh, damn #itsjustasbad

By working from the frequency lists to the keywords and then looking at the collocations for those keywords, the promotional strategies used by celebrities in Twitter could be identified, suggesting that their use of recency in tweeting behaviour was put to a promotional use not typical of all Twitter members (Page 2012).

## Visualisation tools and social networks

### Why text visualisation?

Because social media corpora are typically very large, linguists can often benefit from visualisation tools to aid the interpretation of complicated patterns and thematic trends that they might not be able to observe otherwise (Wise *et al.* 1995, pp.51–2). In addition, some of the metadata available in social media materials, such as the timestamp, geo-spatial information and information about connections in the social network, can open up the possibility of visualising patterns of language use in multidimensional forms. Given that sometimes researchers might be interested in patterns that involve relationships between many textual variables across many contextual dimensions of meaning (such as time, space or network), visualisations can be very useful. Existing techniques commonly used in linguistics, such as statistical analyses of corpus-based data, essentially flatten the text into a countable product, without showing other relationships between contextual features, such as how variation in the frequency of particular words might fluctuate over time, or how particular memes become popular and then disappear from use. Fortunately, advances in computer technology afford us the possibility of annotating, managing and visualising highly complex data. We can now track multiple relationships between variables unfolding in time or along other dimensions. As a result we have the potential to model the unfolding of meaning in text. However, visualisation tools and techniques are not without their problems. As with all forms of computing, 'bad data in equals bad data out'. We have to be careful that we use visualisation strategies that illuminate the kinds of linguistic relationships that we want to explore, which can be based on features that can be clearly identified and which are readily 'countable'. If we do not do this we risk creating a representation that does not accurately reflect the patterns in the texts that we want to understand and which takes on 'a life of its own'.

### What is text visualisation?

The field of visualisation has the potential to provide linguists with some much-needed help by supporting their analytical gaze when they work with texts and large corpora. Visualisation, in general, is concerned with finding methods of representation that best leverage the characteristics of human visual perception to make complex data meaningful. The term "information visualisation" (often abbreviated to "InfoVis") refers to "the use of computer supported, interactive, visual representations of abstract data to amplify cognition" (Card and Mackinlay 1997, p.7). While most visualisation techniques share the general aim of amplifying and enhancing human cognition, they vary considerably in the type of data they seek to represent (e.g. financial data, scientific data, medical data, etc.). There is a large and growing body of visualisations available worldwide and a number of taxonomies are proposed to classify visualisation tools (e.g. Chi 2000; Tory and Moller 2004).

Those interested in visualising text often have a background in both computer science and digital art, bringing both technical and aesthetic skills to the endeavour (for example, see the work of Martin Wattenberg (www. bewitched.com), Ben Fry, (http://benfry.com) and Lee Byron (www.leebyron. com)). Even where the visualisations are not created for the purpose of linguistic research, most visualisation techniques are 'word'-based, as they create their images by training a computer to identify linguistic items at the level of the word (for example, as a string of characters in the text). This focus on lexical features (as opposed to syntax, or to the more complicated variation found in forms of 'languaging' discussed in Chapter 2) is in some respects a limitation. But nonetheless, the importance of words as textual and linguistic units aligns well with the kinds of analysis found in corpus-based approaches. A more straightforward example of a visualisation (rather than the artistic examples mentioned above) includes the word cloud, where the size of the word reflects the frequency with which the word occurred in a particular dataset. Figure 9.2 is a word cloud generated from the words in this chapter by using Freiburg's freeware, Wordle.net. As you can see from this illustration, the most frequently occurring words are shown in a larger size and a darker font than the less frequently occurring words.

Some concordancing software integrates visualisations like word clouds to help the researcher in their process of analysis. For example, WMatrix provides word clouds in conjunction with the verbal frequency and keyword lists. In this case, the differences in the font size can help the researcher see more immediately the more or less frequent items in the list: a visual form of differentiation which eases the burden of searching through and sorting a tabulated list of numerical data. Of course, this interpretive strategy might tend to privilege the larger sized font and therefore the higher frequency items. The researcher has to look more closely to find the smaller items which occur less frequently. So while visualisations can be helpful, we should be aware that, like all parts of the research process, they are forms of interpretation which are not neutral but present information in a particular and selective way.

*Figure 9.2* Word cloud generated from the content of Chapter 9 of this book.

## Social media text visualisation

A common form of social media visualisation can be found in techniques for representing relationships between users (e.g. Heer and boyd 2005). These approaches represent non-linguistic links (e.g. 'friendship' relationships on Facebook or 'following/follower' relationships on Twitter) between users in a social media network. Sometimes they are used as part of Social Network Analysis (SNA), a method for using network theory to analyse social relationships (e.g. Ugander *et al.* 2011). While this form of visualisation can usefully supplement linguistic analysis, linguists are also interested in the more difficult problem of representing 'who is saying what to whom' and the even more challenging problem of representing the meanings being negotiated when someone says something to someone in the putative social network. However, as John Caulfield points out in his case study in this chapter, modelling network connections can be a useful starting point in helping the researcher identify which members of a network might be core participants (and so worth following up with additional forms of analysis) and those who are peripheral (and so might not form the main focus for the analysis).

### Box 9.2 Imagining the Irish language blogosphere: a social network analysis using comments and link data

#### John Caulfield

Irish is a minority language and its survival as an everyday community language is under threat. My research explores how some Irish speakers worldwide use social media to create new forms of language communities online. I aim to describe who's participating, the social processes taking place, and how users have adapted the language to computer-mediated communication. In seeking to visualise the invisible ties formed through interacting online, I turned to social network analysis.

I knew that the cluster of active Irish language bloggers would be small, and I hoped to take a whole network approach. The first challenge was defining what exactly being 'active' and 'Irish language' entailed. Each study sets its own parameters for inclusion. In this case, I included any blogger who had made one post over a three-month period in which Irish was the primary language of communication, and the commenters that responded to these posts. This was admittedly a very low threshold, but it enabled me to expand the network quickly (and later focus analysis on the core of prolific users).

Sourcing the sample was time-consuming and involved six months of participant-observation: writing, reading and searching for Irish language blogs. I expanded the sample by tracing links between blogs and hand-coding them for Irish content. The online researcher is always faced with the niggling doubt that some activity will remain undetected. To overcome this, I continued visiting blogs after my data capture period, and added the small number of newly discovered blogs and commenters that met the criteria to the sample. I could confidently say that the resulting 73 blogs and 68 commenters comprised most, if not all, of the Irish language blogosphere in early 2011.

The next challenge was establishing what would constitute a connection between network members. Again, each study defines ties differently. I set an admittedly low threshold of just one comment, link, blog roll entry (or a few lesser-used functions, like 'likes' and 'notes') between members. In a spreadsheet I compiled an edgelist listing all the individual members, the others they interacted with, and the number of times they interacted. This data was analysed using the igraph package in the statistical software R. I chose the Fruchterman-Reingold layout for my visualisations as it pulls together nodes that are well connected and pushes less well-connected nodes to the periphery. Combining this with colour-coding nodes according to their language use, geographic locations, longevity and subject matter helped reveal patterns of social structure that would have remained hidden in the raw data.

The above approach to social network analysis helped reveal a well-connected core of prolific bloggers who had adapted the features of computer-mediated communication to maintain as monolingual an Irish space as possible. These would later become the focus of discourse analysis.

#advice: Set strict criteria for who is included in your study. It will help you present your findings within very clear parameters.

Figure 9.3 is an example of a networked visualisation taken from Caulfield's study. The square nodes represent blogs and circular nodes represent individual commenters, with edges representing those who interacted across the blogosphere through comments and linking during the data capture period. Arrows show the direction of the interaction. Isolated blogs (those with no interactions) appear unconnected at the edge of the network. In the colour version of this plot, nodes are colour-coded according to their language use, with monolingual blogs/commenters appearing in dark green, and other nodes appearing in other colours according to how much/little Irish they used. The plot indicated that language use affected network position, with monolingual nodes being the most well-connected in the network. Caulfield went on to carry out discourse analysis of core nodes and so identified a number of innovative ways in which core users maintained as monolingual a space as

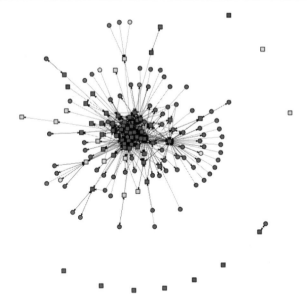

*Figure 9.3* Visualisation of the Irish language blogosphere created by John Caulfield using Gephi software.

possible on their blogs, including hyperlinking from unusual or difficult Irish words to their English language translations. In this way, social network analysis helped identify nodes and themes worthy of further focused analysis, and showed how the partly automated process of quantitative analysis can be complemented with a qualitative approach to other parts of the research project.

Social media text visualisation usually focuses on visualising social text stream data. Because of the limitations of automatic language processing, language-focused social media visualisation tends to concentrate on what is loosely defined as the 'topic' of the communication, in part, because of visualisation's reliance on identifying linguistic features at the level of the word. However, in these social media visualisations, the 'flattened out' dimensions of word frequency are counter-balanced to include visual representation of how the topics relate to other contextual data provided in corpus, such as the geographical or temporal location of the post. Examples include:

• ThemeCrowds, a visualisation that was applied to a micro-blogging corpus "with the goal of identifying groups of users within a large geographical area, who discuss similar topics over time" (Archambault *et al.* 2011, p.81);
• visualisations of the temporal evolution of topics (Kraker *et al.* 2011);

- visualising social media 'events', defined as "a set of relations between *social actors* on a specific *topic* over a certain *time period*" (Zhao and Mitra 2007, p.1);
- Twitinfo, a system design to allow users to visually explore Twitter events base on keyword queries (Marcus *et al.* 2011).

Topic-based techniques have also been used to create social media analytics to support journalistic inquiry (Diakopoulos *et al.* 2010), to represent discourse about climate change (Scharl *et al.* 2013), and explore information propagation (Chien-Tung *et al.* 2011). In addition social media services such as Facebook have begun developing their own in-house visualisation techniques (e.g. Facebook graph search, www.facebook.com/about/graphsearch) to allow users to visually explore their own networks. Visualisations drawn from social media can also have very practical uses in areas such as improving emergency response (Mazumdar *et al.* 2012), and have been used to track how social media sites disseminate knowledge during crises (Procter *et al.* 2013).

### TwitterStreamgraph: an example of social media text visualisation

A visualisation technique that has been used with streaming data is the streamgraph (Byron and Wattenberg 2008). This is an example of a text visualisation technique that allows the researcher to represent visually "usage over time for the words most highly associated with … [a] search word" (Clark 2008). The streamgraph builds on visualisation formats that are familiar from more traditional types of graphs and charts. For example, area graphs represent the frequency of a particular kind of data graphically by blocking out (usually in colour) the portion of a graph that falls beneath the plot line (the larger the blocked out portion of the shape, the greater the quantity of the item being quantified at that point). In packages like Microsoft Excel, for example, it is possible to create simple area graphs by entering numerical data into the spreadsheet and selecting the "Area Chart" format from the menu. The area chart in Figure 9.4 is a visual representation of the number of times that messages were retweeted from a selection of named accounts in the hours following the news reporting the death of former British Prime Minister, Margaret Thatcher, in April 2013.

From Figure 9.4, you can see that some users posted messages that were redistributed as retweets more frequently than others (in this case, the celebrity figures such as the comedian Frankie Boyle, boy band member Harry Styles and television host Piers Morgan were retweeted more often than mainstream news accounts like the BBC or CNN, for example). But while an area graph usually shows a single data series (in the example above, the number of retweets), stacked area graphs can represent multiple data series by stacking one on top of the other. This can be useful if you wanted

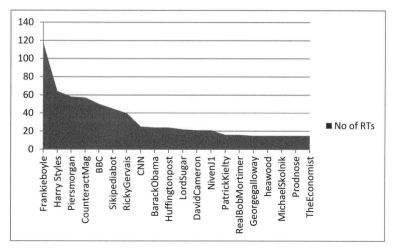

*Figure* 9.4 An area graph for rebroadcast tweets following the death of Margaret Thatcher.

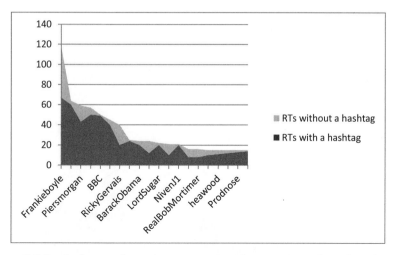

*Figure* 9.5 Stacked area chart showing retweeted messages with and without a hashtag.

to visualise the relationship between two or more different variables. For example, if you wanted to represent how many of those retweeted posts contained a hashtag and how many did not, you could use coloured areas to visualise that difference, as in Figure 9.5. In the chart in Figure 9.5, the proportions of retweeted messages with and without a hashtag are indicated through the relative size of the coloured blocks for each of the different Twitter members. Again, the correlation between size and quantity allows the viewer to see fairly quickly certain correlations (for example the extent to which retweeting and hashtags were used in combination as a means of making a particular tweet more visible).

Streamgraphs build on this established model of stacked area graphs but generate smooth curves for the different data streams by interpolating between points to produce a flowing river of data. An example of a web-based tool for doing limited interactive streamgraph visualisations of lexis occurring in tweets is TwitterStreamgraph[4] (Clark 2008). In the TwitterStreamgraphs, the distribution of the most 'interesting' capitalised words that occur in a database of Twitter messages for either a single Twitter account or a group of Twitter accounts can be represented by combining the size of font (for individual words) with the size of the stacked areas of the chart. For example, Figure 9.6 shows a streamgraph using *linguistics* as a search word.

Other visualisation tools can adapt models of representation that move beyond mathematical visualisations derived from graphs and charts. For example, Brice Russ' study of American dialects in Twitter (see his case study in Chapter 8) used Google Maps to plot the geographical distribution of different lexical variables (such as *soda*, *coke* and *pop* for soft drinks). You can see an example of one of the dialect maps in Figure 9.7, and more on Brice Russ' web pages: www.briceruss.com.

Rather than representing the relationship between the different variables in Russ' study (the lexical variables, *soda*, *pop* and *coke*), and their relationship to geographical location (different towns in America) in a chart, visualising the distribution of the terms across the map more powerfully suggested the clustering of the terms across physical locations.

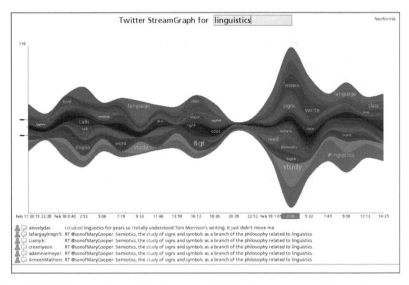

*Figure 9.6* A Twitter StreamGraph generated with the search word *linguistics*.

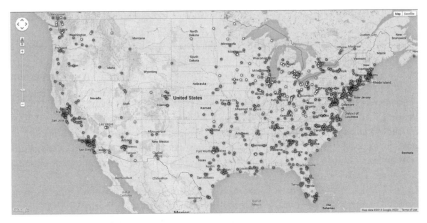

*Figure 9.7* Dialect map showing the distribution of *soda*, *coke* and *pop* (Russ 2012).

As even the brief range of visualisations suggests, there are now a variety of tools and models for making a picture 'tell a thousand words' – or at least represent the frequency of thousands of words! No doubt as time goes by, additional tools for visualisation will emerge. Whether your research project is relatively simple or involves more complex, large-scale analysis of data, it is worth exploring how interpreting your results can be modelled in different ways. All of these visualisations, like any representation of analysis (verbal or visual), will be partial and selective, so just as with all your choices in the research design, from formulating your question through to gathering and analysing your data, make sure that your choice of visualisation is thought through carefully with a clear rationale.

## Notes

1 At the time of writing this POS tagger is available for download here: www.ark. cs.cmu.edu/TweetNLP/.
2 At the time of writing the annotation guideline from which the features in this list were extracted is available here: https://github.com/brendano/ark-tweet-nlp/ blob/master/docs/annot_guidelines.md.
3 Teen Second Life and Second Life are trademarks of Linden Lab.
4 The interactive application is available at: www.neoformix.com/Projects/Twitter StreamGraphs/view.php.

## References

Anthony, L. (2005) 'AntConc: design and development of a freeware corpus analysis toolkit for the technical writing classroom', in *Professional Communication Conference, 2005. IPCC 2005. Proceedings. International*, USA: IEEE, 729–37.
Archambault, D., Greene, D., Cunningham, D. and Hurley, N. (2011) 'Theme-Crowds: multiresolution summaries of Twitter usage', paper presented at the 3rd

International Workshop on Search and Mining User-generated Contents, Glasgow, Scotland, UK.

Baker, P. (2010) 'Corpus methods in linguistics', in Litosseliti, L., ed., *Research Methods in Linguistics*, London: Continuum, 93–116.

Beißwenger, M. and Storrer, A. (2008) 'Corpora of computer-mediated communication', in Lüdeling, A. and Kytö, M., eds, *Corpus Linguistics: An International Handbook* (Vol. 1), Berlin and New York: Mouton de Gruyter, 292–308.

Byron, L. and Wattenberg, M. (2008) 'Stacked graphs–geometry and aesthetics', *Visualisation and Computer Graphics, IEEE Transactions on*, 14 (6), 1245–52.

Card, S. and Mackinlay, J. (1997) 'The structure of the information visualisation design space', in *Proceedings of the 1997 IEEE Symposium on Information Visualisation*, Phoenix: IEEE, 92–9.

Chi, E.H. (2000) 'A taxonomy of visualisation techniques using the data state reference model', paper presented at the Information Visualisation, 2000. InfoVis 2000.

Chien-Tung, H., Cheng-Te, L. and Shou-De, L. (2011) 'Modeling and visualizing information propagation in a micro-blogging platform', *2011 International Conference on Advances in Social Networks Analysis and Mining (ASONAM)*, USA: IEEE, 328–35.

Clark, J. (2008) Twitter Topic Stream, available: http://neoformix.com/2008/Twitter TopicStream.html [accessed 19 February 2012].

Diakopoulos, N., Naaman, M. and Kivran-Swaine, F. (2010) 'Diamonds in the rough: social media visual analytics for journalistic inquiry', *2010 IEEE Symposium on Visual Analytics Science and Technology (VAST)*, Salt Lake City: IEEE, 115–22.

Gimpel, K., Schneider, N., O'Connor, B., Das, D., Mills, D., Eisenstein, J. and Smith, N.A. (2011) 'Part-of-speech tagging for Twitter: annotation, features, and experiments', *Proceedings of the 49th Annual Meeting of the Association for Computational Linguistics*, Portland, 42–7.

Heer, J. and boyd, d. (2005) 'Vizster: visualizing online social networks', *2005 IEEE Symposium on Information Visualisation*, Minneapolis: IEEE, 32–9.

Kraker, P., Wagner, C., Jeanquartier, F. and Lindstaedt, S. (2011) 'On the way to a science intelligence: visualizing TEL tweets for trend detection', in Kloos, C., Gillet, D., Crespo García, R., Wild, F. and Wolpers, M., eds, *Towards Ubiquitous Learning* (Vol. 6964), Berlin Heidelberg: Springer, 220–32.

McEnery, T. and Hardie, A. (2012) *Corpus Linguistics: Method, Theory, Practice*, Cambridge: Cambridge University Press.

Marcus, A., Bernstein, M.S., Badar, O., Karger, D.R., Madden, S. and Miller, R.C. (2011) 'Twitinfo: aggregating and visualizing microblogs for event exploration', *Proceedings of the 2011 Annual Conference on Human Factors in Computing Systems*, ACM, 227–36.

Mazumdar, S., Ciravegna, F., Gentile, A.L. and Lanfranchi, V. (2012) 'Visualising context and hierarchy in social media', paper presented at the International Workshop on Intelligent Exploration of Semantic Data (IESD), Galway City, Ireland.

O'Donnell, M. (2008) 'Demonstration of the UAM CorpusTool for text and image annotation', *Proceedings of the ACL-08:HLT Demo Session (CompanionVolume)*, Columbus, Ohio, June 2008, Association for Computational Linguistics, 13–16.

O'Donnell, M. (in press) 'Between man and machine: the changing face of corpus annotation software', in Yan, F. and Webster, J.J., eds, *Developing Systemic Functional Linguistics*, London: Equinox.

Page, R. (2012) 'The linguistics of self-branding and micro-celebrity in Twitter: the role of hashtags', *Discourse and Communication*, 6 (2), 181–201.

Procter, R., Vis, F. and Voss, A. (2013) 'Reading the riots on Twitter: methodological innovation for the analysis of big data on Twitter', *International Journal of Social Research Methodology*, 16 (2), 197–214.

Rayson, P. (2009) 'Wmatrix: a web-based corpus processing environment', Computing Department, Lancaster University, available: http://ucrel.lancs.ac.uk/wmatrix/ [accessed 27 November 2013].

Russ, B. (2012) 'Examining large-scale regional variation through online geotagged corpora', paper presented at American Dialect Society, Portland, 5–7 January, available: www.briceruss.com/ADStalk.pdf [accessed 27 November 2013].

Scharl, A., Hubmann-Haidvogel, A., Weichselbraun, A., Lang, H. and Sabou, M. (2013) 'Media Watch on climate change – visual analytics for aggregating and managing environmental knowledge from online sources', *46th Hawaii International Conference on System Sciences (HICSS-46)*, 7–10 January 2013, Maui, Hawaii.

Scott, M. (2008) *Wordsmith Tools Version 5*, Liverpool.

Tagg, C., Baron, A. and Rayson, P. (2013) '"I didn't spel that wrong did i. Oops": analysis and standardisation of SMS spelling variation', *Lingvisticæ Investigationes*, 35 (2), 367–88.

Tory, M. and Moller, T. (2004) 'Rethinking visualisation: a high-level taxonomy', paper presented at the Information Visualisation, 2004. INFOVIS 2004.

Ugander, J., Karrer, B., Backstrom, L. and Marlow, C. (2011) 'The anatomy of the Facebook social graph', *arXiv preprint arXiv:1111.4503*, available: http://arxiv.org/pdf/1111.4503v1.pdf [accessed 27 November 2013].

Wise, J., Thomas, J., Pennock, K., Lantrip, D., Pottier, M. and Schur, A. (1995) 'Visualizing the non-visual: spatial analysis and interaction with information from text documents', *Proceedings of the IEEE Information Visualisation Symposium*, Atlanta, Georgia: IEEE, 51–8.

Wittenburg, P., Brugman, H., Russel, A., Klassmann, A. and Sloetjes, H. (2006) 'ELAN: a professional framework for multimodality research', paper presented at the LREC, Fifth International Conference on Language Resources and Evaluation, available: www.lrec-conf.org/proceedings/lrec2006/pdf/153_pdf.pdf [accessed 27 November 2013].

Zappavigna, M. (2012) *Discourse of Twitter and Social Media: How We Use Language to Create Affiliation on the Web*, London: Continuum.

Zhao, Q. and Mitra, P. (2007) 'Event detection and visualisation for social text streams', paper presented at the International Conference on Weblogs and Social Media (ICWSM'2007), Boulder, Colorado, USA.

# Index

Note: page numbers in italic type refer to figures; those in bold refer to tables.

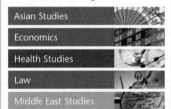